CONVERSATIONS
WITH BOURDIEU

THE
JOHANNESBURG
MOMENT

MICHAEL BURAWOY AND KARL VON HOLDT

WITS UNIVERSITY PRESS

Published in South Africa by:

Wits University Press
1 Jan Smuts Avenue
Johannesburg

www.witspress.co.za

First published 2012

ISBN 978-1-86814-540-9

Edited by Alex Potter
Cover design and layout by Hothouse South Africa
Printed and bound by Paarl Media

CONTENTS

ABBREVIATIONS AND ACRONYMS

ANC	African National Congress
COSATU	Congress of South African Trade Unions
CPF	Community Policing Forum
CWP	Community Work Programme
DA	Democratic Alliance
FLN	Front de Libération Nationale/ National Liberation Front
FOSATU	Federation of South African Trade Unions
MEC	Member of the Executive Council
SACP	South African Communist Party
SWOP	Society, Work and Development Institute
UDF	United Democratic Front

PREFACE

MICHAEL BURAWOY

My four-year stint with the Ford PhDs, which had brought me to the University of the Witwatersrand for three weeks every year, had come to an end. Karl von Holdt, then acting director of SWOP (the Society, Work and Development Institute) invited me to come to Wits for a semester on a Mellon Visiting Professorship. I would work with students and faculty and also give public lectures. There was interest in my giving lectures on the work of Pierre Bourdieu, which I had previously done at the University of Wisconsin. I revised and expanded these lectures from six to eight. As at Wisconsin, the idea was to bring together faculty and students from different departments and develop another side to SWOP's activities.

But Wits would be a different experience altogether, as Bourdieu was not the popular theorist in South Africa that he was in Wisconsin. After all, Bourdieu was not only a theorist of the North and from the North, but more specifically of France and from France, which made him more unfamiliar than Anglo-American theorists. His convoluted style of writing, his elliptical sentences, his erudition and his philosophical grounding – in sum, his deployment of cultural capital – make his work challenging to access.

As I had done in Wisconsin, I sought to interpret Bourdieu by presenting his ideas in relation to Marxism through a series of imaginary conversations between Bourdieu and Marx, Gramsci, Fanon, Freire, Beauvoir, Mills and myself, respectively. Bourdieu makes reference to Marx – indeed, his work is a deep engagement with Marx (as well as Durkheim and Weber) – but Marx never receives a sustained examination. As for

Gramsci, Fanon and Beauvoir, his scattered references and footnotes are contemptuous, while Freire and Mills hardly get a mention. Nonetheless, there are some interesting parallels and convergences with these theorists that more often than not evaporate under closer examination. My endeavour was to rescue these figures buried in Bourdieu with a view to problematising both Bourdieu and Marxism. The Marxists I chose – and I realise Mills had an ambiguous relationship with Marxism – were all concerned with developing a theory of superstructures or ideological domination, and therefore most convergent with what lies at the centre of Bourdieu's opus: the theory of symbolic domination. These theorists also had important things to say about intellectuals and the public face of social science, and here too there was much to debate, as Bourdieu was – and still is – the pre-eminent public sociologist of our era. Like Marxist theory, Bourdieu was always concerned with the relation of theory and practice.

Still, this was South Africa, and even if Marxism had more currency here than in other parts of the world, it was nonetheless flagging; and, moreover, Bourdieu's concerns with symbolic domination seemed removed from the South African situation, where physical violence seemed far more salient – something about which Bourdieu has little to say beyond some of his early writings on Algeria. My original intention was to try and show the significance of Bourdieu to the New South Africa; this was, after all, a time of the struggles between African National Congress Youth leader Julius Malema and Congress of South African Trade Unions president Zwelinzima Vavi, struggles that might be seen as precisely open warfare of a symbolic kind, with Vavi even calling for a 'lifestyle audit' for Malema – effectively questioning the basis of ruling-class 'distinction', a questioning that would be difficult to imagine in France, with its settled symbolic order. It was also the time of preparation for the FIFA Soccer World Cup, a spectacle if ever there were one that absorbed the attention of the entire population, masking the real interests at play. Again, the symbolic world of post-apartheid South Africa could not be disregarded. Still, it could be argued that Bourdieu's significance might be the non-applicability of his ideas to South Africa, i.e. that his ideas are irrevocably Northern or French.

The eight conversations held over a period of six weeks in February and March 2010 brought in crowds from different quarters of the university, and each presentation was followed by heated exchanges. They were made all the more interesting by Karl von Holdt, who consistently defended Bourdieu against Marxist detractors, showing how his ideas do have validity in South Africa. My own attempt to incorporate South Africa into these conversations proved to be paltry and wooden, and so when it came to writing up the lectures, I invited Karl to respond with his own reflections. He has done this in an exceptional manner, in a sense returning Bourdieu to where he began his sociological life – Africa. After all, many of Bourdieu's abiding ideas are taken from his interpretation of the Kabyle kinship society in Algeria. It was from his studies of the Kabyle that he developed the notions of symbolic capital, misrecognition, habitus, male domination and so forth. Bourdieu applied these ideas to French society, and Karl has now taken them back to Africa, pointing to the symbolic dimensions of township violence, the power of the concept of habitus, the disciplinary mode of education and the place of intellectuals in contemporary South Africa.

If I presented a rather arid conversation between Bourdieu and Marxism, Karl has extended the conversational mode to one between Northern and Southern theory, but based on more than three decades of engaged research and contestation in education, labour and community. Karl brings to the forefront a subordinate register in Bourdieu's writings, the dimensions of struggle, crisis and social transformation. He does not, however, engage Bourdieu's writings as a combat sport and he does not dismiss or ignore either myself or Bourdieu, but uses Bourdieu to construct a dialogue about the South Africa of yesterday, today and tomorrow. So we now offer a set of conversations on conversations in the hope of sparking further debate and discussion about the trajectory of South Africa, about the continuing vitality of Marxism and about the relevance of Bourdieu's thought to different contexts.

These conversations have benefitted from many other conversations with colleagues and students: in Berkeley with Xiuying Cheng, Fareen Parvez, Gretchen Purser, Dylan Riley, Ofer Sharone, Cihan Tuğal, and Loïc Wacquant, whose boot camp course opened my eyes to the enormity of Bourdieu's achievements; in Madison with Erik Wright, Gay Seidman, Mara Loveman and Matt Nichter; and in Johannesburg with Bridget Kenny, Oupa Lehoulere, Peter Alexander, Irma du Plessis, Prishani Naidoo, Michelle Williams, Vish Satgar, Eric Worby, Shireen Ally, Tina Uys, Andries Bezuidenhout, Sonja Narunsky-Laden, Ahmed Veriava and Jackie Cock. Especial thanks to Jeff Sallaz, who gave me detailed commentary on both the Madison and the Johannesburg Conversations with Bourdieu, and to an anonymous second reviewer who also gave us excellent comments on the draft manuscript. I have tried to address their criticisms and suggestions in the book. Last, but not least, for the past 45 years I have had the good fortune of listening to, learning from and living with two great interpreters of South Africa – Luli Callinicos and Eddie Webster – and it is to them that I dedicate these conversations.

PROLOGUE
The Johannesburg Moment

KARL VON HOLDT

Forty years ago, in the early 1970s, Durban experienced a ferment of new ideas that were to profoundly shape resistance to apartheid. The central figures in this ferment were two charismatic intellectuals, Steve Biko and Rick Turner. Biko and his comrades founded the Black Consciousness movement and its organisational forms, the South African Students' Organisation and the Black People's Convention, from which emerged a new generation of political activists who went on to organise trade unions, community organisations and the United Democratic Front. Rick Turner's ideas about participatory democracy and the projects he initi-ated to support a nascent black trade union movement, partly in response to the challenge of Black Consciousness, influenced many of those who contributed to the building of the trade union movement.

The Durban ferment was not only about the ideas of intellectuals; it was also about a shift in popular consciousness. In 1973 some 100,000 workers participated in a wave of strikes in Durban, breaking with the quiescence of the 1960s. By the end of the decade both Biko and Turner had been killed by the Security Police. Their ideas, however, continued to shape the resistance movement in different ways throughout the 1980s.

This was what Tony Morphet – drawing on Raymond Williams's idea of a structure of feeling – called the 'Durban moment', constituted by profound shifts in ideas and consciousness among intellectuals and workers, and setting off far-reaching reverberations across South Africa, way beyond the immediate locale of Durban (Morphet, 1990: 92–93; Webster, 1993).

That was the Durban moment. This book is subtitled 'the Johannesburg moment'. What do we mean by this?

At the simplest level, the title is a reference to the fact that the book grew out of a series of lectures on Pierre Bourdieu, the great French sociologist, given at the University of the Witwatersrand in Johannesburg in 2010. The significance of the reference to place is not simply that the lectures took place here, but that they presented an occasion for interrogating the relevance of Bourdieu's work to South Africa – and, more importantly, confronting the meaning of South Africa for Bourdieu's theory. It is through exploring the significance of this interrogation and confrontation that we can arrive at some sense of the possible meaning of a 'Johannesburg moment'.

In contrast to the Durban moment, the Johannesburg moment is a post-apartheid moment; that is to say, it is a moment of political rupture with apartheid – a moment of the new Constitution, democracy, reconstruction and transformation.

Yet in our book – which presents a multilayered conversation, not only between Bourdieu and an array of interlocutors presented by Michael, not only between 'Johannesburg' and Bourdieu, but also between Michael and myself – I argue that this place (Johannesburg and its hinterland) is distinguished by a fractious and turbulent set of social contestations, both small and large, over the shape of an emerging social order in post-apartheid South Africa. So sharp is this contestation, so multi-centred and diverse, that we may speak of multiple local moral orders, a social fragmentation and a profound disordering of society, which are evident in many different ways, among them an argument deep in the heart of our society over the meaning of 'law' and 'order'.

Thus, from the start, the Johannesburg moment is one that disrupts the stark binary of oppression and freedom and the comforting trajectory of transformation and reconstruction. Nor should we imagine that such arguments and contestations take place only on the far peripheries of our city, in places like Trouble (discussed in the main body of the book), from which its towering buildings and twinkling lights cannot even be seen. They take place as well in its heart, in those buildings and their streets, as well as its leafy suburbs.

One of the icons of Johannesburg is the Constitutional Court and the wider Constitution Hill precinct. It symbolises the new post-apartheid order in South Africa – the order of democracy and human rights. The Constitution and its Court are supposed to rise above society, just as they rise above the cacophony of Johannesburg on their hill, and preside over all institutions, deliberating, adjudicating and providing guidance in the construction of a new order.

But in reality, what is the reach of the Constitution and its Court? Trouble itself is only 30 or 40 km away from the Constitutional Court as the highway goes, but the Constitution appears to have little force there, just as the law seems to have little presence. If the Republic is defined by the constitutional order, then Trouble belongs in a different Republic; or, perhaps, Trouble is a place of struggle between contending Republics.

Constitution Hill is home to a moving exhibition on the conditions of the apartheid jails and the role of these jails in securing the apartheid order. Visitors can be forgiven for imagining that there are no longer jails in our constitutional democracy, and that if there are, conditions for prisoners are decent and humane. The truth is very different – our jails are more overcrowded than ever before, and violence and corruption continue to pervade many of them. What role do they play in securing the post-apartheid order? The Constitution no doubt seems remote both to the incarcerated and their jailers.

Nor can the Constitution remain above the fray. The Constitutional Court itself is increasingly at the centre of controversy, ranging from the dispute between Judge Hlope and some Constitutional Court judges to the process of appointing a new chief justice. There can be little doubt that the same contestations, the same battles over the nature of order, the same cacophony of Johannesburg will necessarily penetrate its inner workings. The progressive liberal consensus that characterised its early years may well give way to sharp differences that reflect wider divergences, each with substantial constituencies in society, over such questions as social conservatism or the relative power of the executive branch of government.

Johannesburg is also the city of head offices, and the streets outside the headquarters of the African National Congress (ANC) in 2011 were witness to violent clashes between the police and the supporters of the president of the ANC Youth League, Julius Malema, protesting against the disciplinary hearings brought against him and his executive by the ANC. This provides a dramatic image for 'a profoundly unstable ANC which at the same time exists in a state of profound paralysis' due to the fierce struggles between different factions of the elite, as well as different constituencies of the Tripartite Alliance, over the control and direction of the organisation (Von Holdt, 2011a). Authority and discipline have become extremely unstable and highly contested within the organisation, much as they have in the broader society. Indeed, the ANC general secretary warns that the ANC is 'imploding' because 'chaos and anarchy are good forests for mischief' (*The Star*, 21 September 2011).

Thus, Johannesburg confronts us with all the contradictions and tensions of post-apartheid reality at their most intense. By virtue of its dynamism and scale, the city serves to refract them so that the dynamic interaction between order and disorder, between multiple orders and the jagged edges of ruin, become most visible and most intense in this place. Johannesburg was always at the centre of the making and remaking of the South African order. However, this moment is different, characterised, as noted above, by an historic rupture.

New forces, new problems and new questions come to the fore as we emerge from the ruins of the old. Many of our assumptions are questioned and much of what we took to be true breaks to pieces. We find we have to think again. Clashing narratives provide us with alternative ways of naming ourselves, evident in the multiple meanings assigned to our city. Are we a 'world-class African city' in the making, as the city authorities would have us believe? Is Johannesburg the second-greatest city after Paris, as Johannesburg artist William Kentridge's title so ironically proclaims? Are we a Third World slum? Are we a site of the African Renaissance, or are we another anecdote in the tale of Afro-pessimism? Is London a suburb of Johannesburg, in another of Kentridge's musings (Cameron, Christov-Bakargiev & Coetzee, 1999: 109)? Is Johannesburg a suburb of Lagos, or Harare? Whose story is it in which we play out our roles?

Again, we are reminded of the sharp contrast with the Durban moment. The latter was founded on two binaries – the class binary of worker versus capitalist and the racial binary of the black oppressed versus white domination. Both of these binaries designated the agents of history and located them in master narratives of progress. Both narratives provided for a triumphal ending after long periods of suffering and struggle. The Johannesburg moment is that ending, however, it disrupts those neat binaries. The master narratives and their moral certainties are no longer clear. In its place we have multiple symbolic orders in contention over such matters, paralysis in our present and uncertainty in our future.

It is perhaps inevitable that the situation should give rise to an attempt to assert a new binary – that between order and disorder. Thus, we have the strengthening of social conservatism and the assertion that the erosion of morality and authority must be countered with a new authority, embedded in institutions such as the executive organs of the state or the social structures of patriarchy. We have the increasingly violent responses of the police to both crime and social protest. We have new attempts to control information, to limit the space of the press.

It is easy for progressives to fall back on moralistic responses to this kind of assertion of conservative order and counterpose the progressive values of the Constitution. But we might do better to interrogate more carefully the sources of this response, and to think more deeply about why there is a pervasive sense that morality and authority are in crisis. Many people in places like Trouble long for an orderliness within which to conduct their daily lives. And where the state fails to guarantee that order, we have the forceful authoritarianism of vigilante mobs and xenophobic crowds imposing a very different kind of order on communities.

We explicitly present the Johannesburg moment – like the Durban moment before it – as a moment of theoretical endeavour: indeed, the disruption of master narratives and their attendant certainties makes a fresh engagement with theory imperative. So we turn to Pierre Bourdieu. Bourdieu is primarily a theorist of order and its reproduction. We confront this Bourdieu with the argumentative, unruly and violence-laden social realities of South Africa – with, precisely, the Johannesburg moment. And in this theatre, we conduct a series of conversations between Bourdieu and (mostly) Marxist intellectuals and theorists, exploring the intersections and divergences between their theories and his. This is a doubly appropriate endeavour, because, in contrast to Bourdieu, Marxism is a theory of struggle and change, and because, as a theory of change, it has been hugely influential both in the struggle against apartheid and in the scholarly field in South Africa.

In these engagements, we see theoretical work as a dynamic endeavour, with intellectuals building onto and borrowing from what went before, or demolishing it and making use of the rubble afresh, as they confront the theoretical constructions of their forebears and opponents while attempting to wrestle into coherence the social world around them. The accumulated weight of social order in the West and in the Western sociology of Bourdieu – and of Mills, and in the Marxism of Gramsci and Beauvoir and Burawoy – is contrasted with the making and remaking of social order in the post-colony, where the old order is ruptured and the new order seems unable to come into being, weighed down as it is with the legacies and conflicts of the old, as well as with new and contradictory claims and battles and confusions – a world for which two of our interlocutors, Freire and Fanon, in turn attempt the remaking of Marxism.

Our Johannesburg conversations are not simply a critique of Bourdieu from a Marxist perspective. We explore Marxism as a living encounter between individuals and generations. Fanon wrote that decolonisation, 'which sets out to change the order of the world, is clearly an agenda for total disorder'. The disorder of the Johannesburg moment presents a challenge not only for Bourdieu, but also for Marxists.

Marxism and Bourdieusian theory share their point of origin and their reference points in the development of Western society – they can be seen, in other words, as elements in what Bourdieu called 'the imperialism of reason'. The challenge of the Johannesburg moment is to disorder and reorder Western theory so that it is better able to name our own world. Not only that, though: the point is to so rework theory that it enables a rethinking of the West, a renaming of what appears so solid and dominant. In short, the goal, in the words of Dipesh Chakrabarty (2000), is to provincialise Europe.

This is not a project that limits itself, or can limit itself, to Johannesburg or South Africa. The Johannesburg moment is linked to Mumbai, São Paulo, Istanbul, perhaps Cairo, perhaps Lagos, perhaps Beijing (Yongle, 2010), perhaps Moscow, other cities of the global South, or outside of the West, with the accumulated cultural and intellectual resources to undertake such projects. Indeed, Johannesburg is a latecomer to this scene – we have only recently won our political freedom – but we can draw on resources from our past. Explicit in the work of both Biko and Turner, for example, was a questioning of European 'civilisation'.

Nor is the project limited to a set of questions about theory. These questions have urgent practical implications, and if we develop the wrong answers, the consequences could be disastrous. As an illustration, in the first decade of democracy, the ANC government adopted orthodox Western policy prescriptions regarding economic policy, and at the same time took a radically heterodox position on the nature of HIV and AIDS. The result was the deepening of both inequality and the ravages of disease in our society. If the opposite positions had been taken – medical orthodoxy and economic heterodoxy – South Africa might have found itself in a very different position today.

In this book, we begin a process of putting Western theory through the grinder of Johannesburg, probing and reconstructing it in a way that helps us understand our world and name it afresh. At least, that is our ambition. Readers will have to judge for themselves whether it is successful.

ACKNOWLEDGEMENTS

I would first of all like to express my huge gratitude to Michael for inviting me to participate in this project. It has been a wonderfully exciting and productive journey of exploration that totally disorganised my plans for the two years we have been working on it – but that is just another of the hazards of the Johannesburg moment. I would also like to thank my colleagues on the collaborative research project into collective violence embarked upon by the Society, Work and Development Institute (SWOP) and the Centre for the Study of Violence and Reconciliation – Malose Langa, Sepetla Molapo, Kindiza Ngubeni, Adele Kirsten and Nomfundo Mogapi. I have drawn so much from this research, and from our continuing conversations about its meaning and implications, in my engagement with the work of Bourdieu and the other interlocutors in this book. I want especially to thank Adele Kirsten, my partner, for those many conversations over breakfast or tea in which I first tested some of the ideas that have gone into this book. I am grateful too to the colleagues who took the time to read and comment on various of the pieces I wrote for the book – Khayaat Fakier, Brahm Fleisch, Sarah Mosoetsa and Eddie Webster – as well as the wonderfully engaging audiences at Michael's lecture series at Wits.

Belinda Bozzoli, deputy vice chancellor for research at the time; Tawana Kupe, dean of the Faculty of the Humanities; and the Faculty Research Committee all contributed to making Michael's visit possible, while the award of a Mellon Distinguished Visitor's Grant provided the necessary financial support and Christine Bischoff provided seamless organisation. I would particularly like to thank Veronica Klipp of Wits University Press for her enthusiastic response to the idea of this book, and the other members of her team – Melanie Pequeux, Alex Potter and Tshepo Neito – for so efficiently piloting the processes of production, editing and marketing. To Veronica and Darryl Accone, thanks for inviting me to present the opening address at the 2011 *Mail & Guardian* Literary Festival, so forcing me to present a trial run of the ideas that have gone into this prologue.

Publication of this book is also an occasion to acknowledge my friend and comrade, Moloantoa Molaba. I mourn his untimely death. We worked together as a team for so much of my research into violence and state functioning and our conversations about our experiences were so lively that I cannot think about what I have written in this book without remembering him. *Lala ngoxolo, mtshana.*

CONVERSATION 1

SOCIOLOGY AS A COMBAT SPORT

MICHAEL BURAWOY

Bourdieu Meets Bourdieu

> I often say sociology is a combat sport, a means of self-defence.
> Basically, you use it to defend yourself, without having the right
> to use it for unfair attacks.
>
> Pierre Bourdieu

These sentences are taken from *La Sociologie est un sport de combat*, a popular film produced by Pierre Carles in 2001 about the life of Pierre Bourdieu featuring him at demonstrations, in interviews about masculine domination, in humorous banter with his assistants, in an informal research seminar with his colleagues, in the lecture hall, on television debating with Günter Grass and, in a final dramatic scene, facing the wrath of immigrants. We see Bourdieu voicing opposition to government policies and especially neoliberalism, but we also see him on the defensive – stumbling to explain sociology in simple terms to a confused interviewer, or sweating under pressure of interrogation or intensely nervous when he has to speak in English.

Is this sociology as a combat sport? If so, where are the combatants? We see Bourdieu, but where is the opposition? Where are the other contestants? It's like watching a boxing match with only one boxer. No wonder he can talk of sociology as 'self-defence'; no wonder he can seem so innocent and charming with the opposition absent. Where is the reviled Bourdieu, 'the sociological terrorist of the left', 'the cult leader', 'the intellectual dictator'? Even the Spanish feminist interviewing him about masculine domination lets him off the hook when it comes to his own masculinity – at which point he leans on Virginia Woolf – or when he claims to understand masculine domination better than women do. Significantly, the only time he comes under hostile fire is when young immigrants tell him they are not interested in his disquisitions on oppression – after all, they know they are oppressed – whereupon Bourdieu goes on a tirade against their anti-intellectualism. It seems he has nothing to offer them but words. Here, only at the end of the film, are the first signs of combat.

This absent combat with the absent enemy is not peculiar to the film. Throughout Bourdieu's writings, combatants are slain off-stage with no more than a fleeting appearance in front of the readership. Sociologists, economists and philosophers come and go like puppets, dismissed with barely a sentence or two. What sort of combat sport is this? He says sociology shouldn't be used for unfair attacks, but how fair is it to tie up the enemy in a corner and with one punch knock him/her out of the ring? What is this combat without combat? I've searched through Bourdieu's writings to find elaborations of 'sociology as a combat sport', but to no avail. Minimally, if this is a true combat sport, there should be rules of play that allow all contestants to show their abilities – their strengths as well as their weaknesses. And the rules should apply equally to all. There is not much evidence of fair play either in the film or in his writings.

The purpose of these conversations, then, is to restore at least a small band of combatants who, broadly speaking, are Marxist in orientation. They are there in Bourdieu's 'practical sense' beneath consciousness, circulating in the depths of his habitus, and only rarely surfacing in an explicit and verbal form. To attempt such a restoration is to counter the symbolic violence of their erasure with a symbolic violence of my own. It involves a certain intellectual combat. Still, I restore these Marxists not so much as to issue a knock-out blow (as if that were even possible), but rather to orchestrate a conversation in which each learns about the other to better understand the self. In this opening conversation, however, I will probe the idea of sociology as a combat sport as it applies to Bourdieu's own practice, leading to his contradictory postures in academic and non-academic fields. I will suggest that a better model than combat is the more open and gentle one of conversation – a conversation between Bourdieu the academic theorist and Bourdieu the public intellectual – if we are to unravel the paradoxes of his life's work.

COMBAT VS. CONSENSUS

I am struck by the translation of the film's title into English: *La Sociologie est un sport de combat* becomes *Sociology Is a Martial Art*. There is no warrant for translating combat sport as martial art. Both words exist in French as they do in English, so why this mistranslation? I can only conjecture that this is a manoeuvre to attract an English-speaking – and especially an American – audience for whom labelling an academic discipline as a combat sport would discredit both sociology and the film. It does not suit the self-understanding of US academics and would have an effect opposite to the one in France, where academics do indeed seem to relish the idea of combat sport, where struggles are held out in the open public arena, and where the academic world merges with the public world. In the United States, on the other hand, the academic world is at once more insulated from the public sphere and also more professional. It is dominated by ideologies of consensus formation and peer review. Here, 'martial art', with its connotations of refinement and science, is a more appropriate and appealing metaphor. Academic exchange does not operate according to explicit rules of combat, but with unspoken understandings based on a style of life. Thus, French-trained Michèle Lamont (2009) is fascinated by the exotic 'American' culture of peer assessment based on trust and mutual respect, just as ignominy befalls Loïc Wacquant when he displays French-style combat in the US academy.[1]

We can better understand Bourdieu's milieu and the work he produced by comparing him to Talcott Parsons, who was born and bred American. Both were the most influential world sociologists of their time. Both conquered their national fields of sociology from the summit of their respective academies – Harvard and Collège de France, respectively. Both reshaped the discipline around the world and in their homelands. Both exerted influence on a variety of disciplines beyond their own. Both wrote in difficult prose that only seemed to magnify their appeal. Both generated waves of reaction and critique, dismissal and contempt, as well as ardent disciples.

The parallels extend to the substance of their social theory. Thus, both were primarily interested in the problem of social order, which they tackled with parallel, functionalist schemes – Parsons through the internalisation of common values, Bourdieu through the constitution of habitus – constituting an enduring set of dispositions acquired through participation in multiple fields. Thus, socialisation figured equally prominently in both their accounts of social order. Both had difficulty developing an adequate theory of social change, and their thin theories of history relied on the idea of spontaneous differentiation – in Parsons the rise of subsystems of action and in Bourdieu the emergence of differentiated fields. Neither saw the future as very different from the present: revolutionary change was not part of their conceptual repertoire.

Moreover, both were deeply committed to sociology as a science. Indeed, both conceived of sociology as the queen of the social sciences – other disciplines were a special case of or subordinate to sociology. At the same time, both drew heavily on the vocabulary and ideas of the discipline of economics, just as both were hostile to its reductionism. Despite their claims to universalism, their theories were distinctively products of the society they theorised, in the one case the pre-1960s United States and in the other the post-1960s France. They were both masters of the art of universalising the particular – the particular being the social structure of their own countries as they saw it – as neither took comparative research seriously.

But here the parallels cease. If Parsons's social order rested on *value consensus* that prevented a brutish Hobbesian war of all against all, then Bourdieu's rested on *symbolic domination* that secured silent and unconscious submission. Where Parsons endorsed value consensus as freedom, Bourdieu condemned symbolic domination as debilitating to both the dominant and the dominated. Accordingly, if Parsons was rather complacent about the world in which he lived, Bourdieu was consistently critical of it. If Parsons stood aloof from society, in the final analysis, Bourdieu was always deeply engaged with it. Where Parsons saw science and society as based on consensus, Bourdieu took an agonistic view, seeing society as always potentially contested. Science in particular was an arena of competition and struggle through which truth emerges. Where Parsons brushed aside intellectual and political antagonisms that divided the academy, Bourdieu made them definitive of the academic field, of scientific progress.

Their divergence is most clear in the way they built their theoretical frameworks. Parsons's (1937) voluntaristic theory of action, which, like Bourdieu, sought to transcend the dichotomy of structure and agency, laid claim to a grand synthesis of four canonical thinkers – Durkheim, Weber, Marshall and Pareto. Later, he would incorporate Freud. Parsons not only basked in the glory of canonical figures, but he actually created the canon himself by examining their writings in meticulous detail. He brought Durkheim and Weber to the centre of the US sociological tradition.[2] He is not alone in building on so-called founders: Jürgen Habermas (1984) follows a similar strategy in his two-volume theory of communicative action, building on the work of Marx, Weber, Durkheim, Simmel, Lukács and the Frankfurt School, as well as Talcott Parsons himself.

Bourdieu, by contrast, took a dismissive stance toward his competitors and forerunners, largely silencing the giants upon whose shoulders he was perched. There is rarely a systematic engagement with any sociological work other than his own. Marx, Weber, Durkheim, Lévi-Strauss, Pascal and others lurk in his writings, but he refers to them only in passing, as if to do otherwise might minimise his own contributions. He presents himself as the author of his own tradition, committing the sin he accuses other intellectuals of, namely their adhesion to the 'charismatic ideology' of autonomous 'creation', forgetting that the creator too has to be created (Bourdieu, 1996 [1992]: 167). In recreating sociology, Bourdieu fashioned himself after Flaubert, whom he regarded as the creator of the French literary field because he had such a subtle command of its elementary forces. If sociology is a combat sport, then Bourdieu was its grand master, so effective that the combat is invisible, taking place back-stage.

Parsons was the great systematiser, ironing out differences and contradictions, generating thereby his ever-more elaborate architecture of structural functionalism with its own concepts and vocabulary, liable to collapse under its own weight. Bourdieu, by contrast, refused all systematisation. His works are incomplete, full of fissures and paradoxes, a labyrinth that provides for endless discussion, elaboration and critique. As a gladiator he was the expert at defensive manoeuvres to elude his assailants. Whereas Parsons specialised in grand theory, at home with rarefied abstractions, far removed from the concrete, everyday world, Bourdieu rarely wrote without empirical reference. For all its difficulty – its long and winding sentences that continually double back and qualify themselves – Bourdieu's theorising is deeply engaged with lived experience and follows rich research agendas. Where Parsons's architectonic scheme disappeared without so much as a whimper once its founder passed away, its brittle foundations having lost touch with the world, Bourdieu's ideas outlive their author and are far more flexible in their wrestling with an ever-changing reality.

Unlike Parsons – and more like Marx, Weber and Durkheim – Bourdieu was steeped in the history of philosophy and, like them, his works are relentlessly empirical, ranging from the study of photography, painting, literature and sport to the analysis of contemporary stratification, education, the state and language. His writings straddle sociology and anthropology, including studies of peasant family strategies in the villages of the Béarn, where he was born, as well as his books on Algeria that dwelt on the social order of the Kabyle, written during the period of anti-colonial struggles and marking the beginning of his research career. His methods range from sophisticated statistical analysis to in-depth interviewing and participant observation. His meta-theoretical innovations, relentlessly applied to different historical contexts and different spheres of society, revolve around his notions of field, capital and habitus. Even though Parsons was well versed in anthropology, economics and psychology as well as sociology, in the end even he cannot compete with Bourdieu's originality or scope, nor with his influence across such a range of disciplines in the social sciences and humanities.

Parsons was like a vacuum cleaner, sucking in everything that came into his sphere of influence, whereas Bourdieu was more like a mop, pushing backwards and forwards in all directions. The imagery of the one was consensus building; the imagery of the other was combat; their divergence was reflected in the social theories they developed. Let me turn to that link between sociology as a combat sport and the substance of Bourdieu's social theory.

UNMASKING DOMINATION

Symbolic domination is at the centre of Bourdieu's sociology. It is a domination that is not recognised as such, either because it is taken for granted (naturalised) or because it is misrecognised – i.e. recognised as something other than domination. For Bourdieu, the prototype of symbolic domination is masculine domination that is not generally perceived as such, so deeply is it inscribed in the habitus of both men and women. He defines habitus – a central concept in his thinking – as a 'durably installed generative principle of regulated improvisations', producing 'practices which tend to reproduce the regularities immanent in the objective conditions of the production of their generative principle' (Bourdieu, 1977 [1972]: 78). We are thus like fish swimming in water, unaware of the symbolic domination that pervades our lives, except that the water is not just outside us, but also inside us. Drawing on his fieldwork among the Kabyle, Bourdieu (2001 [1998]) describes the way gender domination is inscribed in daily practices, in the architecture of houses and in the division of labour, so that it appears as natural as the weather.

In modern society, education provides one of Bourdieu's most important examples of symbolic domination (Bourdieu & Passeron, 1977 [1970]; 1979 [1964]). The school appears as a relatively autonomous institution following universal rules and eliciting the active participation of teachers and students in the acquisition of labour market credentials. This meritocratic order obscures the bias of the school, whose pedagogy favours those middle- and upper-class students endowed with cultural capital, i.e. those already equipped with the capacity to appropriate mental and abstract teaching – the symbolic goods on offer. The school advantages the dominant classes and reproduces their domination through the participation of the dominated, a participation that holds out the possibility of upward mobility, thereby misrecognising the class domination that it reproduces as its basis.

More generally, the dominant classes obscure their domination behind the distinction they display in the cultural sphere (Bourdieu 1984 [1979]). Their familiarity with high culture – what Bourdieu calls legitimate culture – is not viewed as an attribute of their class, but a gift of the individual. The dominated are ashamed of their inadequate appreciation of legitimate culture, sometimes pretending to claim knowledge of it that they don't have and endowing it with a prestige that obscures its basis in class-determined cultural capital. Dominated cultures are just that – dominated by material necessity, on the one hand, and by the distinction of legitimate culture, on the other.

We will have reason to interrogate these claims in later conversations, but for now I am concerned with the implications of symbolic domination for Bourdieu's conception of sociology as a combat sport. If society is held together by symbolic domination that misrecognises the grounds of class domination or gives it false legitimacy, then the task of the sociologist is to unmask the true function of the symbolic world and reveal the domination it hides. This, however, proves to be a most difficult task – symbolic domination is rooted in the habitus, i.e. in dispositions that lie deep in the unconscious, inculcated from childhood onwards. Even leaving aside the question of habitus, Bourdieu maintained that the dominant classes have no interest in unmasking domination, whereas the dominated do not have the capacity – the instruments of sociological knowledge – to see through domination:

> The sociologist's misfortune is that, most of the time, the people who have the technical means of appropriating what he says have no wish to appropriate it, no *interest* in appropriating it, and even have powerful interests in refusing it (so that some people who are very competent in other respects may reveal themselves to be quite obtuse as regards sociology), whereas those who would have an interest in appropriating it do not have the instruments for appropriation (theoretical culture etc.). Sociological discourse arouses *resistances* that are quite analogous in their logic and their manifestations to those encountered by psychoanalytical discourse (Bourdieu, 1993 [1984]: 23).

From a theoretical point of view, therefore, dislodging symbolic power would seem to be virtually impossible, requiring 'a thoroughgoing process of countertraining, involving repeated exercises' (Bourdieu, 2000 [1997]: 172), but this never deterred Bourdieu from combatting it wherever and whenever he could.

COMBAT IN THE PUBLIC SPHERE

From early on, Bourdieu's scholarly career went hand in hand with public engagement. Formative of his outlook on sociology and politics was his immersion from 1955 to 1960 in the Algerian war, first enlisted in the army and then as an assistant professor at the University of Algiers. It was here that he turned from philosophy that seemed so remote from the Algerian experience to ethnology, or what we might call a sociology of everyday life. His earliest writings displayed a fascination with the diverse traditions of the Algerian people, but it was not long before he broached the question of the day – the question of liberation – and how colonialism was creating struggles that were transforming the cultural and political aspirations of the colonised.

On his return to France, he would write blistering articles on the violence of colonialism. Soon, however, his sociological research led him away from brutal colonial violence to an analysis of symbolic violence, in particular the way education reproduced class domination. His two books on education, both written with Jean-Claude Passeron, especially the second and better known, *Reproduction in Education, Society and Culture* (1977 [1970]), became controversial for their uncompromising refusal to entertain the view that education can transform society. In the 1970s, rather than write of burgeoning social movements from below, as other sociologists, such as Alain Touraine, were doing, Bourdieu examined the way language and political science conspired to dispossess the dominated, effectively making them voiceless in the political arena. Opinion polls, with their artificial construction of public opinion, served as an archetypal instrument of disempowerment. For Bourdieu, democracy hid the struggle within the field of power among elites whose appeal for popular support was driven not so much by a concern for the dominated, but by manoeuvres within this field of the dominant.

As he ascended the academic staircase, converting his academic capital into political capital, he became more radical. He used his position as professor at the Collège de France, which he assumed in 1981, to draw attention to the limits of educational policy, and began to direct his attacks at the academy. Still, at the same time, he placed his hope in the potential universality of the state and the creation of an International of intellectuals. In the 1990s he deliberately gave voice to the down-trodden in the best-seller *The Weight of the World* (Bourdieu et al. 1999 [1993]), a collaborative work of interviewing immigrants, blue-collar workers and low-level civil servants – in short, the dominated. He joined social struggles, most famously the general strike of 1995 that opposed the dismemberment of the welfare state. He spoke out against the socialist government that was socialist in name, but neoliberal in content. As he aged, so his assaults on neoliberalism and the distortions of the media, especially television, took a popular turn in the book series Liber-Raisons d'Agir. Gone were the long and tortured sentences, and in their place he delivered uncompromising attacks written in an apocalyptic tone. Neoliberalism, he warned, meant the subjugation of education, art, politics and culture to the remorseless logic of the market, not to mention the 'flexploitation' of workers and their ever-more precarious existence.

His combative spirit in the public sphere, however, collided with his theoretical claims. For a long time Bourdieu had been contemptuous of sociological interventions in politics – social movement sociology or 'charitable sociology', as he once called it (Bourdieu, Passeron & Chamboredon, 1991 [1968]: 251). He insisted that sociology had to be a science with its own autonomy, its own language and its own methods inaccessible to all but the initiated. He had dismissed the idea of the organic intellectual as a projection of the habitus and conditions of existence of intellectuals onto the benighted, yet here he was on the picket lines, leading the condemnation of the socialist government. Having insisted on the depth of symbolic violence, how could he work together with the subaltern? Was he just manipulating them for his own ends, as he accused others of doing? If the social struggles of the subaltern are misguided, rooted in a misrecognition of their own position, was Bourdieu being led astray by joining workers in their protests? We don't know – his practice was at odds with his theory, and he never cared to interrogate the contradiction. This is what he writes in *Acts of Resistance*:

> I do not have much inclination for prophetic interventions and I have always been wary of occasions in which the situation or sense of solidarity could lead me to overstep the limits of my competence. So I would not have engaged in public position-taking if I had not, each time, had the – perhaps illusory – sense of being forced into it by a kind of legitimate rage, sometimes close to something like a sense of duty. ...

And if, to be effective, I have sometimes had to commit myself in my own person and my own name, I have always done it in the hope – if not of triggering mobilization, or even one of those debates without object or subject which arise periodically in the world of the media – at least of breaking the appearance of unanimity which is the greater part of the symbolic force of the dominant discourse (Bourdieu, 1998: vii–viii).

Here, Bourdieu is attributing a certain rationality – you might say good sense – to the publics he is addressing that they don't have in his earlier writings.

This is the first paradox, the *paradox of public engagement* – the simultaneous claim of its impossibility and its necessity. It leads to the second paradox, the *paradox of relative autonomy*. In fighting neoliberalism, Bourdieu finds himself defending the very autonomy of educational, cultural and scientific fields that earlier he had claimed were responsible for the reproduction of domination. In the end, he finds himself defending the great institutions of French culture, notwithstanding their role in reproducing domination. A child of the French Enlightenment, Bourdieu claims that these institutions he condemns – the state, the university, literature and art – do have a universal validity and do represent a rich cultural heritage that should be accessible to all.

You might say Bourdieu is defending not the status quo ante, i.e. the relative autonomy of these institutions, but their full autonomy, so that they become the privilege of all. Yet if this is the case, then it is an entirely utopian project, so that the paradox remains: defending the relative autonomy of cultural fields against market invasion is the defence of the very thing he denounces – symbolic domination. But in calling for the defence of the cultural, bureaucratic and educational fields, he can rally the interests of intellectuals, artists and academics – fractions of both the dominant classes and the new middle classes – against market tyranny.

COMBAT IN THE ACADEMIC FIELD

It is easier for intellectuals and academics to attack the excesses of the market than to see themselves exercising symbolic domination over society by virtue of the autonomy they so stoutly defend. While intellectuals denounce physical violence throughout the world, they are reluctant to recognise that they too are the perpetrators of violence, i.e. a symbolic violence that assures a taken-for-granted – what Bourdieu calls 'doxic' – submission to domination incorporated in bodies and language. Thus, although they may see themselves as autonomous, intellectuals are implicated in the state through its monopoly of the legitimate use of symbolic violence, through consecrated classifications and categories.

But intellectuals, academics and social scientists are not all of a piece. While most do not recognise their contribution to symbolic domination, some, like Bourdieu's followers, do spell out the truth of symbolic domination. This division of intellectuals into those who have a good sense and those who have bad sense calls for an analysis of academic fields that reveals what we are up to behind our screens of objectivity and science, pointing to the ways we deceive both ourselves and others. In short, the sociology that we apply to others must equally be applied to ourselves. The purpose of such reflexivity, however, is not to denounce our fellow scientists, but to liberate them from the illusions – scholastic fallacies – that spring from the conditions under which they produce knowledge, namely their freedom from material necessity. Bourdieu criticises his fellow academics for not recognising how their material conditions shape their knowledge production, and so they mistakenly foist their theories onto the subjects whose actions they theorise. For Bourdieu, to better understand the conditions of the production of knowledge is a condition for producing better knowledge.

This sounds very fine in principle, but in practice the scientific field, no less than any other field, is a combat zone in which actors struggle to enforce their view of the world – their theories, methodologies and philosophies. Indeed, Bourdieu (2000 [1997]: 116) refers to the scientific field as one of 'armed competition' in which some actors manage to accumulate capital at the expense of others. He assumes, however, that the rules of such combat ensure the production of truth – or, more accurately, the reduction of falsehood – even though, as he says in his article on the scientific field, there is an ever-increasing concentration of capital with its own conservative tendencies. What happens to that open competition for truth when the scientific field is monopolised by a few powerful actors? What assures the ascendancy of good sense over bad sense, Bourdieusian sociologists over neoliberal economists? Are there rules of combat or does anything go?

In his own practice of science Bourdieu can be quite ruthless in establishing his domination. As already mentioned, he devotes little time to recognising the contributions of others, tending to constitute himself as the soul originator of his ideas. He may be standing on the shoulders of giants, but they are invisible, repressed below the surface. He seems to deploy the recognition of others in footnotes and acknowledgements to maximise the recognition that he receives. His very writing is a form of symbolic violence, trying to impress upon the readers his own distinction through esoteric references, appeals to Greek and Latin, and long-winded sentences, all of which have an intimidating effect. Those who dare to openly disagree with him – if they are sufficiently important – are deemed to suffer from irrationality, weak-mindedness or even psychological disorders manifested in repression and defence mechanisms. Or, more simply, they express the interests that they have by virtue of their place in the academic field. He exercises symbolic violence within the field of science against these infidels, all in the name of the Realpolitik of reason and to unmask symbolic violence in the wider society. Throughout, he is so sure that he is right that any stratagem to vanquish the opposition seems justified. Here, combat often appears not as self-defence, but as 'unfair attacks' on enemy combatants.

While happy to locate others in the academic field and explain their perspectives in terms of that position, he fails to apply the same principle to himself. The nearest we get to such a self-analysis are his claims to outsider status, coming as he did from a peasant background with a 'cleft habitus', that allows him greater insight into the workings of the academy and, indeed, of the world. His *Sketch for a Self-analysis* (Bourdieu, 2007 [2004]) is just that – a sketch that describes his sufferings in boarding school and as an outsider in the École Normale Supérieure, but tells us next to nothing of Bourdieu as a combatant in the scientific field. Indeed, Bourdieu never undertook a sociological investigation of the field of sociology, in which he was indeed a, if not the, central player – the French field. The nearest he gets is *Homo Academicus* (Bourdieu, 1988 [1984]) which is an incomplete examination of the French academic field as a whole – an examination of the relations among disciplines, but not the disciplinary field itself.

Here, then, we come to the third paradox, *the paradox of reflexivity*. On the one hand, he argues that an analysis of the academic field in which one operates is a precondition of scientific knowledge. On the other hand, he himself undertakes neither an analysis of his own place in the field of sociology nor even an analysis of the field of French sociology itself, as if none of his competitors is worthy of serious examination. Bourdieu's interest in reflexivity – i.e. in scientifically assessing the field of sociology and his position in it – clashes with his interests as an actor, namely to accumulate academic capital, which means to elevate the status of sociology and his position within it. To accomplish these ends, Bourdieu mobilises the cultural capital that derives from a philosophy degree at the École Normale Supérieure and builds a school of sociology with its own vocabulary, methodology, theory, journal, etc. It involves disrecognising others and exercising symbolic domination over them, which, if successful, is at odds with the project of reflexivity and endangers the very project of science.

In these three paradoxes – the public engagement of sociologists, the relative autonomy of fields, the reflexivity of scientific analysis – we see the contradiction between theory and practice. But according to Bourdieu's own theory, this is to be expected – there is always a gap between theory and practice. We find this argument in all his meta-theoretical writings from *Outline of a Theory of Practice* (1977 [1972]) to *The Logic of Practice* (1990 [1980]) to *Pascalian Meditations* (2000 [1997]). He shows the necessity of the rupture between sociological understanding and common sense, between theory and practice, and how practice reproduces this separation. If people truly understood what they do, if they understood how their practices reproduce their subordination, then the social order would crumble. But for all his interest in reflexivity, Bourdieu does not turn this analysis back onto *himself* and examine the ways in which *his* theory and practice are at odds with each other. There is no internal conversation between Bourdieu and Bourdieu, between his theory and practice.

The following engagements with Bourdieu, therefore, will study the paradoxical relations among and within the three nodes of Bourdieu's meta-framework: how he condemns symbolic domination, but defends the very institutions that reproduce that domination; how he advocates reflexivity by locating intellectuals within their fields of production, but fails to do the same for himself; and, finally, how he is critical of public engagement and yet this becomes so central to his own identity.

CONVERSATIONS WITH BOURDIEU

Bourdieu's model of sociology as a combat sport certainly casts doubt on the conventional collective self-understanding of scientists as building science through consensus. In his celebrated model, Robert Merton (1973 [1942]) defines the ethos of science as made up of four elements: universalism, communism, disinterestedness and organised scepticism. Competition there is, but this does not take the form of a combat sport in which the goal is to defeat the opposition! Yet of course, inasmuch as science is a field in the Bourdieusian sense, it must have relations of domination and subjugation that play themselves out as combat. To deny those relations of domination, as is the wont of the dominant, is itself a strategy of domination. It is not surprising, therefore, that Parsons and Merton should have a consensus view of science. On the other hand, to endorse the idea of sociology as a combat sport without any further elaboration of the rules of that combat also excuses opportunistic strategies of disrecognition, expropriation and distortion that are inimical to science.

Here I want to consider a third model of science, one based on dialogue. The idea is not to suppress difference in the name of consensus, but to recognise difference as a challenge to existing assumptions and frameworks. Here one challenges not in order to vanquish, but rather to converse in order to better understand others and, through others, learn the limits and possibilities of one's own assumptions and frameworks. A model of dialogue is not exclusive of the other two models. In order to converse, there must be some common ground to make conversation intelligible. An inner circle of agreement is necessary for an outer circle of disagreement. Equally, in order to converse, it is necessary to give voice to subordinate perspectives, which usually requires combat. In a field of domination, conversation cannot be taken for granted, but has to be advanced and defended.

In the conversations that follow, we will bring to life some of the combatants Bourdieu has slain. I will follow Bourdieu's prescription that to read an author it is necessary to first place him or her in the context of the field of production – competitors, allies and antagonists who are taken for granted by the author and invisibly shape his or her practice. I cannot recreate all the academic fields within which Bourdieu was embedded. That would be a task far beyond my capabilities, covering as it would philosophy, linguistics, literature, painting and photography, as well as sociologists and anthropologists – indeed, the entire French intellectual field. So I have chosen a distinctive group of social theorists who wander like ghosts through Bourdieu's opus, because, unlike Bourdieu, they believe the dominated, or some fraction thereof, can indeed under certain conditions perceive and appreciate the nature of their own subordination. I am, of course, thinking of the Marxist tradition that Bourdieu engages, usually without so much as recognising it, and even to the point of denying it a place in his intellectual field. This is ironic indeed, but perhaps not surprising, since these social theorists were all experienced combatants, very much Bourdieu's equals.

In staging these conversations with Bourdieu, I have chosen Marxists with distinctive perspectives on the place awarded to intellectuals in social theory and public life, namely Gramsci, Fanon, Freire and Beauvoir.

I begin with Marx, perhaps the greatest gladiator of them all, whose Achilles heel is undoubtedly the absence of a theory of intellectuals, and I end with C. Wright Mills, no mean combatant himself, who erected a theoretical architecture similar to Bourdieu's.

While Marx did not pay serious attention to the question of intellectuals – their place in society or their labour process – his theory of capitalism as a self-reproducing and self-destroying system of production is nonetheless deeply embedded in Bourdieu's treatment of fields of cultural and intellectual production. The underlying structure of Bourdieu's thought is similar to Marx and Engels's engagement with Hegelian thought laid out in *The German Ideology* (1978 [1845–46]), but Bourdieu carries it forward in a very different direction, toward the study of cultural fields rather than the economic field. From Marx we turn to Gramsci and his theory of intellectuals that turns on the understanding of hegemony – a notion at first glance similar to, but in the final analysis profoundly different from, Bourdieu's symbolic domination. When asked to explain the difference between his own work and that of Gramsci, Bourdieu dismisses the very question. Yet I shall show that this conversation is pivotal to all the others.

Frantz Fanon, whose account of the colonial revolution is in many ways parallel to that of Bourdieu (their stays in Algeria overlapped), suffers the same fate as Gramsci. There is no serious engagement, but only an occasional contemptuous dismissal of Fanon's writings on the colonial revolution as dangerous, speculative and irresponsible. There is no reference to *Black Skin, White Masks* (1967 [1952]), which is an exemplary treatment of the symbolic violence of racism. From Fanon we turn to Freire, whose point of departure is quite similar to Bourdieu's – a deep-seated cultural domination or internalised oppression. But the solution is to develop a distinct pedagogy of the oppressed that liberates them from oppression. Although Freire is not mentioned by name, we can presume that Bourdieu would dismiss him along with other forms of critical pedagogy calling for the transformation of education. Having no confidence in the common sense of the oppressed, Bourdieu would reject a pedagogy that relies on dialogue and focus instead of making the dominant culture accessible to all.

We turn next to Simone de Beauvoir, whose account of masculine domination as symbolic violence predates and surpasses the account Bourdieu offers in his book, *Masculine Domination* (2001 [1998]), which makes only one reference to Beauvoir. The reference is not to *The Second Sex* (1989 [1949]), but to Beauvoir as the unknowing victim of Sartre's symbolic violence. This is a travesty. Beauvoir's account of masculine domination as symbolic domination is not only superior to Bourdieu's, but always seeks emancipatory challenges to that domination, although liberation only comes with socialism. I then turn from Beauvoir to C. Wright Mills, whose accounts of methodology and stratification, and their public engagements are astonishingly parallel, especially when one takes into account the differences in historical and national contexts. We can see that Mills is the American Bourdieu or Bourdieu is the French Mills, both borrowing from, but also careful to separate themselves from, Marxism. I end with a conversation between Bourdieu and myself. Instead of speaking through the voices of other Marxists, I speak in my own voice, bringing my interpretations of domination, based on my ethnographic work in capitalism and state socialism, into dialogue with Bourdieu, reconstructing my own understanding of capitalism and state socialism, while questioning the depth of Bourdieu's symbolic domination.

If Parsons presented the growth of theory as based on consensus, papering over conflicts and emphasising synthesis, and if Bourdieu presented the growth of theory as based on combat, repressing the other, I present the growth of social science as based on dialogue. Here, each side learns about its assumptions and its limits through discussion with others, leading not to some grand synthesis, not to mutual annihilation, but to reconstruction. The growth of Marxism has always relied on an engagement with sociology as its alter ego, and in our era the pre-eminent representative of sociology is Pierre Bourdieu, and so he provides the impetus for the reconstruction of Marxism for the 21st century.

Bourdieu in South Africa

What I find so striking when reading Bourdieu in South Africa is how alert his texts are to the textures of social order, how acutely conscious they are of the accumulated weight of centuries of social structure that define 'the way things are', and how light that weight seems, embedded as it is in language and embodied in practices that have evolved gradually over time. His analysis is fine-tuned to the intimacies of domination and subordination – to the way they are inscribed in bodies, language and psyches.

Our own social reality appears to be the polar opposite – fractured, contested, disputative, disorderly, violent. In contrast to Bourdieu's account of profoundly stable domination, reproduced as it is through the social structure of field, habitus and symbolic violence, we have challenge, reversal and constant shifts in meaning. The order of apartheid was ruptured and overthrown by countless initiatives that entailed not only resistance, but the formation of counter-orders. Symbolic violence is 'a gentle violence, imperceptible and invisible even to its victims' (Bourdieu, 2001 [1998]: 2); South African violence has been throughout its colonial history, and still is, rough, physical, all too visible in battered, punctured and dying bodies, whether it is police violence against strikers, subaltern violence against foreigners or domestic violence against women.

So why read Bourdieu in South Africa?

It may be that Bourdieu's very attentiveness to the question of order helps us to think about the limits of order and the contestation over these limits. One of our problems is how to think about resistance, about social fragmentation, about disorder, about pervasive violence – which should necessarily mean paying attention to different kinds of order as well. Local orders that emerge 'from below', formed by subaltern communities and activities and not infrequently shaped by elements of pre-colonial culture and practice, as well as by new networks and organisational forms, may support or subvert state orders. All too often, it seems that the master categories of sociology – state and society, bureaucracy and industrialisation, class, development, modernity – struggle to encompass our realities, and instead of illuminating them, impose a grid of concepts that leave us dissatisfied and with the sense that something crucial has been left out; not to speak of the sense such sociology gives us that our society is something less than it ought to be, or that we have not yet arrived at our destination, at a place we can feel is somehow whole and explicable.

Bourdieu clearly finds the master categories of sociology inadequate, and so he reworks sociology, inventing and refashioning concepts so as to explore domination, order and social reproduction. To do this, he draws from his ethnographic studies among the Kabyle in Algeria, conducted using a different disciplinary framework – anthropology. This is interesting: whereas sociology and its master categories evolved in a systematic attempt by social scientists in the West to understand their societies' transition to modernity, anthropology was designed as its sister discipline, with the purpose of understanding non-Western 'traditional societies', and to do this it had to adopt a conceptually more flexible, open-ended approach. It had its master categories to be sure, but decolonisation and the post-colonial world challenged its implicit assumptions profoundly.

When the anthropological gaze is turned back on the West, it sometimes sees things freshly and proves itself able to adopt a conceptual inventiveness in ways that sociology may find difficult to do. The discipline that arose to codify the West's view of the 'other' may provide social scientists with a way to look at the West differently, through different categories, precisely as an other – and may even provide social scientists from the South with the tools for 'provincialising' the West and its social science. To some degree, this is what happens with Bourdieu, with his rethinking of the state, for example (1994).

It should also be said that what anthropology lacks – in contrast to sociology – is precisely the firm structure provided by a deep conceptual grid such as the state–society–economy triad. This too is evident as a lack in much of Bourdieu's work – the focus on discrete fields without a theory of civil society; the silence about the dynamics of economic transformations and their impact on social processes, for example.

Leaving these questions aside, though, Bourdieu's focus on the mechanisms of order and the concepts he finds it necessary to elaborate in order to explore this – field, habitus, classification, cultural capital, symbolic domination and symbolic violence – may point us towards exactly the sites that must be examined if we are to think about the limits of order. Symbolic violence may help us to think about physical violence; habitus may help us to think about resistance.

It is also possible that the subtlety of Bourdieu's thinking about domination and order may alert us to the processes of ordering beneath a surface that appears unruly and fragmented, pointing towards deep continuities of domination and racial ordering derived from our colonial and apartheid past, as well as subaltern formations of resistance and counter-order. Many aspects of South African society – from the brutal facts of economic control and the distribution of poverty to the subtle ordering produced in language and symbols – are deeply shaped by this history, but in ways that remain opaque in public discourse precisely as a consequence of symbolic violence.

On the other hand, it may be that Bourdieu's concepts are rendered useless in our social reality, that they flutter about like moths caught in strong sunlight, out of their element, pointing to the need for other concepts. And indeed, one hopes that continuing interrogation of Bourdieu's work by the light of our social reality has the potential not only to generate new insights in our own research, but also to unsettle metropolitan sociology and shake up its master categories, contributing to a robust engagement – whether in the form of combat sport or dia-logue – between centre and periphery, North and South, the West and 'most of the world', as Partha Chatterjee puts it.

These conversations with Bourdieu are set up essentially as a series of dialogues between Marxists and Bourdieu, choreographed by a Marxist, Michael Burawoy. This too resonates with South African sociology, which in its most creative and prolific wing – that is to say, its progressive wing – is Marxist or Marx-inspired. This sociology has concentrated on social transformations, colonisation and its impact on traditional society, industrialisation, state formation, agrarian transformation, urbanisation, class formation, patriarchy, changing labour regimes, trade unionism, urban resistance and so on. This is a rich sociology of transition, trans-formation and struggle. Why, then, contemplate a conversation with Bourdieu? Surely we have within the Marxist sociological tradition in South Africa and within the broader international resources of Marxism sufficient conceptual apparatus to wrestle with our reality?

Our Marxism tends to suffer from a similar problem to our sociology. It too works with master categories through which capitalism is analysed – schemas of change and assumptions about transitions between modes of production, revolution and reform, classes and state, class struggle and ideology, capitalism and socialism, social movements and resistance – which too often are mapped quite crudely onto our social reality. Marxism tends towards reductionism in its analysis of such salient features of our history and our present as colonialism, racism and ethnicity.

Many South African Marxists are currently so intent on finding the signs of a class movement and the prospects for an alternative future that they grapple insufficiently with the contradictions, ambiguities and complexity of the present. The workings of democracy, state efforts at redistribution and development, far-reaching policy innovations, and, on the other hand, working-class xenophobia, popular prejudice, racial and ethnic identities, the intractability of patriarchy, repertoires of violence, social fragmentation, lawlessness, the fragility of authority – these remain little explored, and so the sociology of change seems disconnected from the actual social changes taking place all around us.

To take one example: Marxist analysis of post-apartheid society tends towards a ritualistic denunciation of neoliberalism and the neoliberal state – concepts that are assigned tremendous and far-reaching explanatory power, but which quite ignore other, equally important, dimensions of state functioning. Post-apartheid South Africa has seen an explosion of redistributive social spending by the state, with the building of 2.3 million houses and the dramatic expansion of social grants from 2.5 million recipients in 1996 to 14.5 million in 2010 constituting two of the most obvious achievements. On the other hand, sections of the state are increasingly dominated by processes of elite formation, including patronage and corruption, and by its status as the symbolic site for the assertion of African sovereignty (Von Holdt, 2010a). Neither of these dimensions can be reduced to 'neoliberalism'.

Given these weaknesses within current sociological Marxism in South Africa, dialogue between Marxism and Bourdieu, with his concentration on symbolic domination and the reproduction of social order, may contribute to the regeneration of South African Marxism, inviting it to rethink its assumptions and its ways of seeing.

There is something else as well. Bourdieu, with his emphasis on the construction of scholarly fields and on the necessity for reflexivity regarding scholarly practices, invites us to consider a matter to which we are too often blind: the racial structure of South African sociology and what this may mean for the nature of the analytical narratives it establishes.

The canonical authorities of South African sociology are virtually all white. It may be responded that the white authors of mainstream sociology are mostly progressive and Marxist, aligning themselves broadly with the interests of the oppressed and on the side of democracy. These points may be true as far as they go, but what is the significance of the racial structure of this field for the production of knowledge and the search for truth? Is it not necessarily the case that most white scholars, lacking the experience of racial oppression – and not only that, but experiencing the structures of racial oppression as *dominants*, and therefore as beneficiaries and protagonists of its symbolic violence – are likely to have a limited feel for its place in social reality and therefore in the scholarly analysis of social reality? To take this point further, white scholars have a direct stake, emotional as much as material, in continuing to underplay the significance of racial power.

And indeed, Marxist sociology (in contrast to the communism of the South African Communist Party) has tended to treat national oppression, racism and racial discrimination as epiphenomena in relation to the narrative of capitalist accumulation, class domination and class struggle – something that Marxism allows all too well. Thus, Black Consciousness and the national liberation movement were regarded with a profound scepticism: their focus on epiphenomena was an index of their petty bourgeois class base. In the 1970s many in the white student Left, rejected as 'liberal' by black students who were developing the theories and practices of Black Consciousness at the time, turned to Marxism and involvement in the fledging trade union movement (Ally, 2005). Progressive white scholars took an analogous turn in the scholarly field, writing against white liberal historiography, on the one hand, and the national liberation movement and its associated communist movement, on the other.

It is not only the question of race that is important, however; it is also a question of the extent to which the scholarly field reproduces the hegemony of the Western canon, and with it the symbolic violence of hegemonic rationality against the rest of the world – what Bourdieu calls the imperialism of reason. In this logic, South Africa becomes simply the local site of a global logic of development or, in its Marxist manifestation, of capitalist accumulation and reproduction. This question is not entirely separate from the racial one, since there are a multitude of reasons why white scholars with a settler background might feel more at ease reproducing the Western canon – in which Bourdieu, of course, is a towering figure – than seeking a position of critique founded in the 'periphery'. What is required, in the words of Suren Pillay (2009), is not only a deracialisation of knowledge production, but its decolonisation.

The power of white scholars to define the stakes and rules of the scholarly field, and to shape its analytical narratives, its curricula and its themes may appear to be invisible, but is all too visible to many black students and staff. The symbolic violence of white seniority and authority is alive and replicated in the academy. The scholarly establishment may comfort itself that the new generation of black scholars and researchers will confine themselves to amplifying the sanctified narratives through their better ability to conduct research in townships and workplaces, but already they are subverting, contesting and reconstructing the dominant narratives.[3] Race plays a critical part in this, as do new narratives about our colonial history and post-colonial reality, and a reconsideration of the canon itself, including Bourdieu. New forms of combat in the scholarly fields of sociology and its sister disciplines should therefore be anticipated and welcomed.

NOTES

1   See the responses of Anderson (2002), Duneier (2002) and Newman (2002) to Wacquant's (2002) attack on their work.

2   There is, of course, an element of combat in Parsons too, for example, in the way he deals with Marx at a time when Marxism was enjoying a certain renaissance in US sociology: '[J]udged by the standards of the best contemporary social-science theory, Marxian theory is obsolete' (1967: 132). Marx was a 'social theorist whose work fell entirely within the nineteenth century … he belongs to a phase of development which has been superseded' (1967: 135).

3   For recent interventions, see Ally (2005), Buhlungu (2006), Naidoo (2010) and Pillay (2009).

THEORY AND PRACTICE

MICHAEL BURAWOY

Marx Meets Bourdieu

> *The historical success of Marxist theory, the first social theory to claim scientific status that has so completely realized its potential in the social world, thus contributes to ensuring that the theory of the social world which is the least capable of integrating the theory effect – that it, more than any other, has created – is doubtless, today, the most powerful obstacle to the progress of the adequate theory of the social world to which it has, in times gone by, more than any other contributed.*
>
> Bourdieu (1991 [1984]: 251)

What is Bourdieu saying here? The historical success of Marxism is to have constituted the idea of class out of a bundle of attributes shared by an arbitrary assemblage of people, what he calls 'class on paper'. Aided by parties, trade unions, the media and propaganda – an 'immense historical labor of theoretical and practical invention, starting with Marx himself' (Bourdieu, 1991 [1984]: 251) – Marxism effectively called forth the working class as a real actor in history, an actor that otherwise would have had only potential existence. However, Marxism did not see itself as constituting the working class, but as discovering and then reflecting the prior existence of an objective class that was destined to make history in its own image. Marxism did not have the tools to understand its own effect – 'theory effect' – without which there would be no 'working class'. In short, Marxism did not comprehend its own power – the power of its symbols – and thus missed out on the importance of symbolic domination.

But why does Marxism constitute such a 'powerful obstacle to the progress of the adequate theory of the social world' (Bourdieu, 1991 [1984]: 251) *now*, if before it had been so successful? Here I conjecture the answer to be as follows. In failing to recognise the symbolic world, Marxism fails to anticipate the emergence of fields of symbolic production – fields of art, literature, science, journalism – that engender their own domination effects, overriding and countering Marxism's symbolic power. Marxism cannot understand that a classification or representational struggle has to precede class struggle, i.e. classes have to be constituted symbolically before they can engage in struggle. Unable to compete in the classification struggle, Marxism loses its symbolic power and the working class retreats back to a class on paper, no longer the effective actor that it was. When the economic was being constituted as an autonomous field in 19th-century Europe, Marxism had a firm grasp of reality, but with the rise of cultural, scientific and bureaucratic fields, Marxism lost its grip on reality and its theory became retrograde.

Bourdieu never examines his claims about Marxism, but that is precisely what we will do, starting with Marx himself. I will let Marx respond through a dialogue with Bourdieu, taking as my point of departure their common critique of philosophy. From there I construct a conversation that reveals their divergent theories, showing how the one ends up in a materialist cul-de-sac and the other in an idealist cul-de-sac. Each breaks out of the prison he creates, but in ways he cannot explain, which becomes the paradox of the gap between theory and practice.

THE CRITIQUE OF PHILOSOPHY

Uncanny parallels join Marx and Engels' critique of the 'German Ideology' (Marx & Engels, 1978 [1845–46]) and Bourdieu's critique of 'scholastic reason' in *Pascalian Meditations* (2000 [1997]). In *The German Ideology*, Marx and Engels settle accounts with Hegel and the Young Hegelians, just as in *Pascalian Meditations* Bourdieu settles his scores with his own philosophical antecedents. Both condemn philosophy's disposition to dismiss practical engagement with the world. As Marx writes in the first Thesis on Feuerbach, the German philosophers elevate the theoretical attitude as the 'only genuinely human attitude', while practice is only conceived in 'its dirty-judaical manifestation'. Bourdieu's immersion in the Algerian war of independence and his experience of the raw violence of colonialism made nonsense of his philosophical training at the École Normale Supérieure.

Still, *Pascalian Meditations* is Bourdieu's culminating theoretical work in which Pascal is presented as an inspirational philosophical break with philosophy, centring the importance of the practice of ordinary people, emphasising symbolic power exercised over the body and refusing pure philosophy emanating from the heads of philosophers. *The German Ideology*, by contrast, is not a culminating work, but an originating work that clears the foundations for Marx's theory of historical materialism and materialist history. The different titles reflect their different location in the biography of each of their authors, but the argument against philosophy is, nonetheless, surprisingly similar.

Let us begin with Marx and Engels scoffing at the Young Hegelians who think they are making history, when they are but counter-posing one phrase to another:

> As we hear from German ideologists, Germany has in the last few years gone through an unparalleled revolution. The decomposition of the Hegelian philosophy ... has developed into a universal ferment into which all the 'powers of the past' are swept. ... It was a revolution besides which the French Revolution was child's play, a world struggle beside which the struggles of the Diadochi appear insignificant. Principles ousted one another, heroes of the mind overthrew each other with unheard-of rapidity and in the three years 1842–45 more of the past was swept away in Germany than at other times in three centuries. All this is supposed to have taken place in the realm of pure thought (Marx & Engels, 1978 [1845–46]: 147).

Here is Bourdieu's attack on modern and postmodern philosophers:

> Now, if there is one thing that our 'modern' or 'postmodern' philosophers have in common, beyond the conflicts that divide them, it is this excessive confidence in the powers of language. It is the typical illusion of the *lector*, who can regard an academic commentary as a political act or the critique of texts as a feat of resistance, and experience revolutions in the order of words as radical revolutions in the order of things (Bourdieu, 2000 [1997]: 2).

The argument is the same: we must not confuse a war of words with the transformation of the real world, the things of logic with the logic of things.

But how is it that philosophers mistake their own world for the real world? The answer lies in the fact that they are oblivious to the social and economic conditions under which they produce knowledge. For Marx, it is simply the division of mental from manual labour that permits the illusion that ideas or consciousness drives history:

> Division of labour only becomes truly such from the moment when a division of material and mental labour appears. *From this moment onwards consciousness can really flatter itself that it is something other than consciousness of existing practice*, that it *really* represents something without representing something real; from now on consciousness is in a position to emancipate itself from the world and to proceed to the formation of 'pure' theory, theology, philosophy, ethics, etc. (Marx & Engels, 1978 [1845–46]: 159; emphasis added).

Emancipated from manual labour, upon which their existence neverthe-less rests, philosophers imagine that history is moved by their thought. 'It has not occurred to any one of these philosophers', Marx and Engels (1978 [1845–46]: 149) write, 'to inquire into the connection of German philosophy with German reality, the relation of their criticism to their own material surroundings.' In identical fashion, Bourdieu argues that philosophers fail to understand the peculiarity of the material conditions that make it possible to produce 'pure' theory:

> But there is no doubt nothing more difficult to apprehend, for those who are immersed in universes in which it goes without saying, than the scholastic disposition demanded by those universes. There is noth-ing that 'pure' thought finds it harder to think than *skholè*, the first and most determinant of all the social conditions of possibility of 'pure' thought, and also the scholastic disposition which inclines its possessors to suspend the demands of the situation, the constraints of economic and social necessity (Bourdieu, 2000 [1997]: 12).

The scholastic disposition calls forth the illusion that knowledge is freely produced and that it is not the product of specific material condi-tions. Bourdieu does not limit his critique of the scholastic fallacy – i.e. repression of the conditions peculiar to intellectual life – to philosophers, but broadens it to other disciplines. He criticises anthropologists, such as Lévi-Strauss, and economists for universalising their own particular experience, foisting their abstract models onto the recalcitrant practice of ordinary mortals. Only sociologists, reflexively applying sociology to themselves and, more generally, to the production of knowledge, can potentially appreciate the scholastic fallacy of others, and the necessary separation of theory and practice.

In Bourdieu's eyes – and here I am imputing an argument to Bourdieu that, as far as I know, he never made – Marx contravenes his own critique of idealism and becomes the perpetrator of a scholastic fallacy. He is guilty of inventing the idea of the proletariat that carries the burden of humanity by fighting against dehumanisation to realise another scholastic invention – communism – a world community populated by renaissance individuals, rich in needs and varied in talents. These ideals are but the projection of the intellectuals' sense of alienation from their own conditions of existence. Real workers, Bourdieu would argue, are only concerned to better their material conditions of existence, bereft of such lofty Marxian dreams. Just as Bourdieu could turn Marx against Marx, so, as we will see, Marx could turn Bourdieu against Bourdieu. For the moment, it is sufficient to note that both Marx and Bourdieu insist on a break with the logic of theory by turning to the logic of practice.

FROM HISTORICAL MATERIALISM TO COEXISTING FIELDS

Out of these common critiques of philosophy arise divergent social theories. Since Bourdieu's social theory is so clearly a response to Marx, we should begin with the latter. For Marx, the logic of practice refers to economic practice, understood as the concrete social relations into which men and women enter as they transform nature. These social relations form the mode of production with two components: the forces of production (relations through which men and women collaborate in producing the means of existence, including the mode of cooperation and the technology it deploys) and the relations of production (the relations of exploitation through which surplus is extracted from a class of direct producers and appropriated by a dominant class). The mode of production gives rise to Marx's three histories: (1) history as a succession of modes of production – tribal, ancient, feudal and capitalist; (2) history as the dynamics of any given mode of production as the relations of production first stimulate and then fetter the expansion of the forces of production – a theory that Marx only works out for capitalism; and (3) history as the history of class struggle that propels the movement from one mode of production to another when the material conditions of such a transition are met. Capitalism gives way to communism, which, being without classes and thus without exploitation, is not a mode of production. The key to history lies in the mode of production, but it is only within the capitalist mode of production that the direct producers, i.e. the working class, through their struggles come to recognise their role as agents of revolution.

Bourdieu will have no truck with such economic reductionism, such a theory of history and of the future, this projection of intellectual fantasies onto the benighted working class. But let us proceed step by step. When Bourdieu turns to the 'logic of practice', he goes beyond economic activities to embrace activities in all arenas of life, and furthermore those activities are seen less in terms of 'transformation' and more in terms of bodily practices that lead to and evolve from the constitution of the habitus, the inculcation of dispositions of perception and appreciation. Here is how Bourdieu defines habitus in *Outline of a Theory of Practice*:

> The habitus, the durably installed generative principle of regulated improvisations, produces practices which tend to reproduce the regularities immanent in the objective conditions of the production of their generative principle, while adjusting to the demands inscribed as objective potentialities in the situation, as defined by the cognitive and motivating structures making up the habitus (Bourdieu, 1977 [1972]: 78).

The habitus generates practices that, like moves in a game, are regulated by the regularities of the social structure and in so doing they reproduce these structures. But practices and knowledge are bound together by the body whose importance the intellectualist vision misses. The social order inscribes itself in bodies; that is to say, we learn bodily and express our knowledge bodily – all under the organising power of the habitus, itself largely unconscious.

The notion of habitus gives much greater weight and depth to the individual, who in Marx is simply the effect or carrier of social relations. Nevertheless, in the account of these social relations, Bourdieu's notion of field draws on and generalises certain features of Marx's concept of mode of production, or at least his conception of the *capitalist* mode of production elaborated in *Capital*. Indeed, underlining the parallels, Bourdieu refers to the *political economy of symbolic goods* (science, art, education). As with the capitalist mode of production, so with the notion of field, individuals are compelled to enter relations of competition in order to accumulate capital according to the rules of the marketplace. Bourdieu's fields have the same character, each having their own distinctive 'capital' that agents seek to accumulate, bound by rules of competition that give the field a certain functional integrity and relatively autonomous dynamics. If there is any overall historical tendency of fields, it is toward the concentration of field-specific capital, as when Bourdieu (1975) writes of the scientific field as being dominated by those who increasingly monopolise scientific capital.

However, there are fundamental differences between Marx and Bourdieu. In Bourdieu's field, most fully elaborated for the literary field in *Rules of Art* (Bourdieu, 1996 [1992]), but also in his account of the scientific field, the notion of exploitation, so essential to Marx, is absent. Instead we have a field of domination governing the struggle between the consecrated incumbents and the new challengers, the avant-garde. It is as if capitalism were confined to just the competition among capitalists, which is, of course, how conventional economics thinks of the economy. Indeed, the only book Bourdieu devotes to the economy as such, *The Social Structures of the Economy* (2005), focuses on the role of habitus and taste in the matching of supply and demand for different types of housing. It is all about the social underpinnings of the housing market. There is no attempt to study housing from the standpoint of its production process – from the standpoint of construction workers, for example. The very concept that is definitive of the capitalist economy for Marx, namely exploitation, is absent in Bourdieu's concept of the field.

More to the point, the architecture of fields is profoundly different in the two theories. In Marx, there is essentially just one major field – the capitalist mode of production with its inherent laws of competition leading to crises of overproduction and falling rates of profit, on the one hand, and the intensification of class struggle, on the other. The only thing holding back the demise of capitalism is its superstructure, composed of, you might say, a series of subsidiary fields – legal, political, religious, aesthetic and philosophical. Bourdieu transposes the base–superstructure model into a system of coexisting fields. Although the economic field is, in some undefined sense, still dominant and threatens the autonomy of other fields, Bourdieu pays attention to the inner workings of the 'super-structure' that in Marx is more or less dismissed as epiphenomenal.

No less fundamental is the way they conceive of the relation among fields. If Marx has a *historical succession* of economic fields, Bourdieu has a *functional coexistence* of fields. Bourdieu's multiplication of coexisting fields poses a host of new problems with respect to the relations among fields, which is why one axis of differentiation and struggle within any field is over its autonomy/heteronomy with respect to other fields, usually the economic field. In his later writings, Bourdieu engages in a polemical defence of science and culture, education, and politics against the corrosive influence of the invading economy. The creation of the literary field in 19th-century France required the break from bourgeois literature, on the one hand, and social realism, on the other, to an autonomous literature-for-literature's sake. But autonomy brings with it another kind of relation among fields, a relation of *misrecognition*. The autonomy of the educational field or of various cultural fields leads to the misrecognition of their contribution to the reproduction of relations in other fields, most notably class relations in the economic field. Whether in *distinction* or in *reproduction*, the pre-existence of class structure is taken as given and the focus is on how culture or education simultaneously secure and obscure class domination.

The coexistence of fields raises a further question: that of their effect on the action of individuals as they move across fields. In Marx, individuals are only studied in one field and there they act out the imperatives of the relations in which they are embedded. Bourdieu's analysis is more complex, for he has to ask how individuals nurtured in one field behave in another field – how do students coming from peasant families (as opposed to the urban middle classes) behave within the educational sphere? Does it make no difference or is there something in their cultural capital or their habitus that makes them behave differently? Each field may have its logic, but sometimes the strength of the habitus that agents bring from another field – the peasant who comes to town – may lead to a tension, conflict or even rupture with the new order in what he calls a 'misfiring' of habitus. It is the durability of the habitus that can lead to what Bourdieu calls *hysteresis* – how an individual's inherited and obdurate habitus inhibits adaptation to successive fields.

Bourdieu's favourite example of hysteresis is the devaluation of educational credentials that, in his view, explains the student protest of May 1968. In *Homo Academicus*, Bourdieu (1988 [1984]) describes how the expansion of higher education created an oversupply of assistant lecturers whose upward mobility was consequently blocked. The ensuing tension between aspirations and opportunities not only affected the young assistants, but students more generally, who found that their degrees did not give them access to expected jobs. The result was a discordance between class habitus and the labour market in a number of fields simultaneously, so that their normally disparate temporal rhythms were synchronised, merging into a general crisis conducted in a singular public time and producing an historical event that suspended common sense.

This is a repotted version of the theory of relative deprivation that once informed so much social psychology and social movement theory. It does not take seriously the self-understanding of the actors, nor even the resources they have at their disposal. The disjuncture of habitus and field, expectation and opportunity, disposition and position is always a potential source of change, but we need to know when it leads to adjustment to the field, when it leads to innovation and when it leads to rebellion. In these regards, Bourdieu's theory of habitus has little to offer – even less than Robert Merton's (1968 [1947]) famous essay on social structure and anomie that more systematically examined the consequences of the gap between aspirations and possibilities, namely, rebellion, ritualism, retreatism, innovation and conformity. In Bourdieu's hands, habitus remains a black box, yet one that is nonetheless essential to thinking about the effects of mobility between fields both on the individual and on the transformation of the fields themselves.

We can now put the two models side by side: Marx's succession of modes of production through history with its problematic dynamics and transition, its unjustified linear progress to communism; and Bourdieu's unspecified totality made up of coexisting and homologous fields with unexamined and untheorised interrelationships. If Marx's totality is governed by a richly developed base and a weakly understood superstructure, Bourdieu's unspecified history can at best be seen as the development of a differentiated set of fields with no mechanisms of propulsion, reminiscent of Durkheim's or Spencer's models of differentiation, or Weber's coexisting value spheres. Thus, in Bourdieu's account, the Kabyle form an undifferentiated society without the separate fields that characterise advanced societies, but there is no notion of how one gets from the undifferentiated to the differentiated society. Or, to put it even more crudely: if Marx's theory of history is deeply flawed, Bourdieu has no theory of history, even if his work is historically rooted.

SYMBOLIC DOMINATION: FROM WEAK TO STRONG

Marx's strong sense of social transformation is accompanied by a weak theory of symbolic domination, in contrast to Bourdieu's strong theory of social reproduction, at the heart of which is symbolic domination. Still, there remains an uncanny convergence in the way they both conceive of symbolic domination. Let us return to *The German Ideology* and to the much-quoted passage on ideology:

The ideas of the ruling class are in every epoch the ruling ideas: i.e. the class which is the ruling material force of society, is at the same time its ruling intellectual force. The class which has the means of material production at its disposal, has control at the same time over the means of mental production, so that thereby, generally speaking, *the ideas of those who lack the means of mental production are subject to it* (Marx & Engels, 1978 [1845–46]: 172; emphasis added).

Here, Marx and Engels advance from a dismissal of ideology (in contradistinction to science) to the real effects of those illusory ideas in sustaining the domination of the dominant class. We do not know, however, what they intended when they wrote that the dominated class, i.e. those who don't have access to the means of mental production, are *subject to* the ruling ideas. Bourdieu takes up the issue and sees subjection as deep and almost irreversible:

Symbolic violence is the coercion which is set up only through the consent that the dominated cannot fail to give to the dominator (and therefore to the domination) when their understanding of the situation and relation can only use instruments of knowledge that they have in common with the dominator, which, being merely the incorporated form of the structure of the relation of domination, make this relation appear as natural; or, in other words, when the schemes they implement in order to perceive and evaluate themselves or to perceive and evaluate the dominators (high/low, male/female, white/black, etc.) are the product of the incorporation of the (thus neutralized) classifications of which their social being is the product (Bourdieu, 2000 [1997]: 170).

The parallels are astonishing, except that Bourdieu puts symbolic violence at the centre of his account. For Marx, of course, symbolic violence does not only originate from the superstructure, but is powerfully present within the economic base itself. Exploitation itself is mystified by the very character of production, which hides the distinction between necessary and surplus labour, since workers appear to be paid for the entire work day. Participation in the market leads to commodity fetishism wherein the objects we buy and sell and those we consume are disconnected from the social relations and human labour necessary to produce them. Again, the essence of capitalism is mystified.

For Marx, however, these expressions of ideology – whether ideology is understood as ruling ideas or as lived experience – are dissolved through class struggle, leading the working class to see the truth of capitalism, on the one hand, and their role in transforming it, on the other:

> It is not a matter of what this or that proletarian or even the proletariat as a whole *pictures* at present as its goal. It is a matter of *what the proletariat is in actuality*, and what in accordance with this *being,* it will historically be compelled to do. Its goal and its historical action are prefigured in the most clear and ineluctable way in its own life-situation as well as in the whole organization of contemporary bourgeois society. There is no need to harp on the fact that a large part of the English and French proletariat is already *conscious* of its historic task and is continually working to bring this consciousness to full clarity (Marx & Engels, 1978 [1845–46]: 134–35).

This optimistic teleology is deeply flawed. For the proletariat to rid itself of the 'the muck of ages', as Marx and Engels put it in *The German Ideology* (1978 [1845–46]: 193), is not so easy. Only under unusual circumstances does class struggle assume an ascendant path, intensifying itself as it expands. On the contrary: through its victories, through the concessions it wins, its revolutionary tempo is dampened and its struggles come to be organised, most frequently *within* the framework of capitalism. In this, the state, under-theorised by Marx, plays a key role. In such a context, the symbolic violence of dominant ideologies incorporated in lived experience prevails over the cathartic effect of struggle.

Bourdieu indicts the whole Marxist tradition – and not just Marx – for its revolutionary optimism, labelling it an intellectualist fantasy or scholastic illusion, and then bends the stick in the opposite direction:

> And another effect of the scholastic illusion is seen when people describe resistance to domination in the language of consciousness – as does the whole Marxist tradition and also the feminist theorists who, giving way to habits of thought, expect political liberation to come from the 'raising of consciousness' – ignoring the extraordinary inertia which results from the inscription of social structures in bodies, for lack of a dispositional theory of practices. While making things explicit can help, only a thoroughgoing process of countertraining, involving repeated exercises, can, like an athlete's training, durably transform habitus (Bourdieu, 2000 [1997]: 172).

What this 'countertraining' might look like is never elaborated. Whether class struggle might be a form of 'countertraining' is especially unclear, because Bourdieu never entertains the idea of class struggle or even allows for 'collective resistance' to the dominant culture. The working classes are driven by the exigencies of material necessity, leading them to make a virtue out of a necessity. They embrace their functional lifestyle rather than reject the dominant culture. An alternative culture remains beyond their grasp, because they have neither the tools nor the leisure to create it (Bourdieu, 1984 [1979]: chap. 7).

Having thus written off the working classes as incapable of grasping the conditions of their oppression, Bourdieu is compelled to look elsewhere for ways of contesting symbolic domination. Having broken from a fallacious logic of theory to the logic of practice and having discovered that the logic of practice is no less fallacious, he breaks back to the logic of theory, to the emancipatory science of sociology and to struggles within the dominant class. Let us follow his argument.

FROM CLASS STRUGGLE TO CLASSIFICATION STRUGGLE

In his writings on the period 1848–51 in France, Marx has a complex analysis of the struggles among the fractions of the dominant class that cannot be summarised here. Suffice to say that intellectuals played a significant role. In a succinct paragraph in *The German Ideology*, Marx and Engels wrote of a cleavage within the dominant classes, between its economic part and its intellectual part, as follows:

> The division of labour ... manifests itself also in the ruling class as the division of mental and manual labour, so that inside this class one part appears as thinkers of the class (its active conceptive ideologists, who make the perfecting of the illusion of the class about itself their chief source of livelihood), while the others' attitude to these ideas and illusions is more passive and receptive, because they are in reality the active members of the class and have less time to make up the illusions and ideas about themselves. Within this class this cleavage can even develop into a certain opposition and hostility between the two parts (Marx & Engels, 1978 [1845–46]: 173).

Without referring to Marx, Bourdieu calls these the dominant and dominated fractions of the dominant class, giving the latter a 'chiastic' structure in which one part is well endowed with economic capital (and relatively low in cultural capital), while the other is well endowed with cultural capital (and relatively low in economic capital). Bourdieu, too, recognises the conflict between the two fractions, but casts that conflict in terms of struggles over categories of representation – so-called classification struggles. Recognising that intellectuals are the source of ruling ideology – 'the illusion of the class about itself' – Bourdieu also sees the possibility of their generating a symbolic revolution that can shake the 'deepest structures of the social order':

> Likewise, the arts and literature can no doubt offer the dominant agents some very powerful instruments of legitimation, either directly, through the celebration they confer, or indirectly, especially through the cult they enjoy, which also consecrates its celebrants. But it can also happen that artists or writers are, directly or indirectly, at the origin of large-scale symbolic revolutions (like the bohemian lifestyle in the nineteenth century, or, nowadays, the subversive provocations of the feminist or homosexual movements), capable of shaking the deepest structures of the social order, such as family structures, through transformation of the fundamental principles of division of the vision of the world (such as male/female opposition) and the corresponding challenges to the self-evidences of common sense (Bourdieu, 2000 [1997]: 105).

It is not clear whether this 'shaking' will actually undermine the domination of the dominant class; there is not even a hint that it will create opportunities for the dominated to challenge their subjugation. One has to ask, therefore, what are the interests that lie behind any such 'symbolic revolution'?

As the dominated fraction of the dominant class, intellectuals are in a contradictory position. Certain parts may identify with the dominated classes and, indeed, try to represent the latter's interests. As such, they may even pursue an agenda hostile to the dominant class as a whole. In the final analysis, however, it is an intellectualist illusion that they share interests with the dominated, as there is little basis for an enduring connection between intellectuals born out of *skholé* and workers born into material necessity.

Rather than turning to any presumed universalism from below, Bourdieu commits himself to what he calls the Realpolitik of reason, the pursuit of universality that is wired into the character of the state:

> Those who, like Marx, reverse the official image that the State bureaucracy seeks to give of itself and describe the bureaucrats as usurpers of the universal, acting like private proprietors of public resources, are

not wrong. But they ignore the very real effects of the obligatory reference to the values of neutrality and disinterested devotion to the public good which becomes more and more incumbent on state functionaries in the successive stages of the long labor of symbolic construction which leads to the invention and imposition of the official representation of the State as the site of universality and the service of the general interest (Bourdieu, 2000 [1997]: 124).

In this remarkable passage, written at the very time he is attacking the French state for continuing to violate its public function, in which the (conservative) right hand of the state is displacing the (socialist) left hand, when the state is openly pursuing an aggressive assault on the working class, Bourdieu is also appealing to its 'disinterested devotion to the public good' that will, he claims, eventually assert itself against the state's usurpers. In the long run, therefore, the state will become the carrier of the general interest, but how?

The idea of universality will not prevail simply because it is an attractive ideal – that would be the worst form of idealism – but because there are certain fields that by their very functioning, by virtue of their internal struggles, give rise to a commitment to the universal:

In reality, if one is not, at best, to indulge in an irresponsible utopianism, which often has no other effect than to procure the short-lived euphoria of humanist hopes, almost always as brief as adolescence, and which produces effects quite as malign in the life of research as in political life, it is necessary I think to return to a 'realistic' vision of the universes in which the universal is generated. To be content, as one might be tempted, with giving the universal the status of a 'regulatory idea', capable of suggesting principles of action, would be to forget that there are universes in which it becomes a 'constitutive' immanent principle of regulation, such as the scientific field, and to a lesser extent the bureaucratic field and the judicial field; and that, more generally, as soon as the principles claiming universal validity (those of democracy, for example) are stated and officially professed, there is no longer any social situation in which they cannot serve at least as symbolic weapons in struggles of interests or as instruments of critique for those who have a self-interest in truth and virtue (like, nowadays, all those, especially in the minor state nobility, whose interests are bound up with universal advances associated with the State and with law) (Bourdieu, 2000 [1997]: 127).

Let us recall that Bourdieu sets out on his journey with a critique of scholastic reason that misses the ways in which theoretical models, such as those of 'rational choice' or 'deliberative democracy', are but projections of the very specific conditions under which academic knowledge is produced. After turning from this fallacious logic of theory to the logic of practice and finding there only misrecognition, Bourdieu returns to the same universalities produced in the scientific, legal and bureaucratic fields, universalities that he had earlier called into question as scholastic fallacies – the product of the peculiar circumstances of their production. But now he turns to them as the source of hope for humanity.

We are back with the Enlightenment, with Hegel's view of the state criticised by Marx as portraying a false universality that masks the interests of the dominant class by presenting them as the interests of all. Not just Marx, but Weber too saw the danger that such universality would become a formal rationality and, thus, the perfection of domination. We can see this Enlightenment faith in Bourdieu's proposals for an International of intellectuals, recognising that they are a corporate body with their own interests, but at the same time regarding them as the carriers of universalism and forming a corporatism of the universal. They are what Alvin Gouldner (1979) calls a flawed universal class. Bourdieu was not only organising intellectuals, but paradoxically he was also to be found on the picket lines of striking workers, haranguing them about the evils of neoliberalism – even as he claimed they could not understand the conditions of their own oppression. No different from the people he studied, he too created a gap between his theory and his practice, especially when his theory led him into a political cul-de-sac.

CONCLUSION

Marx and Bourdieu set out from similar positions, but they end up in divergent places. They both start out as critics of intellectualist illusions or scholastic fallacies that privilege the role of ideas in the making of history. They both move to the logic of practice, but where Marx remains wedded to this logic, seeing in it a future emancipation realised through working-class revolution, Bourdieu sees it as a cul-de-sac mired in domination. So he breaks away from the logic of practice back to the practice of logic and to a faith in reason, whether embodied in an International of intellectuals or the universality of the state. In short, if Bourdieu starts out as a critic of philosophy and ends up as a Hegelian, believing in the universality of reason, Marx also starts out as a critic of philosophy, but ends up with material production, but no considered place for intellectuals or for himself. Marx cannot explain how he produced his theory of capitalism, sitting in the British Museum removed from the working class and writing in a place remote from their experiences. We are on the horns of a dilemma: intellectuals without the subaltern or the subaltern without intellectuals.

Each recognises the dilemma and, in his practice, each breaks with his theory: Bourdieu joins workers as allies in the struggle against the state, while Marx battles with intellectuals as though the fate of the world depended on it. Can we bring theory and practice closer together? Gramsci, with his theory of hegemony and intellectuals, seeks to do just that, trying to transcend the theoretical opposition: faith in the subaltern, on the one hand, and in intellectuals, on the other. In the next conversation, we will see how he fares, and where this will leave Bourdieu.

KARL VON HOLDT

Bodies of Defiance

Bourdieu is interested in the subordinated body that the subaltern habitus predisposes to manual labour, as well as to deference, humility and a physical stance of submission. This immediately poses the question of the body in resistance. The body on strike is already a body of defiance, refusing the routines of subordination and of the supervisor's instruction, disrupting authority. Striking workers today chant songs with their roots in the freedom songs of the 1980s, dance the toyi-toyi war dance that originated in the military camps of Umkhonto we Sizwe, and carry sticks that they understand to symbolise acts of fighting or war.

Where does this – the refusal, the defiance – fit into the idea of habitus, which predisposes the dominated to find domination invisible and submit to it? Nor does the body of resistance only come into being at the moment of explicit collective mobilisation. In my study of workers' struggles at Highveld Steel in the apartheid era, workers talked about a continual resistance to the pace of white managers and their machinery, about an 'apartheid go-slow' on the part of African workers. Workers at the Daimler-Benz plant in East London wore wooden AK-47s strapped to their bodies on the production line, symbolising the connection between their struggles and the military struggle of the African National Congress (ANC), while supervisors locked themselves in their offices (Von Holdt, 1990). Can Bourdieu's theory account for the resistant body, the body that refuses the machinery and structures of domination?

According to Bourdieu (2000 [1997]: 182), historical critique is 'a major weapon of reflexiveness' which 'makes it possible to neutralise the effects of naturalisation'. For Bourdieu, it is the scholar who has the time and occupies a location that makes it possible to pursue this task. The first strike I went to after arriving in Johannesburg in 1986 was an occupation strike in a big engineering works. Hundreds of workers were gathered in a solid and disciplined phalanx, toyi-toying slowly up the main roadway between the factory buildings. Many were bearing cardboard shields and steel replicas of spears turned on factory lathes, and in front of them whirled and danced two of the strike leaders, their factory overalls supplemented with animal furs and beads, referencing pre-colonial culture and resistance to colonial conquest.

History is not something that is solely available to social scientists toiling away in scholarly fields; it is available to be appropriated and reinvented and marshalled afresh by subalterns. In the colony, history is embodied. The bodies of the colonised constitute a site of struggle in the form of conquest and resistance, and in the various endeavours of colonial authority to order and subdue the subject body. Racial classification systems – which reached their apogee under apartheid – provide the foundation for physical and symbolic assault. When the railway strikers in 1987 made use of traditional medicine to protect them before going out to confront the guns of the police, they were drawing on all the resources of their history. Rationalists may point out that the bullets drew blood anyway, but if the medicine gave the strikers strength to challenge the apartheid order, is that not how apartheid was brought to the negotiating table?

In the colonial experience, history has a bodily presence that has to be accommodated in any attempt to make use of Bourdieu's concept of habitus or of bodily dispositions; it may not be impossible for anthropologists or sociologists to make similar arguments about the subordinated body in the metropolis.

In Bourdieu, for the most part, habitus and symbolic violence fit the embodied individual – the social body – seamlessly into social structure, so that social reality appears most of the time as ordered and coherent, and domination becomes natural and invisible. This is how Bourdieu resolves the opposition between agency and structure, but he does so in a way that removes agency from the picture. 'The body is in the social world but the social world is in the body', so that the body can only act in accordance with the social world, by which it is *'pre-occupied'* before it acts (Bourdieu, 2000 [1997]: 142, 152). This comes close to constituting a tautological circle that allows little room for agency or volition.

In contrast, the colony poses the question of the *limits* of order and the limits of authority's power to occupy the body. The potentiality of the body for defiance is present within the body of submission, corresponding to the distinction James C. Scott (1990) draws between 'the public transcript' of deference and submission and the 'hidden transcripts' of resistance. It is quite intriguing to read the early Bourdieu on the anti-colonial struggle in Algeria: in his account of settler colonialism, racialised oppression is totally transparent and resistance is inevitable – to the extent that it requires no explanation (Bourdieu, 1962 [1961]). This is, of course, too simple an account of colonial domination, as we shall see in the conversation between Frantz Fanon and Bourdieu, but its interest lies in the contrast with his later work on the invisibility of domination in the West.

Echoes of the Algerian experience do surface at critical moments in Bourdieu's text, particularly when he considers the possibilities of social change and the disruption of domination. Contradictory positions in social structure may generate 'destabilised habitus, torn by contradiction and internal division, generating suffering', and the same effect may occur 'when a field undergoes a major crisis and its regularities (even its rules) are profoundly changed'; this happens 'in situations of crisis or sudden change, especially those seen at the time of abrupt encounters between civilisations linked to the colonial situation or too-rapid movements in social space'. But, strangely, this disjunction does not culminate in collective struggle; instead, Bourdieu emphasises the difficulty agents then have 'in adjusting to the newly established order', and the durability of these now maladjusted dispositions creates the 'Don Quixote effect': the disoriented individual is reduced to tilting at windmills and the possibility of subaltern mobilisation to restructure the field itself is elided (Bourdieu, 2000 [1997]: 160–61).

But the question of subaltern agency reappears several times in Bourdieu's text, mostly as a possibility to be gestured towards rather than something fully explored. Thus, 20 pages from the passage discussed above, we find the following:

> The specifically political action of legitimation is always carried out on the basis of the fundamental given of original acceptance of the world as it is, and the work of the guardians of the symbolic order, whose interests are bound up with common sense, consists in trying to restore the initial self-evidences of *doxa*. By contrast, the political action of subversion aims to liberate the potential capacity for refusal which is neutralised by misrecognition, by performing, aided by a crisis, a critical unveiling of the founding violence that is masked by the adjustment between the order of things and the order of bodies (Bourdieu, 2000 [1997]: 181).

For Bourdieu, it is only intellectuals who can see through the silent 'self-evidences' of the given order of things. But what if in the colonial world it is domination that is self-evident? Then what becomes of subaltern agency and intellectuals' monopoly of the power to understand?

Notwithstanding their ambiguities and briefness, it is these passages in Bourdieu that I read most avidly, gesturing as they do to our history of resistance and contestation, and at the fractured and endlessly subverted reality we inhabit in Johannesburg today – which demonstrates so forcefully the limits of authority in post-apartheid South Africa; and they seem to gain an added charge of theoretical explosiveness precisely because of their sparseness and elliptical brevity, surrounded as they are by the overwhelming accumulated weight of domination that is the main emphasis of his texts, as Michael points out.

When Bourdieusian theory, drawing on anthropological insights into indigenous society in the colonies and elaborated in the advanced capitalism of France, is returned to Johannesburg and South Africa, it is confronted by disjunction, fragmentation and subversion, where passages such as those I have quoted above are the ones that really make sense. They need to be expanded and elaborated on.

Colonial and post-colonial realities that are deeply structured by their 'founding violence', by domination and by the uneven distribution of power suggest that the social world may better be understood as contradictory, inconsistent, polyvocal, paradoxical, and full of tensions and uncertainties than as a coherently structured order. In this case, the habitus too should be regarded as complex and contradictory, where different dispositions may be at odds with one another and a particular disposition may even be dogged by a shadow counter-disposition, to which at times the individual may give way. When considered in this way, the relationship between habitus and social world, while structured, is not seamless. The potentiality of the body of defiance is present within the body of submission.

The subaltern has to be brought back in and theorised as an agent capable of mobilising to change the fields of domination.[1] But what kind of subalterns would these be? Would they be workers in their trade unions, which may bear at least a family resemblance to the labour organisations of classical sociology? Or the residents of informal settlements where the state has a minimal presence and is unable to impose its authority in the face of informal local elites who control land, law and punishment? Or the intellectuals, fighting back against the accumulated weight of the imperialism of reason? Does the agency and mobilisation of subalterns such as these bear any resemblance to Marx's conception of a working class whose historical agency is derived from its essential relationship with capitalism?

NOTES

1   As Jennifer Chun (2009) does in her study of the ways in which casualised workers and their organisations seek to challenge their labour market status in Korea and the United States.

CULTURAL DOMINATION

MICHAEL BURAWOY

Gramsci Meets Bourdieu

> It would be easy to enumerate the features of the life-style of the
> dominated classes which, through the sense of their incompetence,
> failure or cultural unworthiness, imply a form of recognition of the
> dominant values. It was Antonio Gramsci who said somewhere
> that the worker tends to bring his executant dispositions with him
> into every area of life.
>
> Bourdieu (1984 [1979]: 386)

> It's like when these days people wonder about my relations with
> Gramsci – in whom they discover, probably because they have
> [not] read me, a great number of things that I was able to find in
> his work only because I hadn't read him .... (The most interesting
> thing about Gramsci, who in fact, I did only read quite recently,
> is the way he provides us with the basis for a sociology of the
> party apparatchik and the Communist leaders of this period – all
> of which is far from the ideology of the 'organic intellectual' for
> which he is best known.)
>
> Bourdieu (1990 [1986]: 27–28)

This is an additional reason to ground the corporatism of the universal in a corporatism geared to the defense of well-understood common interests. One of the major obstacles is (or was) the myth of the 'organic intellectual,' so dear to Gramsci. By reducing intellectuals to the role of the proletariat's 'fellow travelers,' this myth prevents them from taking up the defense of their own interests and from exploiting their most effective means of struggle on behalf of universal causes.

Bourdieu (1989: 109)

If there is a single Marxist whom Pierre Bourdieu had to take seriously, it has to be Antonio Gramsci. The theorist of symbolic domination must surely engage the theorist of hegemony. Yet I can only find passing references to Gramsci in Bourdieu's writings. In the first reference above, Bourdieu appropriates Gramsci to his own thinking about cultural domination, in the second he deploys Gramsci to support his own theory of politics, and in the third he ridicules Gramsci's ideas about organic intellectuals.[1]

Given the widespread interest in Gramsci's writings during the 1960s and 1970s, when Bourdieu was developing his ideas of cultural domination, one can only surmise that the omission was deliberate. Bourdieu's allergy to Marxism here expresses itself in his refusal to entertain the ideas of the Marxist closest to his own perspective. He openly declares that he had never read Gramsci and that, if he had, he would have made his criticisms abundantly clear. Of all the Marxists, Gramsci was simply too close to Bourdieu for comfort.

Indeed, the parallels are remarkable. Both repudiated Marxian laws of history to develop sophisticated notions of class struggle in which culture played a key role, and both focused on what Gramsci called the super-structures and what Bourdieu called fields of cultural domination. Both pushed aside the analysis of the economy itself to focus on its effects – the limits and opportunities it created for social change. Their interest in cultural domination led both to study intellectuals in relation to class and politics. Both sought to transcend what they considered to be the false opposition of voluntarism and determinism, and of subjectivism and objectivism. They both openly rejected materialism and teleology, and instead emphasised how theory and theorist are inescapably part of the world they study.

If one is looking for reasons for their extraordinary theoretical convergence, their parallel biographies are a good place to begin. Unique among the great Marxist theoreticians, Gramsci – like Bourdieu – came from a poor rural background. They were similarly uncomfortable in the university setting, although for Gramsci this meant leaving the university for a life of journalism and politics, before being unceremoniously cast into prison by the fascist state. Bourdieu, by contrast, would make the academy his home, climbing to its very peak and becoming a professor at the Collège de France. It was from there that he made his sorties into political life. No matter how far removed they became from the rural world into which they were born, neither ever lost touch with that world. They both made the experience of the dominated or subaltern an abiding preoccupation.

Given the similarities of their social trajectories and their common theoretical interests, their fundamental divergences are all the more interesting – closely tied, one might conjecture, to the very different historical contexts or political fields within which they acted. Gramsci, after all, remained a Marxist and engaged with questions of socialism at a time when it was still very much on the political agenda, whereas Bourdieu distanced himself from Marxism, prefiguring what would become a post-socialist world. A conversation between Bourdieu and Gramsci built on their common interest in cultural domination promises to clarify their divergent politics. I begin such an imaginary conversation by tracing the intersection of their biographies with history, and then I draw out the parallels in their frameworks, before examining their divergent theories of cultural domination – hegemony versus symbolic violence – and their opposed theories of intellectuals.

PARALLEL LIVES OF PRACTICE

In seeking to comprehend human political interventions, Bourdieu's concept of habitus – the embedded and embodied dispositions acquired through life trajectories – invites us to examine the intersection of biography and history. The political lives of Gramsci and Bourdieu are the cumulative effects of four sets of experiences: (1) early childhood and schooling that saw each migrate from village to city in pursuit of education; (2) formative political experiences, i.e. Bourdieu's immersion in the Algerian revolution and Gramsci's participation in the politics leading up to the factory council movement; (3) theoretical development – for Bourdieu in the academy, for Gramsci in the communist movement; and (4) final redirections, in which Bourdieu moves from the university into the public sphere, while Gramsci is forced to retreat from party to prison. At each successive moment, Bourdieu and Gramsci carry with them a habitus or, as Gramsci (1971: 353) calls it, the précis of their past, which guides their interventions in new fields.

Both Gramsci and Bourdieu grew up in peasant societies. Gramsci was born in Sardinia in 1891; Bourdieu was born in 1930 in the Béarn in the Pyrenees. Both were children of local public employees: Bourdieu the son of a postman who became a clerk in the village post office; Gramsci the son of a clerk in the local land registry who was imprisoned on charges of malfeasance. Bourdieu was an only child, but Gramsci was one of seven children, all of whom played a major role in his early life. Both were very attached to their mothers – in both instances women from higher-status peasant backgrounds than their husbands. They both shone at school and by dint of willpower advanced from their poor villages to metropolitan centres, each with the support of devoted schoolmasters.

Undoubtedly, Gramsci's life was more difficult. Not only was his family far poorer, but he also suffered from the physical and psychological pain of being a hunchback. Only with his deep reserves of determination and with support from his elder brother could Gramsci in 1911 make his way to the mainland of northern Italy, after winning a scholarship to study philosophy and linguistics at the University of Turin. In similar fashion, Bourdieu would make his way to the preparatory lycée and then enter the École Normale Supérieure, where he studied philosophy, the apex of the French intellectual pyramid.

Coming from rural background to the urban metropolis, whether Turin or Paris, was daunting – both were fish out of water in the new middle- and upper-class milieu of the university. Bourdieu writes of his disjoint habitus: 'the durable effect of a very strong discrepancy between high academic consecration and low social origin, in other words a *cleft habitus*, inhabited by tensions and contradictions' (2007 [2004]: 100). Although they both became brilliant intellectuals and political figures, neither lost touch with the sources of his marginality, his village and his family. Gramsci's devotion to his family and rural mores is captured in his letters from prison, just as Bourdieu remained similarly close to his parents, returning home periodically to conduct field research. Their rural upbringing is deeply embedded in their dispositions and thought, whether by way of an obdurate legacy or a vehement reaction.[2]

Gramsci never finished university, but dived into Turin's working-class politics, which was heating up during the First World War. He began writing for the socialist newspaper *Avanti!* and also for *Il Grido*. After the war he became the editor of *L'Ordine Nuovo*, the magazine of Turin's working class, designed to articulate its new culture and destined to become the mouthpiece of the factory council move-ment and the occupation of the factories of 1919–20. Bourdieu, on the other hand, left university and after a year teaching in a lycée was drafted for national service in Algeria in 1955. He would remain in this war-torn country for five years, conducting field work when his mili-tary service was over, teaching at the university, and through his writ-ing representing the culture and struggles of the colonised, both in town and village. With the clampdown after the temporary setback to the anti-colonial movement in the 1957 Battle of Algiers, Bourdieu's position became untenable and he was forced to leave in 1960. Thus, in their formative years after university, both Gramsci and Bourdieu were fundamentally transformed by struggles far from their homes.

Even during these years, however, Gramsci was politically much closer to his protagonists than Bourdieu, whose political engagement mani-fested itself at a scientific distance. The bifurcated world of colonialism removed Bourdieu from the colonised, just as the class order of Italy thrust Gramsci, although an émigré from the semi-feudal Sardinia, into working-class politics. Accordingly, at this point the two men took very different roads. Following the defeat of the factory councils, Gramsci became a leader of the working-class movement, a founder member of the Communist Party in 1921, and its general secretary in 1924, precisely when fascism was consolidated. He spent time in Moscow with the Comintern and in exile in Vienna, but travelled throughout Italy after 1923 at a time when being an elected deputy gave him political immu-nity. This ended in 1926 when he was arrested under a new set of laws, and in 1928 he was brought to trial. The judge declared that Gramsci's brain must be stopped for 20 years. He was sent to prison where, despite contracting numerous and ultimately fatal diseases, he produced the most creative Marxist thinking of the 20th century – the famous *Prison Notebooks*. Ironically, it was the fascist prison that kept Stalin's preda-tors at bay. Gramsci's health deteriorated continuously, until he died in 1937 of tuberculosis, Pott's disease (which eats away at the vertebrae) and arteriosclerosis, just as an international campaign for his release was gaining momentum.

Bourdieu's trajectory could not have been more different. After Algeria, he passed into the academy, taking up positions in France's leading research centres and writing about the place of education in reproducing the class relations of French society. Bourdieu was to be elected to the prestigious chair of sociology at the Collège de France in 1981, which made him a pre-eminent public intellectual and in later years an inheritor of the mantle of Sartre and Foucault. From the beginning, his writings had political import and bearing, but they took on a more activist and urgent mission in the mid-1990s, especially with the return to power of the socialists in 1997. He publicly defended the dispossessed, attacked the ascendant technocracy of neoliberalism, and above all assailed the mass media and journalists in his book *On Television*. He undertook various publishing ventures, from the more academic *Actes de la Recherches en Sciences Sociales* to the more radical Liber-Raisons d'Agir book series. In his last years he would try to forge a 'collective intellectual' that transcended national and disciplinary boundaries, bringing together progressive minds to shape public debate.

If Gramsci moved from party political engagement to a more scholastic life in prison, where he reflected on the failed socialist revolution in the West, Bourdieu took the opposite path from the scholastic life to a more public opposition to the growing tide of market fundamentalism, even addressing striking workers and supporting their struggles. Gramsci's organic connection to the working class through the Communist Party exaggerated the revolutionary potential of the working class. Thus, in prison he devoted himself to understanding how the elaborate superstructures of advanced capitalism, which included not just an expanded state, but also the state's relation to the emergent trenches of civil society, 'not only justifies and maintains its domination but manages to win the active consent of those over whom it rules' (Gramsci, 1971: 245).

By contrast, Bourdieu's adoption of a more overt political posture toward the end of his life came with an already elaborated theory of cultural domination, one based on an analysis of strategic action within fields and its adjunct concept, habitus. In the late 1990s, finding the public sphere increasingly distorted by the media, Bourdieu assumed a more offensive posture, even to the extent of openly supporting protest movements. His spirited defence of intellectual and academic autonomy and his aggressive attacks on neoliberalism made him one of the most prominent public figures in France.

Gramsci's prison writings reflected on and advanced beyond his political practice. He wrote about the ideal Communist Party – the Modern Prince – but he could never find one in practice. If Gramsci's theory advanced beyond his practice, the reverse was true for Bourdieu in his last years. He burst onto the political scene without any warrant from his theorising, which pointed to actors lost in a cloud of misrecognition. Here, practice moved ahead of theory. To examine the respective disjunctures of theory and practice, we need to put their theories into dialogue with each other.

CLASS, POLITICS AND CULTURE

It is difficult to slice up these two bodies of theory into parallel and comparable segments, since each segment achieves meaning only in relation to the whole. Still, I will make parallel cuts into each body of theory, even at the cost of overlap and repetition. I begin with the two broad frameworks for the study of class, politics and culture that can be found in 'The Modern Prince' (Gramsci, 1971: 123–205) and *Distinction* (Bourdieu, 1984 [1979]). In these writings, both Gramsci and Bourdieu divide a social formation into parallel homologous realms – the economic, which gives us classes; the political-cultural, which gives us domination and struggle; and, for Gramsci, the military, which sets limits on struggle.

For Gramsci, the economy serves to provide the basis of class formation – working class, peasantry, petit bourgeoisie and capitalist class. The economy determines the objective strength of each class, while setting limits on the relations among those classes. But the struggles and alliances among classes are organised on the terrain of politics and ideology, a terrain that has its own logic. The political structure, for example, organises the forms of representation of classes in particular political parties. Each political order also has a hegemonic ideology, i.e. a hegemonic system of ideologies that provide a common language, discourse and normative visions shared by the contestants in struggle. Class struggle is not a struggle between ideologies, but a struggle over the interpretation and appropriation of a single ideological system. Alternative hegemonies emerge in moments of organic crisis, otherwise they have little support. Finally, there is a military order that, in relation to class struggle, for the most part is invisible, entering only to discipline the illegalities of groups and individuals or to restore order in times of fundamental crisis. Gramsci is as much concerned about its political moment, i.e. the subjective state of military personnel, as about the technical preparedness of the coercive forces.

Similarly, Bourdieu has homologous realms, with the major division between the economic and the cultural realm. Again, there is no analysis of the economic as such, and classes, as in Gramsci, are taken as given: dominant classes, petite bourgeoisie and working class. But classes cannot be reduced to the purely economic, and contain a combination of economic and cultural capital, so that the dominant class has a chiastic structure divided between a dominant fraction strong in economic and weak in cultural capital, and a dominated fraction strong in cultural and relatively weak in economic capital. Equally, the middle classes are also divided between the old petite bourgeoisie (emphasising economic capital) and the new petite bourgeoisie (emphasising cultural capital). Finally, the working class has a minimal amount of both types of capital, and so its members are forced into a life governed by material necessity.

Gramsci wheels his classes into the political arena, where their interests are forged and organised. Here we find political parties, trade unions, chambers of commerce and so forth representing the interests of given classes in relation to other classes, each battling to advance its own narrow corporate interests. Two classes – specifically capital and labour – also seek to reach the hegemonic level and represent their own interests as the interests of all. In parallel fashion, Bourdieu focuses on the way the cultural realm masks the class stratification upon which it is founded. Absorption in the practices of the dominant – 'legitimate' – culture hides the class-based cultural resources that make these practices possible. The appreciation of art, music and literature is possible only with a leisured existence and inherited cultural wealth, but it is presented as an attribute of gifted individuals. People are in the dominant class because they are gifted; they are not gifted because they are in the dominant class. All cultural practices – from art to sport, from literature to food, from music to holidays – are ranged in a hierarchy that is homologous to the class hierarchy. The middle classes seek to imitate the cultural practices of the dominant class, while the working class grants legitimacy by abstention – high culture is not for its members. They are driven by functional exigencies adapted to material necessity.

If for Gramsci the cultural realm is a realm of class struggle, for Bourdieu it dissipates class struggle. Struggle takes place within separate cultural fields or within the dominant classes, but it is not a class struggle. It is a classification struggle – a struggle over terms and forms of representation. Bourdieu never goes beyond classification struggles within classes to class struggle between classes, which perhaps explains why military force never appears in his theoretical accounts. These divergences between Gramsci's and Bourdieu's notions of politics require us to attend to the differences between two very different terrains of contestation – civil society and the field of power.

CIVIL SOCIETY VS. FIELD OF POWER

Gramsci's innovation was to periodise capitalism not in terms of the transformation of the economic base (competitive to monopoly capitalism, or laissez-faire to organised capitalism, etc.), but in terms of the rise of civil society – the associations, movements and organisations that are neither part of the economy nor the state. Thus, he was referring to the appearance of trade unions, religious organisations, media, schools, voluntary associations and political parties that were relatively autonomous from, but nevertheless guaranteed and organised by, the state. The 'trenches of civil society' effectively organised consent to domination by absorbing the participation of the subaltern classes, giving space to political activity, but within the limits defined by capitalism. Participating in elections, working in trades, attending school, going to church and reading newspapers had the effect of channelling dissent into activities within organisations that would compete for the attention of the state.

This had dramatic consequences, Gramsci argued, for the very idea of social transformation. Attempts to seize state power would be repulsed so long as civil society was left intact. Rather, it was first necessary to carry out the long and arduous march through the trenches of civil society. Such a *war of position* required the reconstruction of civil society, breaking the thousand threads that connected it to the state and bringing it (civil society) under the direction of the revolutionary movement, in particular its party, which Gramsci calls the 'Modern Prince'. The seizure of state power, i.e. the *war of movement*, was but the culminating act in a long, drawn-out conflict. The century-long struggle against apartheid, especially in the 1980s, the advance of Solidarity in Poland during 1980–81 or even the civil rights movement in the United States – are examples, more or less partial, of a war of position. The point is simple: assault on the state might work where civil society was 'primordial and gelatinous', e.g. the French Revolution or the Russian Revolution, but not in advanced capitalism. Lenin's theory of revolution, which prioritised assault on the state, as formulated in *State and Revolution*, is not a general theory, but reflected the specific circumstances of Russia.

Although it does contain elements of a classification struggle, the idea of a war of position on the terrain of civil society, forging a popular challenge to the social order, finds little resonance in Bourdieu's theory. Strangely for a sociologist, Bourdieu has no notion of civil society. What we find instead are leaders of the organisations of civil society – party leaders, trade union leaders, intellectual leaders, religious leaders – competing with one another in the *field of power above* civil society, employing their representative function to advance their own interests, more or less unaccountable to their followers (Bourdieu, 1991: Part III). Where Gramsci emphasises class struggle – although by no means to the exclusion of struggle within classes, especially within the dominant class – Bourdieu, as we have seen, focuses on classification struggles, i.e. struggles within the dominant class about the dominant classifications. Just as in Gramsci's analysis the state coordinates the elements of civil society, so in Bourdieu's the state oversees the classification struggles through its ultimate monopoly of the legitimate means of symbolic violence.

Classification struggles have consequences for, but are not affected by, the dominated. Bourdieu makes no reference to civil society – for him there is no politics except in the field of power, confined to the dominant classes. Like Weber, the majority are steeped in the stupor of subjugation, manipulated by their spokespeople.

HEGEMONY VS. SYMBOLIC POWER

At first blush, hegemony and symbolic domination appear very similar, assuring the maintenance of the social order not through coercion, but through cultural domination. Indeed, there are places where they appear to be saying the same thing, but that would be to obscure fundamental differences – differences that ultimately reside in the capacity of the dominated to understand and contest the conditions of their existence.

Hegemony is a form of domination that Gramsci famously defined as 'the combination of force and consent, which balance each other reciprocally, without force predominating excessively over consent. Indeed, the attempt is always made to ensure that force will appear to be based on the consent of the majority' (Gramsci, 1971: 80). Hegemony has to be distinguished from dictatorship or despotism, where coercion prevails and is applied arbitrarily without regulatory norms. Hegemony is organised in civil society, but it embraces the state too: 'the State is the entire complex of practical and theoretical activities with which the ruling class not only justifies and maintains its dominance, but manages to win the active consent of those over whom it rules' (Gramsci, 1971: 244). A lot rests on the idea of consent, of a knowing and willing participation of the dominated in their domination.

Bourdieu sometimes uses the word 'consent' to describe symbolic domination, but it has a connotation of much greater psychological depth than hegemony. In *Distinction*, Bourdieu writes of habitus as the 'internalized form of class condition and of the conditioning it entails' (1984 [1979]: 101). 'The schemes of the habitus, the primary forms of classification, owe their specific efficacy to the fact that they function below the level of the consciousness and language, beyond the reach of introspective scrutiny or control by the will' (1984 [1979]: 466). In *Pascalian Meditations*, Bourdieu writes:

The agent engaged in practice knows the world but with a knowledge which ... is not set up in the relation of externality of a knowing consciousness. He knows it in a sense, too well, without objectifying distance, takes it for granted, precisely because he is caught up in it, bound up with it; he inhabits it like a garment [un habit]. He feels at home in the world because the world is also in him, in the form of habitus, a virtue made of necessity which implies a form of love of necessity, amor fati (Bourdieu 2000 [1997]: 142–43).

Thus, symbolic domination does not depend either on physical force or even on legitimacy. Indeed, it makes both unnecessary:

The state does not necessarily need to give orders and to exert physical coercion, or disciplinary constraint, to produce an ordered social world, so long as it is able to produce incorporated cognitive structures attuned to the objective structures and secure doxic submission to the established order (Bourdieu, 2000 [1997]: 178; see also p. 176).

Symbolic domination is defined in opposition to the notion of legitimacy, which is skin deep, but also hegemony, which is based on an awareness of domination, a practical sense that is also conscious. In a telling passage, Bourdieu dismisses the notion of false consciousness, not by questioning the notion of falseness (as is usually the case), but by questioning the notion of consciousness:

In the notion of 'false consciousness' which some Marxists invoke to explain the effect of symbolic domination, it is the word 'consciousness' which is excessive; and to speak of 'ideology' is to place in the order of representations, capable of being transformed by the intellectual conversion that is called the 'awakening of consciousness', what belongs to the order of beliefs, that is, at the deepest level of bodily dispositions (Bourdieu, 2000 [1997]: 177).

Instead of false consciousness, Bourdieu talks of 'misrecognition', i.e. the way in which people spontaneously recognise the world as a misrecognition that is deeply rooted in the habitus and seemingly inaccessible to reflection.

Gramsci couldn't be more different. Instead of misrecognition, we have a knowing, rational consent to domination, and instead of habitus, he develops the notion of 'common sense' that contains a kernel of 'good sense' – practical activity that can lead to genuine understanding – as well as inherited folk wisdom and invading ideologies:

> The active man-in-the-mass has a practical activity, but has no clear theoretical consciousness of his practical activity, which nonetheless involves understanding the world in so far as it transforms it. His theoretical consciousness can indeed be historically in opposition to his activity. One might almost say he has two theoretical consciousnesses (or one contradictory consciousness): one which is implicit in his activity and which in reality unites him with his fellow-workers in the practical transformation of the real world: and one, superficially explicit or verbal, which he has inherited from the past and uncritically absorbed. But this verbal conception is not without its consequences. It holds together a specific social group, it influences moral conduct and the direction of the will, with varying efficacity, but often powerfully enough to produce a situation in which the contradictory state of consciousness does not permit of any action, any decision or any choice, and produces a condition of moral passivity. Critical understanding of self takes place therefore through a struggle of political 'hegemonies' and of opposing directions, first in the ethical field and then in that of politics proper, in order to arrive at the working out at a higher level of one's own conception of reality (Gramsci, 1971: 333).

Here we enter the crux of the difference between Gramsci and Bourdieu. Whereas Gramsci looks upon the practical activity of collectively transforming the world as the basis of good sense and potentially leading to class consciousness, Bourdieu sees in practical activity the opposite – class *un*consciousness and acceptance of the world as it is. Compare the astonishingly parallel passage in Bourdieu:

> To point out that perception of the social world implies an act of construction is not in the least to accept an intellectualist theory of knowledge: the essential part of one's experience of the social world and of the labour of construction it implies takes place in *practice*, without reaching the level of *explicit* representation and *verbal* expression. Closer to a class unconsciousness than to a 'class consciousness' in the Marxist sense, the sense of position one occupies in the social space (what Goffman calls the 'sense of one's place') is the practical mastery of the social structure as a whole which reveals itself through the sense of the position occupied in that structure. The categories of perception of the social world are essentially the product of the incorporation of the objective structures of the

social space. Consequently, they incline agents to accept the social world as it is, to take it for granted, rather to rebel against it, to put forward opposed and even antagonistic possibilities (Bourdieu, 1991 [1984]: 235; emphasis added to underline the parallels with Gramsci).

In other words, for Bourdieu, common sense is simply a blanket of bad sense, seemingly for everyone, except possibly for a few sociologists who miraculously see through the fog, whereas for Gramsci, certain groups in certain 'privileged' places can develop insight into the world they inhabit. Thus, different classes have different potentials for developing good sense. The working class in particular is favoured through its collective transformation of nature, whereas production among the peasantry and petite bourgeoisie is too individualised, while the dominant class does not engage directly in production.

The contrast with Lenin is illuminating. Like Bourdieu, Lenin considered the working class by itself to be incapable of reaching more than trade union consciousness. Lenin concluded that truth – carried by the collective intellectual – has to be brought to the working class from without. From this, Bourdieu recoils with horror – the working class is too deeply mired in submission to be altered by such presumptuous vanguardism, which endangers both intellectuals and workers. Gramsci, on the other hand, argues against Lenin, but from the side of falseness, not consciousness. He grants the working class its kernel of truth that opens the door to intellectuals, who can then elaborate that truth through dialogue. From these profound differences emerge not only contrary views of class struggle, but also of the role of intellectuals.

INTELLECTUALS: TRADITIONAL AND ORGANIC

Unique among classical Marxists, Gramsci devotes much attention to intellectuals and their relation to themselves, to the working class and to the dominant classes. We saw how Marx was not able to explain himself to himself – firstly, how a bourgeois intellectual could be fighting with the working class against the bourgeoisie and, secondly, how and why all his literary efforts mattered for class formation and class struggle. He simply had nothing systematic to say about intellectuals. Gramsci's interest in cultural domination and working-class consciousness led him to take seriously the role and place of intellectuals.

He begins with the important assumption that everyone is a theorist and everyone operates with theories of the world, but there are those who specialise in producing such theories, whom we call intellectuals or philosophers. Of these, there are two types: organic and traditional intellectuals. The first is organically connected to the class it represents, while the second is relatively autonomous from the class it represents. Under capitalism, subordinate classes rely on the first, while dominant classes are advantaged by the second. Let us explore the distinction further.

For the working class to become a revolutionary force, it requires intellectuals to elaborate its good sense within common sense. Such an elaboration takes place through dialogue between the working class and a collective intellectual – the Communist Party; the 'Modern Prince' as permanent persuader. This is not a matter of bringing consciousness to the working class from without, which marks Gramsci off from Lenin, but of building on what already lies within it. The organic intellectual can only be effective through an intimate relation with the working class, sharing its life, which, in some readings of Gramsci, means coming from the working class.

We can see why Bourdieu subjects the idea of what he called the 'myth' of the organic intellectual to withering criticism. Since the common sense of the working class is all bad sense, there is therefore no good sense, no kernel of genuine understanding within the practical experience of the working class, and thus nothing for intellectuals to elaborate. There is no basis for dialogue, which therefore degenerates into populism – an identification with the working class, which is none other than a projection of their own desires and imaginations onto the working class, a class that intellectuals mistakenly claim to understand:

> It is not a question of the truth or falsity of the unsupportable image of the working class world that the intellectual produces when, putting himself in the place of a worker without having the habitus of a worker, he apprehends the working-class condition through schemes of perception and appreciation which are not those that the members of the working class themselves use to apprehend it. It is truly the experience that an intellectual can obtain of the working-class world by putting himself provisionally and deliberately into the working-class condition, and it may become less and less improbable if, as is beginning to happen, an increasing number of individuals are thrown into the working-class condition without having the habitus that is the product of the conditionings 'normally' imposed on those who are condemned to this condition. Populism is never anything other than an inverted ethnocentrism (Bourdieu, 1984 [1979]: 374).

In other words, the intellectual, whose habitus is formed by *skholé* (a world that is not governed by material necessity), cannot appreciate the condition of the members of the working class, whose habitus is shaped by the endless and precarious pursuit of their material livelihood. Temporary immersion into factory life generates a reaction in the intellectual that abhors the conditions of working-class life, while the working class itself, inured to its subjugation, looks on with incomprehension.

Intellectuals, being part of the dominated fraction of the dominant class, experience their lives as subjugation, leading some to identify with the dominated classes. But this identification is illusory. They have little in common with the working class. Intellectuals are much better off explicitly defending their own interests as the interests of all – the universal interests of humanity:

> Cultural producers will not find again a place of their own in the social world unless, sacrificing once and for all the myth of the 'organic intellectual' (without falling into the complementary mythology of the mandarin withdrawn from everything), they agree to work collectively for the defense of their interests. This should lead them to assert themselves as an international power of criticism and watchfulness, or even of proposals, in the face of the technocrats, or – with an ambition both more lofty and more realistic, and hence limited to their own sphere – to get involved in rational action to defend the economic and social conditions of the autonomy of these socially privileged universes in which the material and intellectual instruments of what we call Reason are produced and reproduced. This *Realpolitik of reason* will undoubtedly be suspected of corporatism. But it will be part of its task to prove, by the ends to which it puts the sorely won means of autonomy, that it is a corporatism of the universal (Bourdieu, 1996 [1992]: 348).

We are back with the Realpolitik of reason – a claim that in protecting their own autonomy, intellectuals can at the same time defend the interests of humanity. Bourdieu proposes the formation of an International of intellectuals, but why should we have any more confidence in his 'Modern Prince' than Gramsci's? What ends – what visions and divisions – has Bourdieu in mind for this 'organic intellectual of humanity'?[3] Why should we trust intellectuals – the historic bearers of neoliberalism, fascism, racism, Bolshevism and so forth – to be the saviours of humanity? In dissecting the scholastic fallacies of others, is Bourdieu not committing the greatest fallacy of all, the self-misrecognition of the intellectual as (potential) bearer of a deceptive universality? Bourdieu has replaced the universality of the working class based in production and carried by the political party with the universality of the intellectual based in the academy.

In Gramsci's eyes, Bourdieu's universalistic defence of intellectuals is the ideology of the traditional intellectual, who, through defending autonomy, becomes all the more effective in securing the hegemony of the dominant classes. The latter seek to present their interests as the interests of all, and for that they require relatively autonomous intellectuals who genuinely believe in their universality. Intellectuals that are closely connected to the dominant class cannot represent the latter as a universal class. Even a thoroughgoing critical stance toward the dominant class for pursuing its own corporate interest – to wit, an uncompromising pursuit of profit – can help it toward bourgeois hegemony. Can intellectuals represent their autonomy in opposition to bourgeois hegemony without being accountable to another class? Bourdieu says yes, Gramsci says no. Gramsci's organic intellectual not only elaborates the good sense of the working class, but attacks the claims of traditional intellectuals to represent some true universality.

CONCLUSION

Gramsci and Bourdieu are mirror opposites: Bourdieu attacks Gramsci's organic intellectual as mythical, while Gramsci attacks Bourdieu's traditional intellectual as self-deluding. At bottom, the divergence rests on claims about the (in)capacity of the dominated to understand the world and the (in)capacity of intellectuals to transcend their corporate or class interests. To these two questions, Gramsci and Bourdieu have opposite answers. But that does not mean that conversation is futile. Throughout his prison writings, Gramsci shows how aware he is of the Bourdieusian critique by returning time and again to the difficulties of the organic intellectual in sustaining a reciprocal dialogue between the party and its followers, between leaders and led. As we know, Bourdieu based his own critique of the organic intellectual on Gramsci's reflections on the dangers of the alienation of politics from the rank and file. On the other hand, Bourdieu knows only too well the limitations of intellectuals' claims to universality and the danger of the scholastic fallacies that trap them into a parochial corporatism.

The conversation between Bourdieu and Gramsci becomes even more interesting when we consider Bourdieu's contradictory move toward the working class in the collaborative interview project, published in English as *The Weight of the World*. In France, *La Misère du monde* (1993) was a best seller, giving voice to the dominated and aiming to correct pervasive media distortions. For it is here that he and his collaborators describe the organic connection they develop with blue-collar workers, public employees, the unemployed, immigrants, etc. Moreover, if one reads the verbatim interviews side by side with the interviewers' analyses, one is at loss to understand in what way the respondents suffer from misrecognition. Indeed, quite the opposite, the respondents exhibit a deep sociological understanding of their predicament. The vocabulary of misrecognition and habitus is almost completely missing from this book.

No less astonishing is Bourdieu's methodological statement at the end of the book where he talks of the 'Socratic work' of the interviewer in aiding explanation and where he refers to the sociologist as a 'midwife' who helps people become aware of what they knew all along, i.e. the nature of their subjugation. You might even call it a form of consciousness raising in which the 'implicit' is made 'explicit' and 'verbal'. Indeed, this chapter on 'understanding' can be read as a brilliant elaboration of the techniques and dilemmas of the sociologist as organic intellectual of the subordinate classes. But Bourdieu makes no attempt to reconcile this book with his denunciation of the 'organic intellectual'. Yes, to be an organic intellectual requires sustained work, enduring patience and uncompromising collective self-vigilance, but Gramsci never said it was easy. Indeed, for Gramsci it could never be an individual project; it had to be a collective one.

KARL VON HOLDT

Symbolic Challenge

In Bourdieu, the symbolic violence that works through habitus is linked to the broader symbolic order through which the hierarchies of society and the meanings of those hierarchies are stabilised and made normal.

Just as in Gramsci the state is central to the organisation of hegemony, so in Bourdieu it is central to maintaining and naturalising this commonsense social order. The state is the authority of authorities and, as such, imposes classification systems that sanctify prevailing hierarchies, establishes and reproduces shared symbolic forms of thought, and presides over a symbolic order that is, 'in appearance at least, coherent and systematic ... adjusted to the objectives structures of the social world' (Bourdieu, 2000 [1997]: 176). Just as the state claims a monopoly over physical violence, so it claims a monopoly over the legitimate use of symbolic violence (Bourdieu, 1994).

South Africa presents substantial challenges to such conceptions. Here, social order has not settled into a 'commonsense' shape. Both in society and in the state, the symbolic order is contested, fluid and ambiguous.

Research into the state (Von Holdt, 2010a) suggests a profound contradiction between the Weberian rationales of a modern bureaucracy – which is, formally speaking, what is enshrined in the constitution, legislation, regulations and policies of the government – and informal rationales that constitute the state as the premier site of African sovereignty and black advancement. The result is a deeply racialised instability in the meaning of skill, authority and 'face' within the bureaucracy. Whereas the symbolic order of apartheid stabilised skill as an attribute of whites and fundamentally devalued the skills of blacks, the transition opened up a sharp contestation over the meaning of 'skill': many whites continued to question the skills of blacks at the same time as many blacks questioned the skills of whites who, in their view, had gained their positions because of race rather than skill.

The meaning of skill inside the state has become deeply ambiguous, and in many cases managers have been appointed who lack the experience through which complex technical and managerial skills are developed. Black advancement becomes more important than questions of competence or institutional performance. In such cases, incompetence spreads, as managers who lack the necessary skills appoint others who in turn cannot perform. There are, on the other hand, managers, policy-makers and political heads who view these developments with alarm, and attempt to craft counter-strategies to build a competent and skilled bureaucracy – with considerable success in some sectors of the state. The net consequence, though, is the destabilisation of 'skill' and its symbolic meanings, which opens up new opportunities for struggles over who gets appointed and why, while in too many institutions the state loses technical competence and may be said to be dysfunctional.

Similar processes have destabilised authority (Von Holdt, 2010a). As well as fundamentally challenging the legitimacy of the state, the struggle against apartheid destabilised the racialised authority structures in workplaces in both the private and public sectors (Von Holdt, 2003; Von Holdt & Maserumule, 2005). The transition to democracy has neither stabilised the authority of the state nor the legitimacy of authority structures in many workplaces; on the contrary, authority at many levels of our society remains provisional and contested. In public sector workplaces in particular it is not only that shop stewards and significant groups of workers challenge or reject the authority of supervisors or senior managers, but senior management also appears to have deeply ambivalent attitudes towards the authority of front-line supervisors. In hospitals, for example, front-line supervisors and, indeed, hospital managers have very limited disciplinary authority and are frequently second-guessed by departmental officials ensconced in head offices.

The result is a breakdown of discipline and the erosion of authority in many state institutions. Trade unions prevent education officials from visiting schools to assess performance. According to shop stewards interviewed in some hospitals, the majority of hospital staff participate in one or other form of 'corruption'. Nurses associate this situation with the broader changes brought about by democratisation:

> When the ANC took over, everything became relaxed; you could do anything in the new dispensation .... The lowest categories control the hospital. Since the unions were introduced the shop stewards have been running the hospital, but they cannot even write their names! They get out of hand and it is difficult to handle. Management is scared to discipline and control. The shop stewards confront and victimise the nurses. We also belong to a union but we do our job. Everyone barks at us. We have no dignity; we are degraded. There is supposed to be democracy, but not in the manner of [name of hospital] (Von Holdt & Maserumule, 2005: 450).

Such a breakdown of authority coexists with a culture of extreme deference towards the administrative and political leadership within the state. Elaborate rituals of deference are linked to the necessity of defending African sovereignty in the face of a hypercritical 'racial gaze'. In an extreme case, a white doctor, hearing the KwaZulu-Natal member of the executive council (MEC) for health tell staff that white doctors are only interested in profit, threw a picture of the MEC into a dustbin. The doctor was suspended pending a disciplinary enquiry, the MEC publicly accused white doctors of being racist, while the health minister told reporters that the incident 'smells of anarchy' (*Mail & Guardian*, 25 April–1 May 2008; 2–8 May 2008; *Business Day*, 6 May 2008). In this case, the picture had become a highly charged symbol of respect and face. From one side the incident appears as a typical case of how the concern with face overshadows crucial delivery concerns, while from another an agent of the racial gaze is deliberately undermining the authority and credibility of the state (Von Holdt, 2010a).

The instability and contestation within state institutions over the state's meaning and purposes undermine its ability to establish and sustain a coherent structure of symbolic domination. Skills and authority are not simply technical matters, but are crucial dimensions of a classification system and its symbolic order; if the state is internally divided with respect to such dimensions of symbolic order, there is very little possibility that it will be able to enforce and stabilise symbolic order throughout society.

Turning from state institutions to society, our research into community protests and the subaltern crowds that take to the streets of townships and informal settlements suggests that in post-apartheid South Africa, social order has not settled into 'commonsense' shape and that subaltern consciousness exists in a complex relationship with authority, social hierarchy and the state.

Typically, community protests start with a cycle of mass gatherings, marches and petitions. Responses by the authorities are generally inadequate and at some point police violence sparks running street battles between police and crowds of youths, and state buildings such as libraries, clinics and halls are burnt down. Informants – among them protest leaders, youths involved in the street battles and violence, and ordinary community members – provide a variety of contradictory views regarding the destruction of community facilities such as libraries and clinics.

So, for example, in a particular town, one of the protest leaders, a churchman, maintained that the clinic that had been burnt down 'belonged to the apartheid regime' and that the municipal officials had misappropriated money meant for it. The community felt that 'we deserve much better'. As for the library, 'It was a library by name only. You go inside, there is no content'. Asked about the community hall, he answered: 'The community hall? That was excitement. You burn one, you burn them all.' Other informants endorsed his views, but elderly women residents of the township contradicted him: the clinic was conveniently located, and 'to burn it down for us old ladies with high blood pressure and bad knees ...

it was a big mistake'. School students expressed a similar opinion about the burning of the library, which they were accustomed to using as a place to study and do homework. Another protest leader said that the burning of the buildings was wrong, because they belonged to the community, while a third said it was the action of criminals. A teenage school student probably came closest to describing the meaning of this action for protesters: 'People said, this is the municipality, we are going to burn it down' (Dlamini, 2011: 37).

Clearly, a library or a clinic, and the act of burning it down, have different meanings for different actors in the community. For many, it is a public amenity with important practical uses, even if it is inadequate. For others, its manifest inadequacy shows that little has changed since apartheid and government is failing the community. Its practical usefulness is immaterial. Indeed, when the protesters claim that 'nothing had changed' in the library, this was untrue: it had been equipped with 20 new computers, which were all burnt or stolen in the protest (Langa, 2011: 64; Von Holdt, 2011a: 26).

There is a continuity between the apartheid past and the democratic present in the symbolic meaning of library or clinic as a structure that represents authority – an authority that is indifferent to subaltern voices. Burning it down is a symbolic disruption of that authority, an assertion of the anger and grievances of the community. However, protest leaders who are more prominent figures, occupy positions of responsibility and are mindful of the importance of 'public opinion' do not attempt to defend the action of the crowds, but blame it on 'criminals' – even though in all probability they anticipate the action and share in its symbolic assertion.

It is a symbolism that is well understood, both by communities and by authorities, since it was central to the struggle against apartheid authority. Yet its meaning has shifted with the establishment of democracy. Whereas in the 1980s the destruction of state property symbolised the rejection of the apartheid state and the ambition to destroy it, in the democratic era it is intended as a message to the highest levels of authority in the state: 'The Premier undermines us. He'll see by the smoke we're calling him' (Dlamini, 2011: 35–36). Symbolically, such actions both disrupt the authority of the state *and* reaffirm its authority by calling for those at the apex of its structure to ensure that their grievances are responded to.

Such contradictions are accentuated by the fact that in many community protests, at least some of the protest leadership are themselves members of the dominant political formations of the Tripartite Alliance, including the ANC, the ANC Youth League and the South African Communist Party, and are protagonists in internal struggles within the ANC and the Alliance over access to political and administrative positions in local government, and access to jobs and tenders for business contracts. Instability and contestation within the ANC are linked to similar processes within government and the community.

As these studies show, in a situation of historical upheaval and change such as South Africa's, it is not only the state that is the source of symbolic order: subalterns too construct symbolic orders from below in their struggles to appropriate, disrupt or reshape dominant meanings. Just as the post-apartheid state does not hold a monopoly over material violence, so it is unable to monopolise symbolic violence. In South Africa today, very little is self-evident, established or settled. Indeed, what we have is not so much a classification struggle in the Bourdieusian sense, but a classification crisis, a symbolic crisis. 'Decolonisation, which sets out to change the order of the world', writes Frantz Fanon, 'is clearly an agenda for total disorder' (Fanon, 2004 [1961]: 2).

This brings us to the next chapter.

NOTES

1   In another reference, Bourdieu (1991: chap. 8) opportunistically turns Gramsci's warnings about the dangers of the trade union oligarchy – 'a banker of men in a monopoly situation' – and of the sectarian politics of the party apparatus, cut off from its followers, into a blanket denunciation of 'organic intellectuals' as deceiving both themselves and the class they claim to represent. It is curious that Bourdieu here draws on Gramsci's more obscure political writings, while avoiding the *Prison Notebooks* and their key ideas of hegemony, civil society, intellectuals and the state.

2   Reflecting their very different intellectual positions and dispositions, they diverge fundamentally in their relation to their class origins. In the film *La sociologie est un sport du combat*, which is a portrait of Bourdieu's academic and political life, there is a scene in which Bourdieu describes his revulsion for the dialect of his home region in the Pyrenees, illustrating the class habitus he developed in the academic establishment, whereas Gramsci writes moving letters from prison to his sister imploring her to make sure that her children do not lose their familiarity with folk idioms and vernacular.

3   Even Bourdieu is led to the appropriation of the idea of the organic intellectual: 'All this means that the ethno-sociologist is a kind of organic intellectual of humanity, and as a collective agent, can contribute to de-naturalizing and de-fatalizing human existence by placing his skill at the service of a universalism rooted in the comprehension of different particularisms' (Bourdieu, 2008b [2002]: 24). But it is an organic intellectual of an abstract entity (i.e. humanity) – the very antithesis of Gramsci's organic intellectual; indeed, the apotheosis of Gramsci's traditional intellectual.

CONVERSATION 4

COLONIALISM AND REVOLUTION

MICHAEL BURAWOY

Fanon Meets Bourdieu

But above all I wanted to get away from speculation – at that time [1960s], the works of Frantz Fanon, especially The Wretched of the Earth, *were the latest fashion, and they struck me as being false and dangerous.*

Bourdieu (1990 [1986]: 7)

What Fanon says corresponds to nothing. It is even dangerous to make the Algerians believe the things he says. This would bring them to a utopia. And I think these men [Sartre and Fanon] contributed to what Algeria became because they told stories to Algerians who often did not know their own country any more than the French who spoke about it, and, therefore, the Algerians retained a completely unrealistic utopian illusion of Algeria ... the texts of Fanon and Sartre are frightening for their irresponsibility. You would have to be a megalomaniac to think you could say just any such nonsense.

Pierre Bourdieu, interview in Le Sueur (2001: 282)

Bourdieu's stance toward Marxism becomes more hostile as we move from Marx to Gramsci and now to Fanon. Bourdieu is prepared to acknowledge the insights of Karl Marx and, indeed, so many of his ideas find an echo in the writings of Marx. As I suggested in Conversation 2, his theory of cultural domination can be seen as an extension of Marx's political economy from material to symbolic goods. While Bourdieu wants to distance himself from his opposite number in the Marxist tradition, he nonetheless shows a grudging respect by turning Gramsci against Gramsci.

When it comes to Frantz Fanon, the gloves are off, as we see in the rare quotes above, taken from two interviews. I have found no other explicit commentary on Fanon in Bourdieu's works. As with other Marxists, once we allow Fanon to respond, we see both astonishing parallels and glaring divergences. Bourdieu's enmity towards Fanon – there is no evidence that Fanon even knew Bourdieu – is perhaps all the deeper because their lives in Algeria overlapped. But they were worlds apart: the one a scientific observer from the metropolis sympathetic to the plight of the colonised, attempting to give them dignity by recognising their distinctive traditions; the other a psychiatrist from Martinique trained in France and dealing directly with victims of violence on both sides of the colonial divide. The one was attached to the university and ventured into communities as research sites, while the other worked in a psychiatric hospital before committing himself to the liberation movement (the Front de Libération Nationale/National Liberation Front or FLN).

Still, the enmity is especially interesting, given how similar are their accounts of colonialism and its effects, namely those found in Fanon's *The Wretched of the Earth* (1963 [1961]) and Bourdieu's less-well-known works written while he was in Algeria or soon thereafter – *The Sociology of Algeria* (1958), *Work and Workers in Algeria* (written with Alain Darbel, Jean-Pierre Rivet and Claude Seibel) (1963), and *The Uprooting* (written with Abdelmalek Sayad) (1964).[1] Certainly, the two writers refract their writings through different theoretical lenses – modernisation theory and Third World Marxism – which reflect serious disagreements, but it cannot account for Bourdieu's venomous hostility, especially as within his modernisation theory there is more than a whiff of Marxism.

We need to look elsewhere for the source of Bourdieu's contempt for Fanon, namely their places in the French political and intellectual scene. The two men were not only located on different sides of the colour line within the political field of war-torn Algeria, but, just as significantly, they occupied opposed positions within the different, but connected French political field. When Bourdieu moved back to France, he entered a very different intellectual world – that of the metropolis rather than the colony. There, despite his sympathies for the colonised, he positioned himself in opposition to the Third Worldism associated with Sartre and others, and expressed most vividly in the writings of Fanon. We must not forget that the Algerian question created a virtual civil war within France itself, with positions ranging all the way from fervent defence of the anti-colonial revolution to uncompromising support for the settler regime. Indeed, the extremes were organised militarily within France. Bourdieu vacillated in the middle, but he certainly did not take the side of Fanon and Sartre.

It is significant, then, that with immersion in the French political field, Bourdieu breaks with his own 'revolutionary' writings on Algeria to offer a completely different rendering of Algerian society. His best-known Algerian writings are not the early ones, but the heavily theorised treatises *Outline of a Theory of Practice* (1977 [1972]) and the subsequent version, *The Logic of Practice* (1990 [1980]). Based on a timeless, context-free construction of the rural Kabyle[2] – an anthropological mythology if ever there was one – it is here that Bourdieu develops the concepts of symbolic capital, habitus, doxa and misrecognition, which are then used to paint France in functionalist colours. Here lies Bourdieu's brilliance (and, one might say, his limitations) – to take the elementary forms of a fabricated Kabyle social life as the building blocks for studying advanced capitalism. What differentiates the latter from the former is the coexistence of differentiated fields – a notion notably absent in his writings on the Kabyle.

Physical violence is, thereby, relegated to the colony, while *symbolic* violence is pinned to the metropolis – but, ironically, through the extrapolation of a self-reproducing, harmonious, autochthonous Kabyle society. But, curiously, Bourdieu's analysis of France exhibits uncanny parallels with Fanon's first great work, *Black Skin, White Masks* (1967 [1952]), which describes the symbolic violence of the French racial order. But where Fanon stresses the *psychoanalysis* of internalised oppression in the context of the French racial order, Bourdieu undertakes the *socio-analysis* of outward distinction, supported by the undeveloped psychology of habitus. Equally important, however, is their inverse trajectory: Fanon moves from symbolic violence to social revolution, whereas Bourdieu moves in the opposite direction, from social revolution to symbolic violence.

This, then, is how I will construct Fanon's response to Bourdieu's violent denunciations. I begin with their convergent biographies – from margin to centre to margin – and from there explore their parallel accounts of colonialism, showing how they inflect those accounts with different theories, before finally comparing their reverse trajectories leading to Bourdieu's *critical pessimism* with regard to symbolic violence in France and Fanon's revolutionary optimism with regard to colonial violence in Algeria.

CONVERGENT BIOGRAPHIES: FROM MARGIN TO CENTRE TO MARGIN

Bourdieu and Fanon overlapped in Algeria, during the period of intensive strugglers for national liberation (1954–62). Bourdieu arrived in 1955 to do his military service, whereupon he became absorbed by the fate of the Algerian people. He stayed on, taking a position at the University of Algiers, turned from philosophy to ethnology and sociology, and dived into research on all facets of the life of the colonised. Wading into war zones with his research assistants, he became a chronicler and witness to colonial subjugation and the evolving struggles. By 1960 his presence had become politically untenable and he left Algeria for France, where he embarked on his illustrious career as a sociologist, but indelibly marked by his Algerian experiences.

Fanon arrived in Algeria in 1953, two years before Bourdieu, also from France, where he had recently completed a degree in medicine and psychiatry. In Algeria, he was appointed head of the Blida-Joinville Psychiatric Hospital and through his patients he vicariously experienced the traumas of colonial violence. He concluded that psychiatry was no solution to the suffering and so he became involved in the liberation struggle, leading to his expulsion from Algeria in 1956. He went to Tunis, where he continued his psychiatric work, and then to Accra, where he became a roving ambassador for the FLN in different parts of North and West Africa. He died of leukemia in 1961, just before Algeria achieved independence, but not before he had finished *The Wretched of the Earth*, the bible of liberation movements across the world.

In their different ways, both Bourdieu and Fanon were well prepared to develop original interpretations of their Algerian experiences. They both made the uncomfortable journey from periphery to centre. Bourdieu grew up in a small village in the Béarn, where his father graduated from sharecropper to postal employee. Only Bourdieu's brilliance and the support of his teachers took him all the way to the École Normale Supérieure. Fanon grew up in Martinique in a Creole family with middle-class aspirations, before entering the Free French Army in 1943. He served in North

Africa, witnessing colonial oppression of a sort he had never seen before, and then in eastern France, where he discovered the meaning of metropolitan racism. He was back in France in 1946, studying to be a doctor in Lyon. Both Bourdieu and Fanon had bitter experiences of marginalisation in France: the one based on class, which Bourdieu describes in *Sketch for a Self-analysis* and the other based on race that Fanon exposed in *Black Skin, White Masks*. Both were well equipped to be horrified by the abominations of settler colonialism, although their race and political propensities would position them differently within the colonial order.

The transition from centre to periphery, from France to Algeria, demanded a wholesale reorientation of the schemes of understanding they had acquired in their formal training in France. They both converged on a sociology of colonialism – Bourdieu from philosophy that was far too removed from what he saw in Algeria and Fanon from psychiatry that couldn't grasp the structural features of colonial domination. Their accounts of colonialism are remarkably similar.

SEVEN THESES ON COLONIALISM: BOURDIEU EQUALS FANON

Notwithstanding their convergent trajectories from periphery to centre to periphery, given their divergent positions and dispositions, one would expect Bourdieu the French *normalien* and Fanon the Martiniquan psychiatrist to have clashing understandings of the colonial condition. Such an expectation of divergence is only intensified if one takes into account Bourdieu's later denunciation of Fanon's writings as 'speculative', 'irresponsible' and 'dangerous'. It is all the more surprising, therefore, to discover striking parallels in their analysis of colonial domination, anticolonial struggles and the supersession of colonialism. As evidence, let me draw on two texts, both written in 1961, one year before Algeria's independence – Bourdieu's 'Revolution within the revolution'[3] and Fanon's *The Wretched of the Earth*.

1. *Colonialism is a system of domination held together by violence.* In his familiar evocative way, Fanon writes:

> Their first encounter was marked by violence and their existence together – that is to say the exploitation of the native by the settler – was carried on by dint of a great array of bayonets and cannons (Fanon, 1963 [1961]: 36).

Bourdieu is equally clear:

> Indeed, the war plainly revealed the true basis for the colonial order: the relation, backed by force, which allows the dominant caste to keep the dominated caste in a position of inferiority (Bourdieu, 1962 [1961]: 146).

Bourdieu avoids the concept of race, reluctant to use it not only in his analysis of colonialism, but also of French society, where he is far more comfortable deploying class as his critical concept.

2. The colonial situation is fundamentally one of segregation of colonisers from colonised. In Fanon's terms, colonialism follows the principle of 'reciprocal exclusivity', admitting of no compromise:

> The zone where the natives live is not complementary to the zone inhabited by the settlers. The two zones are opposed, but not in the service of a higher unity. Obedient to the rules of pure Aristotelian logic, they both follow the principle of reciprocal exclusivity. No conciliation is possible, for of the two terms, one is superfluous (Fanon, 1963 [1961]: 38–39).

Bourdieu continues to use the term 'caste' to grasp the structural character of colonialism, but this misses out on the experiential moment of race that remains central in Fanon's writings:

> In short, when carried along by its own internal logic, the colonial system tends to develop all the consequences implied at the time of its founding – the complete separation of the social castes (Bourdieu, 1962 [1961]: 146).

3. Colonialism dehumanises the colonised, demanding its reversal. Parallels in their description of colonial domination appear in their accounts of the subjective experience of colonialism. Fanon writes:

> [Colonialism] dehumanizes the native, or to speak plainly turns him into an animal .... [The native] knows that he is not an animal, and it is precisely at the moment he realizes his humanity, that he begins to sharpen the weapons with which he will secure its victory (Fanon, 1963 [1961]: 42–43).

Similarly, Bourdieu (1962 [1961]: 151) writes that 'respect and dignity' are the first demand of the dominated, because they have experienced colonialism as 'humiliation or alienation'. Echoing Fanon he writes:

> The colonial situation thus creates the 'contemptible' person at the same time that it creates the contemptuous attitude; but it creates in turn a spirit of revolt against this contempt; and so the tension that is tearing the whole society to pieces keeps on increasing (Bourdieu, 1962 [1961]: 134).

4. Colonialism uses its domination to dispossess the peasantry of their land. Both Fanon and Bourdieu concentrate on the destruction of the peasantry through the expropriation of land, the very foundation of their existence. Fanon writes:

> For a colonized people the most essential value, because the most concrete, is first and foremost the land: the land which will bring them bread and, above all, dignity (Fanon, 1963 [1961]: 44).

Here is Bourdieu's parallel assessment of the centrality of land:

> The peasant can exist only when rooted to the land, the land where he was born, which he received from his parents and to which he is attached by his habits and his memories. Once he has been uprooted there is a good chance that he will cease to exist as a peasant, that the instinctive and irrational passion which binds him to his peasant existence will die within him (Bourdieu, 1962 [1961]: 172).

While the land is key in both, Bourdieu and Sayad's (1964) analysis in *The Uprooting* is far richer. There they study the resettlement camps created during the Algerian war, the result of forced removals conducted in the name of protecting the colonised from the national liberation movement, but clearly aimed at flushing it out of the rural areas by denying it the support of the people.

5. Only through revolution can the colonial order be overthrown. Fanon here stresses the importance of violence, absolute violence. The order is held together by violence and, therefore, has to be overthrown through violence. This is how he puts it:

The native who decides to put the program into practice, and to become its moving force, is ready for violence at all times. From birth it is clear to him that this narrow world, strewn with prohibitions, can only be called into question by absolute violence (Fanon, 1963 [1961]: 37).

While Bourdieu's idea of a caste system perhaps implies a more harmonious order than Fanon's racial order, he also has no doubt that the colonial system sows the seeds of its own destruction – a 'great upheaval', in which 'the great mass of peasants ... have been carried along in the whirlwind of violence which is sweeping away even the vestiges of the past' (Bourdieu, 1962 [1961]: 188). Only revolution can achieve the end of colonialism:

> That only a revolution can abolish the colonial system, that any changes to be made must be subject to the law of all or nothing, are facts now consciously realized, even if only confusedly, just as much by members of the dominant society as by the members of the dominated society .... Thus it must be granted that the primary and indeed the sole radical challenge to the system was the one that system itself engendered; the revolt against the principles on which it was founded (Bourdieu, 1962 [1961]: 146).

6. *The anti-colonial revolution transforms consciousness, liquidating all forms of localism to build a national solidarity.* For Fanon, violence has a cathartic and unifying effect:

> We have said that the native's violence unifies the people .... Violence is in action all-inclusive and national. It follows that it is closely involved in the liquidation of regionalism and of tribalism .... At the level of individuals, violence is a cleansing force. It frees the native from his inferiority complex and from his despair and inaction; it makes him fearless and restores his self-respect (Fanon, 1963 [1961]: 94).

In Bourdieu's language, the war dissolves 'false solicitude'. Attempts at conciliation and all forms of concession are merely tactics of the dominant to hold on to their power: 'attempts at trickery or subterfuge are at once revealed in their true light. The war helped to bring about a heightened awareness' (Bourdieu, 1962 [1961]: 153). Repression and war lead to the spiralling of hostilities and the deepening of the schism between the two sides. The war becomes a cultural agent, dissolving resignation and replacing symbolic refusal of colonial domination, for example, in the insistent wearing of the veil – what Bourdieu calls traditional traditionalism – with aggressive demands for rights to welfare and education. Pride, he says, replaces shame:

> The feeling of being engaged in a common adventure, of being subject to a common destiny, of confronting the same adversary, of sharing the same preoccupations, the same sufferings and the same aspirations, widened and deepened the sentiment of solidarity, a sentiment which was undergoing at the same time a veritable transformation as the idea of fraternity tended to lose any ethnical or religious coloration and became synonymous with national solidarity (Bourdieu, 1962 [1961]: 162).

This is the 'revolution within the revolution', the revolutionary transformation of consciousness, the substitution of an assertive solidarity for a resentful deference. How different is this revolution within the revolution from Fanon's account of the national liberation struggle?[4]

7. The anti-colonial revolution leads either to socialism or barbarism. Fanon recognises two paths out of colonialism: either national liberation based on peasant revolution leading to a socialist participatory democracy, or the taking of a national bourgeois road that will bring progressive degradation to the political order, ending in dictatorship and repression:

> The bourgeois leaders of underdeveloped countries imprison national consciousness in sterile formalism. It is only when men and women are included on a vast scale in enlightened and fruitful work that form and body are given to that consciousness. ... Otherwise there is anarchy, repression, and the resurgence of tribal parties and federalism (Fanon, 1963 [1961]: 204–5).

Bourdieu, too, discovers a fork in the post-colonial road: not Fanon's struggle for socialism or dictatorship, but an indeterminacy of immediate outcome – socialism or chaos:

> A society which has been so greatly revolutionized demands that revolutionary solutions be devised to meet its problems. It will insist that a way be found to mobilize these masses who have been freed from the traditional disciplines and thrown into a chaotic, disillusioned world, by holding up before them a collective ideal, the building of a harmonious

social order and the development of a modern economy capable of assuring employment and a decent standard of living for all. Algeria contains such explosive forces that it could well be that there now remains only a choice between chaos and an original form of socialism that will have been carefully designed to meet the needs of the actual situation (Bourdieu, 1962 [1961]: 192–93).[5]

Both allow for the possibility of socialism, but for Fanon it is a long historical project, whereas for Bourdieu it is a spontaneous occurrence.

The two critics of colonialism converge to a surprising degree in their assessment of colonialism and its denouement. If Fanon was 'speculative', 'dangerous' and 'irresponsible', then surely Bourdieu was no less so. The main difference, one might surmise, is that Fanon did not live to change his mind. Investigating further, however, we can see that their common understandings are located within very different theoretical-political frameworks – the one is a dissident within modernisation theory and the other a dissident within Marxism.

BOURDIEU: BETWEEN TRADITION AND MODERNITY

Perhaps it is surprising to place Bourdieu in the camp of modernisation theory, given his concern with colonial domination. Nonetheless, his work exhibits close parallels with Durkheim's Manichean worlds of mechanical and organic solidarity. At one extreme, Bourdieu constructs a harmonious order of self-reproduction through rituals of gift exchange and lifecycle, and the unconscious reproduction of masculine domination as expressed in the division of the Kabyle house. This order, unsullied by colonialism, is dominated by a strong collective consciousness. This romantic redemption of ethnic culture has been defended by Bourdieu and his followers as reversing the contempt of colonialism for the culture of its subjects. Paul Silverstein (2004) refers to this as a structural nostalgia that can be a weapon in an anti-colonial struggle.[6] More curious, it is from this vision of 'traditional' society that Bourdieu draws many of his concepts – habitus, symbolic domination, misrecognition – to analyse French society.

Very different from this harmonious order was modern Algeria, beset by colonialism that created a stable but potentially revolutionary working class, a disoriented subproletariat and a dispossessed peasantry. Here we find Durkheim's abnormal forms of the division of labour that generate disorganisation and conflict. On the one hand, there is the forced division of labour and the imposition of unequal conditions on the colonised, depriving them of opportunities for advancement and, indeed, leading to the anti-colonial struggle. On the other hand, there is the anomic division of labour expressed in the confusion of those caught between two opposed worlds – what Bourdieu later calls the 'split habitus' – generating outbursts of irrational, messianic behaviour:

> All these contradictions affect the inner nature of 'the man between two worlds' – the intellectual, the man who formerly worked in France, the city dweller – is exposed to the conflicts created by the weakening of the traditional systems of sanctions and by the development of a double set of moral standards ... this man, cast between two worlds and rejected by both, lives a sort of double inner life, is a prey to frustration and inner conflict, with the result that he is constantly being tempted to adopt either an attitude of uneasy overidentification or one of rebellious negativism (Bourdieu, 1962 [1961]: 142–44).

These ideas of cultural lag – incomplete adaptation to modernity being caught between the old and the new – lie at the core of 1960s modernisation theory of Clifford Geertz, Alex Inkeles and Edward Shils, not to mention Talcott Parsons's pattern variables.[7] To explain the plight of so-called 'new nations' and the impediments to 'modernity', these authors invoked the heavy weight of tradition and primordial attachments (kinship, tribe, religion). Bourdieu, no less than they, provides precious little evidence to back up his claims about this state of anomie.[8]

More original is Bourdieu's adaptation of Weber's, *The Protestant Ethic and the Spirit of Capitalism*. Drawing on Husserl's philosophy of time, Bourdieu (1979 [1963]) argues that modernity is an orientation to a rationally planned future, whereas tradition is encased by the repetition of the same patterns. He pins modernity onto the Algerian working class, which has the stability to think rationally and imaginatively about future alternatives, as opposed to the peasantry, who are stuck in the eternal present, what he calls a *traditional traditionalism*. The unstable, marginal, semi-employed or unemployed urban 'subproletariat' and the rural proletariat displaced from their lands into resettlement camps live from hand to mouth. They exhibit a *traditionalism of despair*, oriented to the here and now, but cognisant of alternative futures that they are denied.

Curiously, this leads Bourdieu, via Durkheimian notions of anomie, to the orthodox Marxist position that the Algerian working class, because it is rooted in stable employment, is revolutionary – in contrast to the uprooted peasantry or urban subproletariat who can only break out into spontaneous, senseless revolt:

> On the one hand, there is the revolt of emotion, the uncertain and incoherent expression of a condition characterized by uncertainty and incoherence; on the other hand, there is revolutionary radicalism, springing from the systematic consideration of reality. These two attitudes correspond to two types of material conditions of existence: on the one hand the sub-proletarians of the towns and the uprooted peasants whose whole existence is constraint and arbitrariness; on the other hand the regular workers of the modern sector, provided with the minimum of security and guarantees which allow aspirations and opinions to be put into perspective. Disorganization of daily conduct prohibits the formation of the system of rational projects and forecasts of which the revolutionary consciousness is one aspect (Bourdieu, 1979 [1963]: 62).

The uprooted may be a 'force for revolution', but not a 'revolutionary force' that self-consciously promotes and rationally organises the transformation of society. The latter possibility is reserved for the working class:

> To those who have the 'privilege' of undergoing permanent and 'rational' exploitation and of enjoying the corresponding advantages also belongs the privilege of a truly revolutionary consciousness. This realistic aiming at the future (*l'avenir*) is only accessible to those who have the means to confront the present and to look for ways of beginning to implement their hopes, instead of giving way to resigned surrender or to the magical impatience of those who are too crushed by the present to be able to look to anything other than a utopian future (*un futur*), an immediate, magical negation of the present (Bourdieu, 1979 [1963]: 63).

What a contrast to the French working class depicted in *Distinction* or *Pascalian Meditations*, whose members are driven by necessity, symbolically dominated and misrecognising their conditions of existence. Not one to be disturbed by contradictions, Bourdieu never explains this most obvious inconsistency. What is the source of the difference? Does it lie in the political structures of the two countries – the effects of symbolic as opposed to colonial violence – or does it lie in Bourdieu's positions in the political-intellectual fields of the two countries? A comparison with Fanon sheds light on both these possibilities.

FANON: BETWEEN CAPITALISM AND SOCIALISM

If Bourdieu analyses Algeria with the Manichean categories of modernity and tradition, Fanon sees Algeria through the bifocal lens of capitalism and socialism; if Bourdieu analyses Algeria from the standpoint of a romantic past, Fanon sees Algeria from the vantage of a romantic future. They meet on the terrain of the present.

For Fanon, colonialism was a space of struggles. National independence is a struggle against the colonial power, Gramsci's *war of movement* conducted with violence, but it is also a struggle over post-coloniality, a *war of position* within the colonised between, on the one hand, the followers of the national bourgeoisie who fight to *replace* the colonisers and, on the other hand, the militants of the national liberation movement who fight also to *transform* the class structure.[9] The war of position for the future exists uneasily alongside the anti-colonial war of movement, but if the former is displaced by the latter and the denouement of colonialism is left to look after itself, democratic socialism will never be victorious. So argues Fanon.

Bourdieu not only failed to separate the two moments of the anti-colonial revolution, but he also did not pay sufficient attention to the idea of class as a potential political force. Fanon, again following Gramsci, examined the balance of class forces behind the reformist national bourgeoisie and the revolutionary national liberation movement. At the heart of the national bourgeoisie lay traders, merchants and small capitalists, together with their intellectuals recruited from teachers, civil servants, lawyers, nurses and other professionals. The national bourgeoisie also had the support of the albeit-small colonial working class, which in Fanon's view was pampered and parasitic. It is here that Bourdieu and Fanon diverge dramatically: relative stability of the working class for Bourdieu meant revolutionary potential, while for Fanon it meant reformism.[10] As we know from South Africa, in reality, the situation is rather more complex – different fractions of the working class become revolutionary at different times.

For Fanon, the revolutionary struggle depended on the dispossessed peasantry, because the latter had nothing to lose. Bourdieu considered this to be 'pretentious foolishness' (cited in Le Sueur, 2001: 284). The peasantry was 'overwhelmed by the war, by the concentration camps, and by the mass deportations', and so to claim that it was revolutionary was 'completely idiotic' (Le Sueur, 2001: 284). Bourdieu attempted to put the picture right with his book, *The Uprooting*, written with Abdelmalek Sayad (1964), which dealt with the crisis of the displaced. Fanon was not as ignorant as Bourdieu made out, as he had done his own field work among the Kabyle (Macey, 2000: 234–36). He considered instinctive rebelliousness to come precisely from the expropriation of their land, which Bourdieu had himself recognised as the source of 'revolutionary chiliasm and magical utopias' (1979 [1963]: 70).

The more substantial difference between them comes with the next step in Fanon's argument. For the peasantry to be a revolutionary force, its volcanic energy had to be disciplined by intellectuals. They would be in plentiful supply – radicals expelled from the towns for exposing the venality of the native elites. Opposed to the bourgeois road, they join the peasantry to forge a revolutionary movement. To Bourdieu, the idea of symbiosis between intellectuals and peasantry is a fantasy of the intellectual that not only cannot work, but is also dangerous and irresponsible. It is very different from Bourdieu's own position as an engaged intellectual supporting the colonised from a healthy, objective distance.

Be that as it may, Fanon continues his analysis of the balance of class forces. There are two projects vying for the support of the colonised classes: the national bourgeois road centred on the native bourgeoisie and the working class, and the national liberation movement centred on the peasantry embracing and embraced by radical intellectuals. Fanon asks which of these two projects will succeed in winning the support of vacillating classes: traditional leaders in the countryside who are reformist by nature, a screen for the colonisers, but who are also accountable to their ever-more militant followers, and the urban lumpenproletariat, recently uprooted from their villages, a volatile group easily manipulated by leaders who grant them the smallest concessions. The colonisers play their own role in shaping the balance between these two tendencies, and when they see the writing on the wall, they throw their weight behind the less threatening national bourgeoisie.

This analysis of the future, so alien to Bourdieu's backward-looking sociology, continues with Fanon's pessimistic, but prophetic anticipations. Should the national bourgeoisie win the struggle for leadership of the anti-colonial struggle and come to power, they will not be able to build a true hegemony, which would require resources that they do not possess. They will become a dominated bourgeoisie – dominated by the metropolitan bourgeoisie – only capable of becoming an imitative and parasitical class, making up for its backwardness by conspicuous consumption and the reversion to tribalism and racism:

> Because it is bereft of ideas, because it lives to itself and cuts itself off from the people, undermined by its hereditary incapacity to think in terms of all

the problems of the nation as seen from the point of view of the whole of that nation, the national middle class will have nothing better to do than to take on the role of the manager for Western enterprise, and it will in practice set up its country as the brothel of Europe (Fanon, 1963 [1961]: 154).

The national bourgeoisie starts out by copying Western institutions – political constitutions and outward manifestations of its economy – but degenerates from a multiparty democracy to a one-party state, and then to a one-man dictatorship. Fanon expressed vividly what would indeed come to pass in post-colonial Africa. This was no empty speculation; it was how things turned out.

By painting the national bourgeois road in such dire colours, Fanon hopes to convince us that the only progressive road is that of national liberation – the revolutionary transformation of the class structure and the realisation of democratic socialism. But how feasible was this? Even if the revolutionary forces won hegemony, could they bring about democratic socialism? Leaving aside colonial legacies that cannot be simply swept aside – the argument of Bourdieu and others – what about international forces? Fanon rather optimistically argued that post-colonial Africa can insist on and enforce reparations from Western capitalism, because the latter needs what Africa has to offer – not just its natural resources, but also its consumer markets. Fanon was naive about the possibilities of democratic socialism, but the naiveté sprang from a desperation that saw the pitfalls of the national bourgeoisie.

Both Bourdieu and Fanon have a fascination for the peasantry and deploy that fascination for a critical analysis of contemporary societies. Bourdieu creates a romantic anthropology of the Algerian peasantry that becomes the basis for his functionalist analysis of symbolic domination in French society. Fanon projects the peasantry as a revolutionary class that will usher in democratic socialism, formulated to highlight the degeneration of post-colonial Africa if it follows the national bourgeois road.

BETWEEN REVOLUTIONARY OPTIMISM AND CRITICAL PESSIMISM

The conversation between Fanon and Bourdieu shows how theoretical influences circulate between colony and metropolis, but especially the influence of the colony on the metropolis. Nor are these isolated examples. Some of the great French intellectuals were shaped by experiences in colonial Africa – Foucault spent two formative years in Tunisia; Derrida and Camus grew up in Algeria – and the Algerian question continues to exert a powerful influence on French intellectual life, even now, almost 50 years after independence.

Thus, the conversation between Fanon and Bourdieu becomes more interesting if we extend it backwards and forwards in time beyond the Algerian experience to examine the theoretical effects of their personal trajectories between colony and metropolis. Here, we see a striking and unexpected convergence in their understandings of French society, especially if placed in the frame of colonialism. The very notion of symbolic violence, at the centre of Bourdieu's corpus on France, implies a contrast with the physical violence of colonialism, especially Algerian settler colonialism. Symbolic violence works through the habitus – the cumulative introjection of social structure into the human psyche and the inscription of social structure onto the body.

The parallels with Fanon are uncanny. *Black Skin, White Masks,* written about Fanon's experience of metropolitan racism, is a psychoanalytical understanding of the internal dynamics of racial domination in which the colonised internalises the social structure and wrestles to find his or her place in that structure. It is a futile struggle of inter-racial sexual liaisons and exaggerated efforts to be the perfect Frenchman/-woman that only further endorses their inferiority. This is not the physical violence of colonialism, but the deeper symbolic violence of metropolitan racial domination. For Fanon, as indeed for Bourdieu, there is simply no effective response to symbolic violence, and so both end up with a critical pessimism with respect to France, which contrasts so vividly to the revolutionary optimism they both exhibit in Algeria.

The parallels become more even intriguing if one probes Bourdieu's great book of symbolic domination – *Distinction.* Here, the dominant classes are blessed with cultural capital, some more than others, and the dominated classes are bereft of such capital, but the middle classes – the petite bourgeoisie – are the great pretenders, aspiring to legitimate culture, over-conforming in their attempt to emulate the class to which they don't belong. The petit bourgeois is indeed the bourgeois 'writ small':

> Even his bodily hexis, which expresses his whole objective relation to the social world, is that of a man who had to make himself small to pass through the strait gate, which leads to the bourgeoisie: strict and sober, discreet and severe, in his dress, his speech, his gestures and his whole bearing, he always lacks something in stature, breadth, substance, largesse (Bourdieu, 1984 [1979]: 338).

Bourdieu's contempt for the petite bourgeoisie who seeks admission to an inaccessible world is strikingly parallel to Fanon's contempt for blacks who try to enter white society by trying to make themselves less black. Although he is never explicit, Fanon is not writing about the working class, but about members of the black middle classes, like himself, who emigrate to France to become professionals of one sort or another. It is as if their own histories of exclusion, seared into their psyches, lead the one (Bourdieu) to be a self-hating petit bourgeois and the other (Fanon) a self-hating black. This might also explain the venom behind Fanon's denunciation of the colonial national bourgeoisie as an imitative bourgeoisie, just as it might also explain Bourdieu's hostility to Fanon, whose revolutionary ardour is the intellectual's attempt to escape his habitus, to jump out of his skin.

There is, however, a profound asymmetry in the trajectories of these two intellectuals. Whereas Fanon starts out in France as a critical pessimist to become a revolutionary optimist in Algeria based on a romantic radical vision of the peasantry, Bourdieu starts out in Algeria as a revolutionary optimist to become a critical pessimist in France by drawing on a romantic conservative vision of the peasantry. Each reacts against his previous experience. Fanon leaves behind the symbolic violence of racism in France primed to participate in revolutionary catharsis against colonial violence. Equally, Bourdieu is all too ready to abandon his equivocal revolutionary optimism, so that when he enters France he rejects Third World Marxism and adopts a critical pessimism based on another form of violence – symbolic violence. Toward the end of his life he breaks out of his critical pessimism by joining the calumniated working class, attacking the symbolic order associated with neoliberalism and forging new bonds with African intellectuals – a return of the repressed, but without theoretical warrant.

Violence

The conversation between Fanon and Bourdieu raises questions of violence and colonialism, and the relation between them. Despite the insight and sympathy with which Bourdieu grasped the realities of colonial domination and resistance in Algeria, these were not the insights he was to take back to France and use in the elaboration of his theory of social order. Rather, what he took back to France to work into a suite of theoretical innovations for understanding society were the insights he drew from his study of rural indigenous society. In consequence, his work has very little to say about social change, transformation, resistance and revolution beyond those occasional and suggestive passages we noted in Conversation 2, frequently marked by references to Algeria or colonisation more broadly. On the face of it, therefore, Bourdieu should have little to say to South African social reality.

But the division between Fanon and Bourdieu – real violence in the colony, symbolic violence in the metropolis; revolution in the colony, invisible and unchallengeable domination in the metropolis – may be too stark. The relationship between symbolic violence and physical violence is much closer than such dichotomies make it appear. And as with symbolic violence, the relationship between the state, the law, and popular violence in communities is a complex and reciprocal one.

This reflection proceeds through a discussion of seven propositions regarding physical violence, drawn from ongoing research into the dynamics of social change in South Africa.

Collective violence on the part of subalterns is frequently a response to the symbolic violence that works to silence them.

Fanon certainly thought so: one reason why subaltern violence was necessary was that it was the only way to break the internal chains of oppression. South Africa's Steve Biko and other intellectuals of the Black Consciousness movement also argued that the first necessity in the struggle for freedom was that blacks should overcome the internal complex of inferiority fostered by white racism. The symbolic violence of racism, in other words, has enormous force in the colonies. It has been argued by some that popular violence in South Africa, particularly ethnic and xenophobic violence, has roots in the self-denigration fostered by the symbolic violence of racism.

Our research into community protests suggests, too, that violence is a last resort when the authorities have repeatedly refused to consult with communities or failed to respond to their grievances. Violence then becomes a refusal to accept the symbolic violence of marginalisation and lack of voice, and an assertion of popular agency and the right to have grievances and to be heard.

Physical violence always has a symbolic dimension.

As Bourdieu (2000 [1997]: 172) remarks, even naked force 'has a symbolic dimension'. When police gather in force to stop a demonstration and shoot protesters with rubber bullets, they are not only attempting to control 'rioters'; they are asserting the symbolic authority of the state to deploy violence in maintaining 'order'. In South Africa, however, this kind of symbolic display is apt to ring with undertones that subvert its official meaning. For the crowds of community protesters, police action of this sort conjures up a different symbolic universe, undermining the authority of the state: the casspirs[11] 'remind us of apartheid, that we are not free in this democracy. We don't need casspirs. We need police that respect human rights' (Langa, 2011: 63).

For their part, when protesters burn down municipal buildings, they are challenging the symbolic authority of the state with a symbolic power of their own, as we saw in Conversation 3. During the struggle against apartheid, burning collaborators to death with the dreaded 'necklace' – a tyre drenched in petrol – was a way of 'purifying' the community. While in some cases xenophobic violence deliberately focuses on killing foreign nationals and even on occasion burning them to death, in many more cases it is limited to looting or the destruction of property, suggesting degrees of restraint on the part of xenophobic crowds.

Building on this, we see that subaltern violence is embedded in its own structures of symbolic meaning that shape its rules and repertoires. This is signalled by a woman worker, discussing strike violence:

> There's no sweet strike, there is no Christian strike ... a strike is a strike. You want to get back what belongs to you. You want the response must be positive and quick. You won't win a strike with a Bible. You do not

wear high heels and carry an umbrella and say 1992 it was under apartheid, 2007 is under ANC. You won't win a strike like that (Von Holdt, 2010b: 141).

The contrast drawn by the striker between Christian behaviour and strike behaviour signals a shift in moral register: a strike has its own moral codes distinct from those of Christianity. And a community protester uses almost exactly the same words to describe protest action against dirty municipal water supplies, suggesting that they resonate with a common sense of popular justice shared among diverse subaltern groups: 'I am a Christian, but when the strikes[12] start you put the Bible down and then you fight. It is necessary to use force. The water is clean now because of the strike' (Langa, 2011: 62).

Subaltern violence is ambiguous, with both emancipatory and corrosive dimensions.

Deployed against unjust authority, subaltern violence disrupts the symbolic order that elevates such authority above the people, and not infrequently it delivers concrete results – clean water, higher wages. Violence, it is clear from our respondents, and as Fanon argues, constitutes an assertion of popular agency and a celebration of popular power. Yet it has its dark side, to which Fanon pays too little attention. Frequently, its victims are other subalterns and it effects a terrible trauma in their lives. Xenophobic attacks provide a dreadful illustration of this.

Moreover, repertoires of violence expand and become embedded in organisational practices. Violence corrodes democracy, both within organisations where disputes or factional struggles are settled through violence (see the discussion under *'Democracy and violence are both ways to structure power'*, below, for an example of this), and in the broader body politic, where violence becomes an alternative to the democratic act of voting: 'Violence is the only language that our government understands ... we became violent and problems were immediately resolved. It is clear that violence is a solution to all problems' (Langa, Dlamini & Von Holdt, 2011: 49).

A brief vignette of the death of one of our respondents illustrates the complex way cycles of violence reproduce themselves over time. During the 1980s Mr T had participated in battles between local self-defence units and vigilante gangs sponsored by the apartheid security apparatus in which several people had been killed. At the time our research team met him, Mr T was a taxi owner and chairperson of the local taxi association. The taxi association had been racked by internal conflict that had recently turned violent, again with deadly consequences.

The current community protests against the town council in his community were violent, and this man formed part of a delegation of elders who went to the ANC head office to request an urgent response to resolve the conflict. He was, he told our researchers, motivated by the desire for peace, fearing that the protests would reignite the taxi war. He spoke about the importance of exploring non-violent methods in dealing with community problems, so that the mistakes of the past in which people start killing each other were not repeated. He also mentioned that since being elected chairperson of the taxi association, there had been three attempts to kill him.

A few days later Mr T was gunned down and died on the scene. His life and death had paradoxical meanings in the community. At his funeral, gunshots were fired in the air, celebrating a fallen hero and soldier. Mourners sang revolutionary songs referring to the activities of the self-defence units. He was spoken of as a hero, and also as a man who had brought peace to the community: 'We have peace in our time because of Mr T', said one speaker (Langa, Dlamini and Von Holdt, 2010).

Violence, democracy, and peace are entwined in perplexing and complex ways in societies such as ours, characterised by a legacy of colonialism and the turbulence of transition. Bourdieu's concept of symbolic violence – and its relation to the broader symbolic order – provides rich insights; however, it needs to be expanded and brought into relationship with structural and physical violence if it is to help us make sense of this social reality.

Democracy and violence are both ways to structure power.

Democracy and violence have a complex and shifting relationship with each other.

The crucial element in the popular resistance to apartheid was the building of popular democratic organisations, such as trade unions and residents associations. This was an innovation, the possibility of which was considered by neither Fanon nor Bourdieu in their analysis of the Algerian revolution, and it constituted a very different form of empowerment on the part of the colonised than the strategies of violence advocated by Fanon. Indeed, it provided a durable structure of empowerment through which subalterns could challenge not only the apartheid regime, but also their own leaders over questions of strategy and tactics, and it would be sustained into the post-apartheid period.

While popular democratic organisation enabled workers and residents to negotiate with the authorities, it did not eliminate violence; indeed, the context for building this type of organisation was an intrinsically violent one, characterised by street battles, the destruction of property, massacres, assault and detentions, judicial repression, and guerrilla operations. Under such conditions, democratic organisation also entailed a coercive element. My research into the internal dynamics of trade union organisation during the 1980s at Highveld Steel provided insight into the relationship among democracy, coercive violence and power.

As union militancy at Highveld Steel increased, the shop steward committee, directly elected by union members in each department of the steelworks, designated a number of militant and active members who were not shop stewards to form a 'strike committee', with the informal understanding that this would mobilise workers, identify strikebreakers and apply 'punishment' to the latter, usually in the form of beatings with a sjambok.[13] This was understood as a way of teaching and enforcing the 'union law' regarding solidarity. Although the shop stewards committee expected the strike committee to be subordinate to its overall direction, a struggle for power rapidly developed between the two committees, as the strike committee came to believe that the compromises entailed by negotiating with management were a sign that shop stewards were 'selling out'. Violence escalated, strikes were accompanied by more and more widespread and serious assaults, and eventually the union split into two.

Underlying this split was the way internal organisational democracy and the complex procedures governing relations between the union and management empowered workers differentially: the more articulate, educated and skilled residents of the township proved to be highly effective shop stewards, in contrast to the illiterate and less educated rural migrant workers in the hostels, and so it was the former who tended to be elected and re-elected. This led to bitterness among the hostel dwellers, particularly as they had initially established the union.

Democracy disempowered them. The violence of the strike committee was a way of taking the union back. For the strike committee and its constituents, it was the sjambok that had built the union. For the shop stewards and their constituencies, it was democracy that had built the union and the sjambok that was destroying it. Both sides mobilised symbolic power in the struggle over the meaning, practices and leadership of the organisation. When the union split, it was into 'the union of the hostels' and 'the union of the township'. Although the two were eventually reunited into one union, deep fissures, buttressed by memories of violence, continued to surface at times of stress (Von Holdt, 2003: 147ff).

As this study showed, democracy does not do away with all violence: every democracy has its 'law' and every law has its coercive dimension. Furthermore, democracy, even within subaltern organisations, does not empower everyone equally, but itself constitutes a structure of differential power. For those who are marginalised and disempowered, violence provides an alternative strategy for reconfiguring the structures of power. However, violence also proves to be profoundly corrosive within subaltern organisation, undermining democracy, producing a climate of fear and the withdrawal of members, division and splits. Violent repertoires have a long life, reproducing themselves within organisational structures and cultures, where they are always available as a resource in future conflict. Democratic leadership stands revealed as an extremely complex and demanding practice.

These dynamics, explored in a small case study of democracy from below, are repeated within large-scale democratic political systems, such as South Africa's after apartheid. Strike violence, for example, persists. Partly this is an enduring repertoire from the anti-apartheid period: as one worker put it, 'Since I was born, I have seen all strikes are violent. There are no such strikes as peaceful strikes.'

Partly, though, there is a deep sense that South African democracy masks great inequalities and that workers have not experienced the promises of liberation (Von Holdt, 2010b). Workers, in other words, are acutely aware of the structural violence that continues to oppress them, which brings us to the next proposition.

Symbolic violence is also interconnected with structural violence.

A national constitution, according to Bourdieu, 'is merely a founding fiction designed to disguise the act of lawless violence which is the basis for the establishment of law'. Symbolic violence thus originates with a process of usurpation, 'the inaugural violence' in which the law is rooted (Bourdieu, 2000 [1997]: 168). This inaugural violence would include what Marx called primitive accumulation in the advanced capitalist countries, as well as the wars and 'pacification' of the populace entailed in the formation of nation states. In the colonies, colonial conquest and land dispossession constitute crucial dimensions of the 'inaugural violence'; in South Africa, this violent process of land dispossession continues to underpin the new post-apartheid constitution, often lauded as one of the most progressive in the world.

But Bourdieu's almost exclusive focus on domination and symbolic violence within the elite, such as takes place within the scholarly, bureaucratic and cultural fields, provides him with a curiously bloodless sense of symbolic violence; it is only when he turns to discuss briefly the symbolic violence experienced by workers in the workplace that he finds it to be based on 'structural violence' derived from the fear of losing their jobs. The symbolic violence experienced by subalterns, then, is bound up with the structural violence – a concept pretty much unexplored by Bourdieu – of their location in society, unlike the symbolic violence experienced in elite fields. The domination experienced by a junior academic in the scholarly field is very different from the domination experienced by a mineworker or by the residents of informal settlements such as Orange Farm.

'Popular justice' may displace the state's monopoly over violence.

In South Africa, the post-apartheid state does not have a monopoly over either symbolic or physical violence. Research into popular crime-fighting initiatives, xenophobic violence, and strike violence reveals the tension between subaltern organisation and the state over the deployment of coercion and the law, which is simultaneously a contestation over physical and symbolic violence.

In a place called Trouble, an area of Reconstruction and Development Programme houses and shacks in Gauteng, the local Community Policing Forum (CPF) attempts to support policing and reduce criminal activities (Von Holdt, 2011b). The grassroots volunteers in the CPF, though, find themselves squeezed between the violence of criminals, community vigilantism, and lacklustre and sometimes corrupt local police. A young woman street patroller in the shack section of Trouble told us that people are scared to talk about crime because of the danger of retaliation by the criminals. As an example, she told us about a rapist who had been apprehended by her street patrollers and who was now sending messages from his jail cell, where he was awaiting trial: '"Tell that girl and her group that I will be out very soon and I will deal with her." So somewhere, somehow, you feel what is the use of patrolling? I do not have any protection.'

As a result, the membership of the CPF is dwindling. She commented bitterly about corruption in the criminal justice system:

I would like to put a big no, the law doesn't exist, the law doesn't work for us. As long as you have money, you can live the way you want in this country of ours. You rape a kid, you have money, you don't even go to court, you are out. I am talking from what I have seen. As long as you have money, then you are free man.

Because of this fear and ineffectual police presence, there has been a rise in community vigilantism:

> What they do is they catch a criminal, they won't come to me, they will whistle their whistle and the community gets up and the next thing you go there, the guy is already beaten up. The community does not care as long as he is dead, a criminal is a criminal. You steal other people's things, you deserve to die, they do not give a damn.

CPF members try to prevent mob justice, believing that it is the state's role to enforce the law, but they sometimes have to withdraw because of the danger to themselves.

Such interviews make it clear that there is an argument deep within communities over legality and the community enforcement of codes of behaviour – over the state and extra-state action. The same argument was apparent in Trouble during an outbreak of xenophobic conflict. Foreign nationals had used guns to repel an attack by South African residents and there was a strong argument from some quarters in the community that residents should arm themselves and retaliate. The CPF and the local ANC branch combined forces to persuade the community not to pursue such a course of action. An ANC office bearer explained that 'As the people, we cannot take our own decision, but the government will come ... We cannot just take the law into our own hands whilst the government is there.' The chairperson of the CPF explained: 'it is part of law enforcement to prevent crime and prevent violence .... It is in the nature of the CPF to be against violence and to stop wrong things.'

In this case, organisations such as the ANC branch and the CPF engage in formative efforts to defend the legitimacy of the state and its monopoly over coercion and law enforcement, against informal groups who advocate taking the law into their own hands.[14] The success of these organisations in this particular case may be related to the fact that foreign nationals were well armed and clearly capable of deploying their own extra-state violence. It is not impossible, though, that the argument will swing the other way in the light of the failure of the police to protect the community from violent crime more generally, or to make any effort to seize the weapons of the foreigners as they had promised. Where the state fails to demonstrate its monopoly over coercion, popular justice is likely to fill the vacuum.

Apartheid and the struggle against it undermined the legitimacy of the state and its laws. The new democratic state has not been able to securely re-establish the legitimacy of the law, with the result that the law tends to receive a qualified and provisional acceptance in many quarters; consider the comments of a striker explaining why the law of the majority ('the law of the union') requires breaking the law of the state:

> I do not think the law is wrong as such. Law is supposed to defend the right to strike and the rights of those not on strike. But how can we follow that law? How are we going to be successful in winning our demands? *Umthetho oyaphulwa, oyenzelwe oko phulwa.*[15] We must follow the majority. The majority vote for a strike (Von Holdt, 2010b: 142).

Seldom, if ever, are violent strikers brought before a court of law. In practice, then, the law of the state has less force than the law of the strike and the symbolic power of the state is further eroded.

Social order is jointly constructed by the state and citizens.

The discussion under the previous proposition illustrated a profound argument and contestation within communities that suggest that the authority of the law and the state are not simply imposed from above on the citizenry, but are actively constituted by citizens, indicating that there is a substantial constituency that supports such a project against both the criminal erosion of law and order, and the protagonists of vigilantism and 'popular justice'.

In exploring this proposition, we turn to a case study (Langa & Von Holdt, 2011) of the community of Bokfontein, near Brits, where an innovative state intervention to establish a community-shaped public work programme has been introduced, and of the way in which this has empowered the community both to bring an end to intra-community violence and to resist calls for xenophobic pogroms. Bokfontein is the product of the removals of two separate communities from land earmarked for development by private and public developers, and consists of some 5,000 residents living in shacks at a site far from towns and work opportunities, and with no public amenities. The people who live there were traumatised, angry, and bitter, and the result was violent and deadly conflict between the two communities.

The Community Work Programme (CWP) is a public employment programme that offers participants two days of work per week, at a minimum of R60 per day, for as long as they wish to remain on the programme. The community decides on the socially useful work to be performed, and the work is organised by work teams and a project leadership selected from the community. In Bokfontein, CWP projects include the building of an access road; planting trees throughout the community; drilling a borehole and installing water piping; establishing a community park and vegetable gardens, the produce of which is used to cook daily meals for the children of vulnerable families; and providing home-based care programmes for vulnerable households, including the chronically ill and AIDS sufferers. The CWP, which employs about 800 participants from the community, has not only improved household incomes, but also allows the community to reimagine itself as a place with public amenities, public goods, and public spaces, and as a caring community that assists the vulnerable and values socially useful labour.

Not only that, but the CWP, and the community building process that preceded it, enabled participants to confront their trauma and the intra-community violence, and establish a new sense of solidarity:

> It helped us deal with the pain of our eviction and also the lines that were dividing us as communities.

> It made it possible for us to know each other. And it brought us together to accept each other as human beings.

The community-building process also enabled foreign nationals, of whom many live in Bokfontein, and South African citizens to discuss discrimination and violence, and to explicitly understand more about each other's histories and cultures. When a nearby community attempted to mobilise Bokfontein residents to take part in xenophobic pogroms, the community as a whole resisted this. The community leadership also explicitly rejects strategies of protest and toyi-toying in favour of negotiating with authorities and business, and forging their own community development strategies: 'So when we toyi-toyi we become violent. What are we teaching our children? Are we not teaching them to also be violent?' (Langa & Von Holdt, 2011).

In Bokfontein, an innovative state intervention has empowered the community to reimagine itself and its future in a collaboration that has created the elements of a new symbolic order in the community, one that both restores the authority of the state and the law, and sustains an active and confident citizenry in a partnership oriented towards development and the future. Here we can see the constituency identified in Trouble, which seeks a new kind of state authority and a peaceful and violence-free community, coming into a power that has both symbolic and material dimensions.[16]

NOTES

1 The English versions to which I will refer are *The Algerians* (1962 [1961]) and *Algeria*, 1960 (1979 [1963]), which is an abridged version of the French *Work and Workers in Algeria* (1963).

2 For an important set of essays on the contradictions and paradoxes of Bourdieu's Algerian writings, see Jane Goodman and Paul Silverstein (2009), especially the chapter by Fanny Colonna, who criticises Bourdieu for his poor stylised fieldwork that misses the realities of daily life and for his unsubstantiated claim that the Kabyle misrecognise what they are up to.

3 First published in *Esprit*, 1, January 1961; English translation appeared in Bourdieu (1962 [1961]: chap. 7).

4 Bourdieu (2000 [1998] writes of the difficulty of changing the habitus, calling for all sorts of bodily retraining. Fanon is saying the same, i.e. that the internalisation of oppression is so deep that the colonised can only transform themselves through violence.

5 Writing with Sayad in 1964, Bourdieu analyses the possibilities of socialism very much in terms familiar from Durkheim and Mauss. They cast doubt on the feasibility of self-organised, decentralised socialism based on autonomous peasant organisation of the farms vacated by colonialists, just as they fear the possibility of a centralised authoritarian socialism imposed from above. Like Fanon, they hope for an educative leadership responsive to needs from below. They easily fall back, however, on the cultural legacies of tradition to explain economic and political regression.

6 We find this vision laid out in the earliest writings of Bourdieu (1962 [1961]) a secondary account of the cultures of different ethnic groups, and then in the self-consciously theoretical works written in France, most notably *Outline of a Theory of Practice* (1977 [1972]).

7 Bourdieu does try to mark his distance from one of the modernisation theorists of the day – Daniel Lerner (1958) – by criticising his psychological characterisation of modernity as the recognition of other, the expression of empathy and as a rationality freely chosen. As orientations to the world, 'tradition' and 'modernity' are not freely chosen, says Bourdieu, but spring from specific material contexts, the clash of unequal civilisations under

colonialism (Bourdieu, 1962 [1961]: 117, 119–20). But the concepts of tradition and modernity are never called into question, simply redefined.

8 Bourdieu (2000) relies on the much misused case of the Kabyle cook – a man who moves from one job to another. There is little evidence that this is a sign of anomie or that he is beholden to some traditional habitus. Instead, the cook shows great entrepreneurial adroitness in adapting to the exigencies of urban life under colonialism.

9 Gramsci seemed to think that the war of position either preceded the war of movement (in the West, where civil society was strong) or followed the war of movement (in the East, with its undeveloped civil society, where socialism would be built after the revolution). Fanon understood the dangers of postponing the struggle for socialism until after independence.

10 Interestingly, Fanon and Bourdieu held opposite views about the working class in advanced capitalism: for Fanon, it was potentially revolutionary; for Bourdieu, it was not. Although there is no sign that Fanon had read Gramsci, he had a very Gramscian view of the West with a developed civil society and a bourgeoisie able to make concessions, all of which was absent in the periphery (Fanon, 1963 [1961]: 38, 108–9, 165, 175).

11 Armoured police vehicles.

12 The word 'strike' is used to describe not only industrial action, but forceful community protest.

13 A sjambok is a rawhide whip.

14 In other sites of our research, both the local ANC branch and organisations such as civic associations and CPFs adopted a very different stance, either supporting or turning a blind eye to xenophobic attacks.

15 'The law is made to be broken.'

16 The CWP has already been rolled out into some 70 communities nationally with a total of 90,000 people employed, and is sparking a discussion about a national employment guarantee.

PEDAGOGY OF THE OPPRESSED

MICHAEL BURAWOY

Freire Meets Bourdieu

> *Thus, in a society in which the obtaining of social privileges depends more and more closely on possession of academic credentials, the School does not only have the function of ensuring discreet succession to a bourgeois estate which can no longer be transmitted directly and openly. This privileged instrument of the bourgeois sociodicy which confers on the privileged the supreme privilege of not seeing themselves as privileged manages the more easily to convince the disinherited that they owe their scholastic and social destiny to their lack of gifts or merits, because in matters of culture absolute dispossession excludes awareness of being dispossessed.*
> Bourdieu and Passeron (1977 [1970]: 210)

For Bourdieu, education is symbolic domination par excellence. In a society where the dominant class can no longer invoke rights of blood to pass on their inheritance nor appeal to ascetic virtue as a justification of success, academic certification becomes the vehicle to justify and transmit its domination. Education attests and consecrates the merits and gift of the bourgeoisie, while concealing their distinction as an outgrowth of their privilege – concealing it, that is, not only from themselves, but also from the dominated, who see themselves as undeserving because unmeritorious. *Reproduction*, which brought Bourdieu and Passeron into the public eye both in France and abroad, offers a deeply pessimistic account of the role of education in reproducing domination through simultaneously privileging and hiding the cultural capital inherited by the dominant. It is designed to dispel illusions that schooling can be a vehicle of social transformation, although that still didn't stop Bourdieu using his place in the education world to advocate change.

Paulo Freire's *Pedagogy of the Oppressed* – the originating, most popular text of critical pedagogy – appeared in 1970, the same year that *Reproduction* was published in France. Neither makes any reference to the other, yet they both embark from a similar criticism of conventional pedagogy and its optimism about formal education's progressive contribution to social change. Freire also sets out from the assumption that the dominated have internalised their oppression, and that this domination is reinforced through a 'banking' system of education in which teachers pour knowledge into the supposedly empty minds of their students. There is, however, an alternative pedagogy, Freire argues, based on dialogue between teacher and student around problems originating with the latter. This requires working with students outside of formal education, i.e. bringing education to their communities, neighbourhoods and villages.

Bourdieu and Passeron may not refer to Freire by name, but they condemn all such 'populist pedagogies' as misguided. Rather than challenging domination, these pedagogies effectively consolidate symbolic domination. Their own solution, to which they refer in the conclusion to their earlier book, *The Inheritors* (1979 [1964]), but all but abandon in *Reproduction*, is 'rational pedagogy' – the attempt to counteract inequalities in the cultural preparation of different classes, not by making concessions to subjugated cultures, but by inculcating dominant culture into disadvantaged groups. They freely admit this to be a utopian project in the context of class domination, but the *attempt* to realise it would have the benefit of unmasking the inequity of cultural preconditioning.

Here, then, are two antithetical approaches to the same problem – i.e. the way in which education reproduces domination. Where Bourdieu can only conceive of a countering of domination by creating universal access to the cultural achievements of bourgeois society, i.e. by extending bourgeois civilisation to all, Freire, on the other hand, sees in this the perfection of domination. He seeks an alternative pedagogy that extricates and cultivates the good sense that remains within the oppressed despite internalised oppression – a pedagogy that starts out from their lived experience.

In the conversation that follows, I first examine the argument of Bourdieu and Passeron, and then construct Freire's antithesis, before seeking a synthesis in Gramsci's writings on education and politics. Gramsci, after all, believed in the 'common school' that would induct everyone into the dominant culture, arming potential organic intellectuals with the wherewithal to identify, elaborate and protect the good sense of the working class. In this view, Freire's separatist solution underestimates the power of ideological hegemony – a power that calls for contestation on its terrain as well as the development of an alternative culture.

SCHOOLING AS SYMBOLIC DOMINATION

Bourdieu had a continuing interest in education throughout his life, which is perhaps fitting for a reflexive sociologist whose career was made by excelling in the academic world. This abiding fascination with education was surely triggered by his own life of upward mobility – an anomaly his theory could not explain. His self-portrait – a son of a rural postal worker who made good through education – subscribes to the ideology of 'merit' and 'gift' that his sociological writings systematically discredit. Not surprisingly, he returns again and again to the question of education, which was central to his own life, but also to French society in general.

In 1964, only four years after he had returned from Algeria, Bourdieu joined Jean-Claude Passeron to publish *The Inheritors*, which examined the critical, but hidden role of cultural capital not only in selecting students for university, but also in subjecting them to a pedagogy that privileged the culturally advantaged. They made the argument – provocative at the time – that even if there were equality of opportunity, even if the children of the wage labourer had the same chance of entering university as the children of the senior executive, still the university would reproduce the domination of the latter over the former. Teaching in the university presupposes and reinforces the privileged upbringing of the middle and upper classes.

For those who are looking for origins, *The Inheritors* prefigures so much in Bourdieu's corpus – the relationship of different classes to culture as laid out in *Distinction* (Bourdieu, 1984 [1979]), the self-delusions of the academic world elaborated as scholastic fallacies, the idea of social structure as a game presented in *Pascalian Meditations* (Bourdieu, 2000 [1997]), the battle of the disciplines worked out in *Homo Academicus* (Bourdieu, 1988 [1984]) and the strategies through which the dominant class reproduces itself through the Grandes Écoles presented in *State*

Nobility (Bourdieu, 1996 [1989]). But most significantly, *The Inheritors* is a prolegomenon to its theoretical deepening and detailed elaboration in *Reproduction in Education, Society and Culture*. Written with Jean-Claude Passeron, *Reproduction* is an uncompromising critique of education that brought both fame and infamy to its authors.

Education exemplifies symbolic domination. Schooling *secures* the active participation of students and teachers in the pursuit of credentials that entails the learning of legitimate culture, while *obscuring* the reproduction of class domination that is the effect of such participation. Securing participation is education's technical function (inculcation), while obscuring class domination is its social function (class selection) (Bourdieu & Passeron, 1977 [1970]: 164–67). Thus, Bourdieu and Passeron criticise economists for emphasising the technical functions of education at the expense of its social functions and critical theorists for focusing on the social at the cost of the technical functions of education. At the heart of symbolic domination is the *combination* of enthusiastic participation and systematic misrecognition. To examine one without the other is to misunderstand the symbolic power of education.

Central to their model of reproduction is the way the relative autonomy of the educational system has the effect of naturalising its two-fold arbitrariness: the imposition of a cultural arbitrary (legitimate culture) through an arbitrary power (class domination). The source of relative autonomy lies with the cadres of teachers, specially trained and recruited as professionals and thus vehement defenders of the autonomy of their practice, but also on the standardisation and routinisation of education; in other words, subjection to its own principles of regulation. Relative autonomy gives the (false) impression of neutrality with respect to class, rendering class bias invisible and all the more profound.

The argument rests on the assumption that primary pedagogical work (PW) in the family produces an enduring and irreversible primary habitus that sets the conditions for subsequent schooling:

> Insofar as PW is an irreversible process producing, in the time required for inculcation, an irreversible disposition, i.e. a disposition which cannot itself be repressed or transformed except by an irreversible process producing in turn a new irreversible disposition, primary PA [pedagogic action] (the earliest phase of upbringing), which is carried out by PW without any antecedent (primary PW), produces a primary habitus, characteristic of a group or class, which is the basis for the subsequent formation of any other habitus (Bourdieu & Passeron, 1977 [1970]: 42).

The primary habitus inculcated by the dominant classes bestows cultural advantages on their children. The primary pedagogical work in the family transmits linguistic and cultural dispositions that take advantage of the symbolic mastery – abstract bookish learning – taught at school. The children of the dominated classes, having received a more functional, utilitarian upbringing, face an alien school environment and pedagogy. Although it appears neutral and universal, school learning presupposes the cultural capital of the dominant class and disparages the culture of the dominated. The power of the school system is redoubled by the labour market, which rewards academic success and in turn further consecrates the legitimate capital of the already privileged and denigrates the dominated culture:

> The more unified the market on which the value of the products of the different PAs [pedagogic actions] is determined, the more the groups and classes, which have undergone a PA inculcating a dominated cultural arbitrary, are likely to have the valuelessness of their cultural attainment brought home to them both by the anonymous sanctions of the labour market and by the symbolic sanctions of the cultural market (e.g. the matrimonial market), not to mention the academic verdicts, which are always charged with economic and symbolic implications. These calls to order tend to produce in them, if not explicit recognition of the dominant culture as the legitimate culture, then at least an insidious awareness of the cultural unworthiness of their own acquirements (Bourdieu & Passeron, 1977 [1970]: 28).

To be sure, there are those, like Bourdieu, who manage to overcome their class background, but they only serve to intensify the obsession with achievement while further mystifying the relation between education and class. Such upward mobility also turns attention away from the more pervasive phenomenon characterising education, namely the exclusion of so many from education at different levels, many of whom quietly eliminate themselves rather than go through the humiliation of being eliminated.

ALTERNATIVE PEDAGOGIES

The picture painted here is very different from that of Paul Willis (1977), for example, who argues that some working-class children do indeed rebel against the middle-class culture thrust upon them in school, embracing their own down-to-earth manual practical culture (with all its problematic sexism and racism); and, furthermore, it is this hostility to middle-class school culture that makes them enthusiastic to re-enter the working class. This rebellion exhibits what Willis calls a 'partial penetration' – the lads clearly understood the bias of the school, but ended up reproducing their own subordination. Willis proposes the creation of schools where teachers would validate working-class culture, elaborating it into a full-blown critique of capitalism. Bourdieu and Passeron dismiss any such sociological relativism as a populist illusion:

> This could lead students to demand that the parallel cultures of the disadvantaged classes should be given the status of the culture taught by the school system. But it is not sufficient to observe that school culture is a class culture; to proceed as if it were only that, is to help it remain so (Bourdieu & Passeron 1979 [1964]: 72).

The populist illusion recognises the social function of education, but misses the technical function, namely the inescapable importance of acquiring credentials that can be utilised for survival. Increasingly, those working-class jobs will not be available to working classes who do not have basic schooling. Thinking perhaps of himself, Bourdieu mocks the very idea of endorsing working-class culture as paternalistic and insulting to the ambitions and capacities of the dominated.

If *popular* pedagogies that celebrate class cultures of the dominated end up channelling the disadvantaged back to the bottom of society, *soft* pedagogies that focus on alternative ways of teaching ignore and further mystify the importance of class:

> ... the ideologies of PA [pedagogic action] as non-violent action – whether in Socratic and neo-Socratic myths of non-directive teaching, Rousseauistic myths of natural education, or pseudo-Freudian myths of non-repressive education – reveal in its clearest form the generic function of educational ideologies, in evading, by the gratuitous negation of one of its terms, the contradiction between the objective truth of PA and the necessary (inevitable) representation of this arbitrary action as necessary ('natural') (Bourdieu & Passeron, 1977 [1970]: 13).

The soft pedagogies become ideologies that do not recognise the role they play in the reproduction of class domination. As we shall see, Freire's problem-based dialogic pedagogy, although not mentioned explicitly, is

clearly one of those ideologies that hide from themselves their own implication in class domination.

So what then is the solution? It is what Bourdieu and Passeron call
'rational pedagogy', which must not only cancel out the inequality of
access to education, but also counteract the advantages of the domi-
nant-class habitus by inculcating the relevant aspects of that habitus in
all classes:

> It may be wondered whether a type of secondary PW [pedagogical work]
> which, conversely, took into account the distance between the pre-exist-
> ent habitus and the habitus inculcated, and was systematically organized
> in accordance with the principles of an explicit pedagogy, would not
> have the effect of erasing the boundary which traditional PW recognizes
> and confirms between the legitimate addressees and the rest. Or, to put it
> another way, whether perfectly rational PW – i.e. PW exerted ab novo in
> all domains on all the educable, taking nothing for granted at the outset,
> with the explicit goal of explicitly inculcating in all its pupils the practi-
> cal principles of the symbolic mastery of practices which are inculcated
> by primary PA [pedagogic action] only within certain groups or classes,
> in short a type of PW everywhere substituting for the traditional mode
> of inculcation the programmed transmission of the legitimate culture –
> would not correspond to the pedagogic interest of the dominated classes
> (the hypothesis of the democratization of education through the ration-
> alization of pedagogy). But the Utopian character of an education policy
> based on this hypothesis becomes apparent as soon as one observes that,
> quite apart from the built-in inertia of every educational institution, the
> structure of power relations prohibits a dominant PA from resorting to
> a type of PW contrary to the interests of the dominant classes who del-
> egate its PAu [pedagogic authority] to it (Bourdieu & Passeron, 1977
> [1970]: 53–54).

What Bourdieu and Passeron present as the only solution in *The Inheritors*
– true democratisation of education – they now dismiss as utopian. Even
utopias have their function in alerting us to the true nature of reality, but
in *Reproduction*, Bourdieu and Passeron bend the stick in the opposite
direction to demonstrate that there cannot be any alternative education
so long as the class structure is what it is. This sounds like a call for
revolution, but of course there is never a hint of that in their writing –
so different from Paulo Freire, for whom education and revolution are
intimately connected.

PEDAGOGY OF THE OPPRESSED

Paulo Freire began his interest in education through the development of literacy campaigns so that peasants could participate in Brazilian education. *The Pedagogy of the Oppressed*, which first appeared in 1970, is a manifesto for Third World revolution that parallels Fanon's *The Wretched of the Earth*. You might say that it is an elaboration of the relation between radical intellectuals and peasantry that we found so unelaborated in Fanon. Like Fanon, Freire had far more faith in the revolutionary potential of the peasantry than the working class, which 'lack revolutionary consciousness and consider themselves privileged' (Freire, 1970: 148). For Freire, critical pedagogy is a necessary part of revolution.

Freire and Bourdieu start out from similar places – domination – although Freire uses a word with a more revolutionary connotation – oppression. Where Bourdieu thematises symbolic violence in France, as opposed to physical violence in the colonies, Freire thematises internal, as opposed to external, oppression. The counterpart to symbolic violence is *internal oppression* – the introjection of the oppressor into the psyche:

> The very structure of their thought has been conditioned by the contradictions of the concrete, existential situation by which they were shaped. Their idea is to be men; but for them, to be men is to be oppressors. This is their model of humanity. This phenomenon derives from the fact that the oppressed, at a certain moment of their existential experience, adopt an attitude of 'adhesion' to the oppressor. Under these circumstances they cannot 'consider' him sufficiently clearly to objectivize him – to discover him 'outside' themselves. This does not necessarily mean that the oppressed are unaware that they are downtrodden. But their perception of themselves as oppressed is impaired by their submersion in the reality of oppression (Freire, 1970: 45).

Leaving aside the question of masculinising the oppressor and oppressed, at first glance this is no different from Bourdieu's notion of social structure being inscribed on the body or internalised in the habitus. Yet, of course, whereas Bourdieu does not see how education could ever liberate the dominated, for Freire this is exactly the purpose of critical pedagogy.

Still, they agree that formal education only reproduces domination/ oppression. But here they begin to diverge, since for Bourdieu, class domination is socially invisible, being the product of formally neutral education, whereas for Freire it lies in the pedagogy itself – the so-called banking model, in which knowledge is deposited in student as object, and in which teacher is teacher and student is student, and what unites them is a relation of unidirectional authority that inhibits creativity, promotes adaptation, isolates consciousness, suppresses context, nurtures fatalism, and mythologises and naturalises domination. Students are subject to a cultural invasion by professionals so that 'the invaded come to see their reality with the outlook of the invaders' (Freire, 1970: 153). For Bourdieu's socio-analysis, Freire substitutes a heavy dose of psychoanalysis.

But Freire is much more optimistic than Bourdieu, for he sees within the psyche two selves, the humanistic individual and the oppressor; the true self and the false self:

> The oppressed suffer from the duality which has established itself in their innermost being … They are at one and the same time themselves and the oppressor whose consciousness they have internalized. The conflict lies in the choice between being wholly themselves and being divided; between ejecting the oppressor within and not ejecting them; between human solidarity or alienation; between following prescriptions or having choices; between being spectators or actors; between acting or having the illusion of acting through the action of the oppressors …. This is the tragic dilemma of the oppressed which their education must take into account (Freire, 1970: 48).

For Freire, then, critical pedagogy must eject the oppressor within, which can only be accomplished through a problem-centred dialogue between teacher and student, in which each learns from the other – for the educator too must be educated. When placed in their own context, tackling their own problems, the oppressed can develop critical faculties through collaboration with others. The interrogation of the folk theory (or thematic universe) of the oppressed leads from problems (or generative themes) to a decoding that focuses on context and thus the historical totality. At the heart of such a pedagogy is the dialogue not only between intellectual and oppressed, but between action and reflection. To veer in one direction or another – activism or verbalism – is to threaten the critical process. Liberation comes through acts of solidarity and collective attempts at social transformation guided by an emergent understanding of historical constraints and possibilities. As in Marx and Fanon, ultimately it is struggle that dissolves inner oppression.

All too little is said about the teacher, who must forge a pedagogy *with* and not *for* the oppressed. Freire does acknowledge the danger that, coming from the oppressor class, teachers bring with them prejudices about the oppressed:

> ... certain members of the oppressor class join the oppressed in their struggle for liberation, thus moving from one pole of the contradiction to the other. Theirs is a fundamental role, and has been so throughout the history of this struggle. It happens, however, that as they cease to be exploiters or indifferent spectators or simply the heirs of exploitation and move to the side of the exploited, they must always bring with them the marks of their origin: their prejudices and their deformations, which include a lack of confidence in the people's ability to think, to want, and to know. Accordingly these adherents to the people's cause constantly run the risk of falling into a type of generosity as malefic as that of the oppressors ... [They] truly desire to transform the unjust order; but because of their background they believe that they must be the executors of the transformation. They talk about the people but they do not trust them; and trusting the people is the indispensable precondition for revolutionary change (Freire, 1970: 60).

Through Bourdieu's eyes, 'the pedagogy of the oppressed' is a dangerous fantasy of intellectuals who think they can overcome, firstly, their own habitus as intellectuals (a dominated fraction of the dominant class) and, secondly, and even more difficult, foster the transformation of the habitus of the dominated. Critical pedagogy is an intellectualist illusion that privileges 'conscientisation' (consciousness raising). It misunderstands the depth of oppression, for it conspires to do what educational ideologies generally do, i.e. focus on the pedagogic relation and thereby obscure its class underpinnings. Freire might retort that Bourdieu is focused on the transmission of the dominant culture and cannot see beyond a banking model of education. When education is taken to the dominated, conducted on their terrain, and working from their problems and issues – rather than enrolling the dominated into the alien schools of the oppressor class – then emancipatory action is possible. Is there a resolution between these mutually opposed positions? I am going to seek one in an unlikely place – the writings of Antonio Gramsci.

GRAMSCI'S COMMON SCHOOL AND THE WAR OF POSITION

If one had to place Gramsci within this conversation between Freire and Bourdieu, it would most likely be on Freire's side. Like Freire, Gramsci's optimism lies in the postulated good sense of the dominated qua working class that springs from its place in production. Cultural invasion there is, but never to the extent of blotting out that good sense at the core of common sense – a good sense that needs elaboration by organic intellectuals engaged in dialogue with the working class, i.e. dialogue not in formal schooling, but in the workplace, in the community. Despite manifest differences in their views about the revolutionary potential of peasantry and proletariat, the centrality of the political party, civil society, and much more, largely due to Gramsci's far richer contextualisation of struggle, nonetheless Gramsci and Freire do share a faith in the capacity of the dominated to see through their domination and engage in struggle to oppose that domination. This shared revolutionary optimism contrasts with Bourdieu's critical pessimism, especially in *Reproduction*.

Therefore, one may be astonished to discover Bourdieu and Passeron's ideas prefigured in Gramsci's notes on education that were written in the context of the fascist regime's call, on the one hand, for vocational education and, on the other, for an active pedagogy that downplays conventional instruction. Gramsci reasserts the importance of instruction, calling for the introduction of the 'common school', which would bestow classical education (Bourdieu's legitimate culture) on all to close the cultural gap between classes. Anticipating Bourdieu and Passeron, Gramsci writes:

> In a whole series of families, especially in the intellectual strata, the children find in their family life a preparation, a prolongation and a completion of school life; they 'breathe in', as the expression goes, a whole quantity of notions and attitudes which facilitate the educational process properly speaking. They already know and develop their knowledge of the literary language, i.e. the means of expression and of knowledge, which is technically superior to the means possessed by the average member of the school population between the ages of six and twelve. Thus, city children by the very fact of living in a city, have already absorbed by the age of six a quantity of notions and attitudes which make their school careers easier, more profitable, and more rapid (Gramsci, 1971: 31).

Gramsci goes even further down Bourdieu and Passeron's road in calling attention to the bodily hexis that gives the intellectual classes advantage in the school:

> Undoubtedly the child of a traditionally intellectual family acquires this psycho-physical adaptation more easily. Before he[1] ever enters the class-room

he has numerous advantages over his comrades, and is already in possession of attitudes learnt from his family environment; he concentrates more easily, since he is used to 'sitting still', etc. (Gramsci, 1971: 42).

Being a hunchback from a poor rural family, Gramsci is perhaps even more aware than Bourdieu of the inherited disadvantages of class – not just the economic, but the cultural disadvantages that he emphasises here. Perhaps Gramsci was thinking of himself and the enormous discipline it took to write the *Prison Notebooks* – so meticulously presented and worked out – when he wrote about the importance of bodily training early on in life:

In education one is dealing with children in whom one has to inculcate certain habits of diligence, precision, poise (even physical poise), ability to concentrate on specific subjects, which cannot be acquired without mechanical repetition of disciplined and methodical acts. Would the scholar at the age of forty be able to sit for sixteen hours on end at his work-table if he had not, as a child, compulsorily, through mechanical coercion, acquired the appropriate psycho-physical habits? (Gramsci, 1971: 37).

Gramsci may have prefigured the argument of *Reproduction*, but his response was very different. Where Bourdieu and Passeron pose the idea of a 'rational pedagogy', only to dismiss it is as utopian, Gramsci builds the idea into a concrete conception of the 'common school', whose raison d'être is to equalise cultural capital across classes:

In the basic organization of the common school, at least the essentials of these conditions [of the families of intellectuals] must be created – not to speak of the fact, which goes without saying that parallel to the common school a network of kindergartens and other institutions would develop, in which even before the school age, children would be habituated to a certain collective discipline and acquire pre-scholastic notions and attitudes. In fact, the common school should be organized like a college, with a collective life by day and by night, freed from the present forms of hypocritical and mechanical discipline; studies should be carried on collectively, with the assistance of teachers and the best pupils, even during periods of so-called individual study, etc. (Gramsci, 1971: 31).

We note here a Freirean flavour with the emphasis on collective discipline and collaborative studies, which is not without significance for the future society Gramsci is imagining. Not surprisingly, and again anticipating the arguments of Bourdieu and Passeron, Gramsci points to the centrality of the teacher – the pivotal conveyor of the dominant culture to the children of the dominated classes:

> In the school, the nexus between instruction and education can only be realised by the living work of the teacher. For he must be aware of the contrast between the type of culture and society which he represents and the type of culture and society represented by his pupils, and conscious of his obligation to accelerate and regulate the child's formation in conformity with the former and in conflict with the latter (Gramsci, 1971: 35–36).

We see that the idea of the common school is not as far-fetched as Bourdieu and Passeron claim. Indeed, examples of such schooling could begin with the notorious boarding school, normally the privilege of the dominant classes, one of which Bourdieu himself attended. He may have hated it – who said remedial education would be fun? – but it seemed to have worked, bringing him from culturally deprived Béarn to the pinnacle of French higher education. Why does he not reflect sociologically on his own schooling as a flawed expression, but an expression nonetheless of rational pedagogy, instead of bemoaning the humiliations he suffered? After all, Bourdieu himself writes that changing habitus requires a comprehensive process of counter-training involving repeated exercises (Bourdieu, 2000 [1997]: 172). This can't be much fun.

Moving farther afield, one might recall the not unsuccessful attempts to reverse class differences in the Soviet Union, or the more thorough-going kibbutzim. The passage above with its reference to a network of 'kindergartens and other institutions' and the collective life of learning anticipates such modern-day experiments as the Harlem Children's Zone, which cordons off an urban area and provides children and their families with extensive social services to counteract cultural disadvantage. Better to examine the attempts to realise a rational pedagogy and the obstacles it confronts as demonstration of the limits of possibility – and the truth of one's theory – than to dismiss it as a worthless utopia!

Their insights into education are very similar, but the projects of Gramsci and Bourdieu are very different. Bourdieu and Passeron are contemptuous of those who harbour the illusion that schooling can be a 'mechanism of change' capable of 'creating discontinuities' and 'building a new world' (1977 [1970]: 65). Yet this is precisely what Gramsci has in mind, which is why he wants to subject everyone – not just the children of intellectuals and the dominant classes – to classical education.

He wants everyone to learn Latin as a way of developing objectivity and disinterestedness, as an appreciation of logic, but also of a sense of history, so we can recognise who we are. Schools can play a progressive role in countering folk beliefs and 'localistic' ties inherited from a feudal world that refuses to disappear, thus preparing citizens for their role in the modern world of politics and civil society:

> Scientific ideas were intended to insert the child into the *societas rerum*, the world of things, while lessons in rights and duties were intended to insert him into the State and into civil society. The scientific ideas the children learnt conflicted with the magical conception of the world and nature which they absorbed from an environment steeped in folklore; while the idea of civic rights and duties conflicted with tendencies towards individualistic and localistic barbarism – another dimension of folklore (Gramsci, 1971: 33–34).

Gramsci envisions the common school as a school for democracy, 'forming [the child] during this time as a person capable of thinking, studying, and ruling – or controlling those who rule' (Gramsci, 1971: 40).

Gramsci was not only concerned to bring children into the modern world, but also to advance the project of social transformation, which brings him into direct engagement with Freire. In the field of education, we might say that Freire represents a war of movement that seeks revolutionary opposition to oppression, which is appropriate where civil society is less developed. The advance of a war of position in worlds with a strong civil society requires an extended battle on the terrain of bourgeois hegemony, and for that one needs the weapons of a classical education. The struggle for the common school, therefore, is part of such a war of position. It would be the crucible of the organic intellectuals of the future – intellectuals who would not only elaborate the good sense of the working class, but contest the bourgeois ideologies that they had imbibed at school.

CONCLUSION

Bourdieu and Passeron make every effort to debunk any notion that the school can be a vehicle of social transformation. Their critique of Freire would focus on his failure to see the broader importance of class domination within which schooling takes place and how the pedagogy of the oppressed leaves that domination unchanged. Moreover, Bourdieu and

Passeron would be very sceptical that members of the dominant class could ever leave their habitus behind when they turn to the peasantry or that the habitus of the peasantry could be transformed.

Recognising Bourdieu and Passeron's critique of the 'pedagogy of the oppressed', namely the penetration of capitalist culture, Gramsci would call for the common school as part of a war of position in civil society, forging intellectuals who are equally at home with legitimate culture and the culture of the dominated class. Gramsci himself, even when in prison, never lost touch with his rural family and his working-class associates. But that did not prevent him from being steeped in the dominant Italian culture, so that much of the *Prison Notebooks* can be seen as a dialogue with Croce, Gentile, Pirandello, Machiavelli and others. This idea of deploying dominant culture against the dominant classes is a familiar aspect of South African history. African nationalist leaders such as Mandela and Tambo were in no way deceived by their missionary education, but used it as a sort of 'common school' that armed them for the struggle against apartheid. Interestingly, Robben Island became known as a 'university of struggle', a school to so many of the leaders of the anti-apartheid movement.

Gramsci also understood that you cannot extricate schooling from broader historical processes. The fight for the common school was part of a fight for the broader transformation of society. Again, this is not a strange idea in South Africa, where schools and universities have been at the forefront of the transformation of society. The Soweto rebellion was organised against the dominant culture and became a catalyst in the struggles to overthrow apartheid. Even if Bourdieu and Passeron would make colonial societies an exception, we only have to turn to May 1968 to see the ways in which French students could be a force for social change and challenge the existing order. It is fascinating to note that neither in *Reproduction*, which appeared in 1970, nor in the epilogue to *The Inheritors*, written in 1979, do Bourdieu and Passeron refer to May 1968. For all the talk of the devaluation of credentials and the bamboozling of a generation in the original text of 1964, this epilogue seeks to show how student frustration was accommodated and class reproduction secured. Only in *Homo Academicus*, written in 1984, does Bourdieu address the student revolt, relying on the same framework of the devaluation of credentials, and the mismatch of objective chances and subjective expectations, opportunities and aspirations, while downplaying the self-understanding of the participants and the ideologies that galvanised the rebellion. Still, finally, there is an attempt at studying the place of education in what was the unfolding crisis of French society.

Once we adopt a broader theoretical canvas and forsake dry statistics for historical process, we quickly grasp the ways in which education becomes a terrain of struggle that fosters both social change and social reproduction. Despite himself, Bourdieu must have believed this, as he was so deeply committed to the advance and teaching of sociology as a progressive form of education, whether in school, university, the pages of *Le Monde* or his own widely read books. Once again, Bourdieu's practice was at odds with his theory.

KARL VON HOLDT

Discipline

My own involvement in the struggle for democracy started in the early 1980s in the adult literacy movement inspired by the work of Paulo Freire. We worked in the huge informal settlement of Crossroads outside Cape Town, where thousands of Africans from the poverty-stricken hinterlands of the Eastern Cape had settled, breaking the pass laws and under constant threat of mass eviction by the police. Every evening we taught to the hiss of gas lamps – there was no electricity – in the classrooms of the local school.

Our practices were participatory and democratic, using pictures and stories to elicit dialogue through which, we hoped, the structural violence of apartheid and capitalism would be exposed. Instead of rows of pupils with the teacher standing in front, we sat in a circle, with the 'coordinator' – as we called the teacher – sitting in the circle with the learners. The learners entered gamely into this process, but at times they were frustrated and perplexed by the endless litany of questions they were asked about the blindingly obvious hardships they faced.

One evening, one of our learners, a strong and intelligent woman who had spent five or six years in formal schooling, came in bearing a stick.

When the session started, she rose and came to the front with the stick, turned and faced the circle of learners, and said, 'This is how we want you to teach', wielding the stick fiercely in the direction of the rest of the class.

We were crestfallen. 'The old ways die hard', we told ourselves. But the incident did make us wonder whether we were serious enough about teaching the rules and structures of language, and whether our approach was too loose and open-ended. How astute she was about the significance of discipline and authority in education, I think now, after reading Michael's dialogue between Paulo Freire and Pierre Bourdieu (and Antonio Gramsci).

After some time, we concluded that Freire did not work – at least as he had envisaged. We could not transcend the authority of the teacher, especially (but not only) when the teacher was white, and the exchange of views and knowledge was not equal. Perhaps Freirean pedagogy might work in the case of intellectuals living among and working with the peasantry they taught, but not in our case, where the relationship was built around pedagogy alone. We concluded that consciousness could not be raised in any meaningful sense in this way, where the learners were scattered individuals and not part of any collective, and that the solution was to work with those who were already involved in popular organisation. From then on we concentrated on working with the members of trade unions.

It strikes me that Freire's strategy may have failed to work in Brazil as well. In the end, it was not the peasantry that provided the main force in the struggle against dictatorship, but the working class organised in trade unions and communities, just as it was in South Africa.

So, in some ways, our experience seems to endorse Bourdieu rather than Freire in this debate. Bourdieu recognises the bodily training and mental discipline required by education. Yet his advocacy of schools that systematically make the legitimate culture available to the children of the subaltern classes and inculcate it in them seems insufficiently critical. Discipline necessarily entails subordination, and the question then becomes, subordination to what? In schools organised according to the logic of the legitimate culture, this must mean subordination to constituted authority – the teachers, the school authorities and the many layers of dominant authority beyond that – as well as to the sanctified texts of the dominant culture. Here we come back to our learner with the stick. This was exactly what she was invoking – the authority of the teacher, the discipline of learning, and the necessity of rules and punishment. Force is integral to education, she was saying.

How, then, could being steeped in the dominant culture be in any sense liberating or empowering, as it turned out to be for Bourdieu (and Gramsci), and how could it provide any basis for critical thought, as it did for Bourdieu (and Gramsci)? In order to account for this, we need to think about education as a contradictory process – and not only in terms of a contradiction between technical and social dimensions, but also within these dimensions. Thus, discipline entails subordination to material and textual authority, but it also provides the tools for self-discipline and rigorous critical thought. Disciplining the self may enable the critical self to emerge. Learning the dominant culture involves submission to its rules and the symbolic order it sanctifies – but dominant culture itself is sufficiently polyvocal and contradictory to provide subversive insights and the possibility of rebellion, at least to those disposed to respond to such insights. On the bookshelves of the libraries, the curious student will find Karl Marx, Antonio Gramsci, Simone de Beauvoir and Frantz Fanon.

This brings us back to Freire and the difference between his concept of a contradictory self and Bourdieu's concept of habitus. Freire's critical pedagogy allows us to think through the contradictions of legitimate culture and pedagogical practices, and think therefore about the formation of critical thought. If we bring Freire, Bourdieu and Gramsci together, we might think about critical pedagogy not as something that can only take place in an alternative informal educational context, but as a constant potentiality within the schools and universities of the official educational system.

It was precisely this recognition of the subversive potentiality of 'legitimate culture' that led the apartheid regime to ban books and destroy independent missionary education – through which many of the greatest leaders of the liberation movement gained access to 'legitimate culture' and forged habits of mental and physical discipline – and bring all black schools under its control, creating a special 'Bantu education' that would not permit blacks to foster false ideas about their prospects; as was famously said by one of the regime's ideologues, blacks were destined to be 'hewers of wood and drawers of water' in white South Africa. Despite this, the massive expansion of black secondary schooling in the townships provided the seedbeds of the youth revolts in 1976 and the 1980s; schools were unsuccessful in inculcating black subservience to apartheid or suppressing the idea of what a 'good education' might look like.

Nonetheless, Bantu education has left a terrible legacy for post-apartheid South Africa in the form of numerous poorly trained teachers – teachers who not only lack technical skills, but also the habits of self-discipline and commitment to pedagogy that are so important for teaching.

While the purpose of Bantu education was to discipline the body and mind for menial work and domination by whites, preventing access to the canonical texts of the dominant culture, post-apartheid education in many schools in poor black communities is unable to install physical or mental discipline. Neither does it provide access to any canonical culture, whether Western or African, since recent educational reforms deny the relevance of 'canon' in favour of 'outcomes'.

As a consequence, in many of the worst-performing schools, the new generations of schoolchildren growing up in a free and democratic South Africa come through ten or 12 years of schooling without the basic skills of reading, writing and numeracy, and lacking as well the social skills of self-discipline and learning. What kind of habitus do children and teenagers emerge with from such a blighted education, with what kind of dispositions towards society, solidarity, work and family? What kind of symbolic violence does this experience constitute? Are the young adults that emerge from this system capable of understanding what our learner tried to teach us – that knowledge and mastery of the world requires discipline and a degree of force?

Another question strikes one forcibly when reading Bourdieu in Johannesburg. What do we make of his argument that access to 'legitimate culture' provides the resources to enter the world of reason located in the values of truth and emancipation – in a word, Enlightenment – and its correlates, democracy and human rights? This formation of reason in the fields of modern education and social and natural science provides the basis for Bourdieu's conception of liberatory politics shaped by intellectuals –'the Realpolitik of reason' (2000 [1997]: 70–72).

In the colonies and post-colonies, legitimate culture mostly means Western culture, the culture of the colonising nations, or now, after colonialism, the nations that currently dominate the world order, and this is a culture that negates the world of the native as something non-modern and 'backward'. As Bourdieu notes, the 'imperialism of reason' generally serves 'to justify the established order, the prevailing distribution of powers and privileges – the domination of the bourgeois, white, Euro-American heterosexual male', thus imposing the dominant values of the dominant nations on the rest of the world. Bourdieu condemns the 'abstract universalism' through which the non-Western world is found lacking and is therefore denigrated, and argues for mobilisation and struggle through which those who are denied access to the universal can claim and realise such access (Bourdieu, 2000 [1997]: 71–73, 77–78).

What might this mean for education in a country such as ours? Is the 'universal' something that can be separated from the dominant culture in which it is embedded? Modernity was constituted in South Africa through violence: colonial conquest, dispossession, slavery, forced labour, the restriction of citizenship to whites, and the application of violent bureaucratic routines to the marshalling, distribution and domination of the black population. Knowledge, reason, rationality, science and the state were racially constituted structures of violence. Is it possible to separate reason from the domination of the West and its implication in colonisation?

There are those who argue that Western culture is intrinsically racist and hostile to the rest of the world – that it is inherently a form of symbolic violence that can only be oppressive. Would the teaching of Latin and French and Voltaire and Shakespeare in South African schools be a way of making the world culture of reason available to all and therefore an emancipatory endeavour, or would it perpetuate oppression? Should it instead be a priority to teach Sesotho or isiXhosa (the teaching of which is still rather rudimentary) and construct a new canon drawing on Steve Biko and Ngugi wa Thiong'o as part of a project to value indigenous culture, knowledge and resistance, and draw from them in constituting a new post-apartheid democratic culture, as against a project of Eurocentric universalism?

Put differently, could it be that some of the self-limiting perspectives of the national liberation movement that make it susceptible to the prevailing orthodoxies of global capitalism have been derived from the influence of the very missionary education that made so important a contribution to the formation of generations of its leadership?

NOTES

1   Gramsci's use of the male pronoun throughout jars with contemporary sensibilities and leads him to miss the gender side of education, which is as important as the class dimension. Bourdieu and Passeron are more sensitive to contemporary usage, but they too are primarily focused on the significance of class.

CONVERSATION 6

THE ANTINOMIES OF FEMINISM

MICHAEL BURAWOY

Beauvoir Meets Bourdieu

*If the scholarly principle of her literary 'vocation', of her emotional
'choices' and even of her relation to her own status as a woman
offered to us by Toril Moi have but little chance of appearing as
Simone de Beauvoir, this is because she is separated from this
by the philosophy of Jean-Paul Sartre to whom she delegated,
in a way, her capacity to do philosophy .... There is not a better
example of the symbolic violence that constitutes the traditional
(patriarchal) relationship between the sexes than the fact that
she will fail to apply her own analysis on relations between the
sexes to her relationship with Jean-Paul Sartre.*

*She loves this destiny [aggrégation in philosophy] like she loves
he who embodies the realisation of what she would long to be:
Normalien, instituted by the rite of the concours in a superman
socially authorised to despise the inferior castes ... a philosopher
who is sure of being one – sure to the point of destroying, for the
sole pleasure of shining or of seducing, which are the same thing,
this is the project of Simone de Beauvoir.*

Bourdieu (1995: viii)

Bourdieu very rarely refers to Beauvoir, but when he does it is with undisguised contempt, reminding us of his treatment of Fanon. Of course, both had a close relation to Jean-Paul Sartre, Bourdieu's imagined combatant and intellectual nemesis. The passages above are drawn from Bourdieu's preface to the translation of Toril Moi's biography of Simone de Beauvoir. In this preface written under the mocking title, 'Apology for a dutiful woman',[1] Bourdieu claims that Beauvoir had no ideas of her own independent of Sartre, and then reduces her to a project of his own (Bourdieu's) projection – to be a philosopher dismissive of those beneath her.

This strategy of *reductionism* justifies the silencing of Beauvoir. If her ideas are an emanation of Sartre's, then there's no need to take them seriously. Bourdieu thereby exercises the very symbolic violence he condemns, namely the masculinist practice of *silencing* women. The final move in this denigration is to *appropriate* Beauvoir's ideas from *The Second Sex* (1989 [1949]) – a foundational classic in the analysis of masculine domination as an expression of symbolic violence. Bourdieu's *Masculine Domination* (2001 [1998]) is but a superficial and diminutive gloss on *The Second Sex*. Reductionism, silencing and appropriation are three stages in the labour of producing one's own distinction through the conquest and erasure of others. In this conversation, I attempt to recover Beauvoir's voice so that she can enter into a conversation with Bourdieu.

ON SILENCING BEAUVOIR

These strategies of combat, doubtless not fully conscious, but deeply embedded in Bourdieu's academic habitus, come into full view in *Masculine Domination* – a book that is full of references to a diverse array of second-wave feminists. Bourdieu confines Beauvoir to a single dismissive footnote:

> For a specific illustration of what is implied by this perhaps somewhat abstract evocation of the specific forms that masculine domination takes within the educational institution, see Toril Moi's analysis of the representations and academic classifications through which Sartre's hold imposed itself on Simone Beauvoir (Bourdieu 2001 [1998]: 86, footnote 11).

Once again he opportunistically exploits Toril Moi's biography of Beauvoir. He focuses on Moi's first two chapters, which do indeed place Beauvoir in her relation to Sartre and then in relation to the French intellectual field, but he ignores Moi's subsequent chapters devoted to the interpretation and original contributions of *The Second Sex*.

Moreover, Bourdieu claims that Beauvoir does not analyse her relation to Sartre, yet *The Second Sex* contains precisely that. Whether one looks at the chapter on love or on the independent woman, she is examining her own relation to Sartre, or her imagined relation to Sartre. Her prize-winning novel, *The Mandarins*, is a thinly veiled dissection of her two major relations, one with Sartre and the other with the American poet Nelson Algren. And then there are the four volumes of memoirs. Moreover, even as she undertakes such a self-analysis, she does not make the mistake of universalising her own situation as an intellectual woman, but recognises how different is the plight of others, trapped in domesticity. If there is one thing one cannot accuse Beauvoir of, it is a failure of reflexivity. Paradoxically, it is Bourdieu, the great exponent of reflexivity, who systematically fails the test of reflexivity. We never discover any reference to, let alone analysis of, his relations with women (or men), even in his own sketch for a self-analysis.

Of course, Bourdieu is not alone in this silencing of Beauvoir, as Moi (1994: chap. 7) has herself shown. When *The Second Sex* first appeared in 1949 it became an instant national scandal. There was public outrage at the bluntness with which Beauvoir – the leading woman intellectual in France of her period – dealt with male domination and female complicity. Everyone seemed incriminated in her uncompromising indictment of the oppression of women. Subsequently, feminists have been loathe to refer to her work, no matter how much they borrowed from her. It became a sacrilegious text of unpleasant revelations, whose reading took place only in secret. Plagiarise from it, yes, but to take it seriously is to taint one's intellectual and/or feminist reputation. Influential though it was for second-wave feminism, homage to Beauvoir was all too often paid in silence.

Why then is Bourdieu, the advocate of reflexive sociology, complicit in this collective amnesia? It is especially surprising, given that the silencing of women is precisely a strategy of domination that he explicates, and seemingly condemns, in *Masculine Domination*. In a section fittingly entitled, 'Masculinity as nobility', Bourdieu (2001 [1998]: 59) writes of 'the virtual denial of their [women's] existence' in which 'the best intentioned of men (for symbolic violence does not operate at the level of conscious intentions) perform discriminatory acts, excluding women, without even thinking about it, from positions of authority'. He denounces the silencing of women, but that does not give him pause to invoke Beauvoir's supposed 'dutiful' relation to Sartre to justify his own suppression of her understanding of masculine domination.

That would be bad enough, but he would at least be following the crowd in expunging her work from the recognised intellectual field. Bourdieu, however, is doubly guilty in that Beauvoir not only prefigured so much of second-wave feminism, but also so much of what Bourdieu himself had to say about masculine domination 50 years later. Moreover, she does so in far richer, more complex, subtle detail and, as we shall see, always seeking paths beyond masculine domination. Yet not a single acknowledgement of *The Second Sex* finds its way into Bourdieu's *Masculine Domination*, although there are ample references to second-wave feminism, particularly the Anglo-Saxon feminists who took so much from Beauvoir.

The argument of this conversation, therefore, is that *Masculine Domination* is a pale imitation of the ideas of *The Second Sex*.[2] Nor should such a convergence be surprising. After all, both Bourdieu and Beauvoir were implacable enemies of domination, always seeking to reveal its hidden and manifest contours. Both were uncompromising in their denunciation of the mythologies of the naturalisation and eternalisation of domination. Both were vocal enemies of identity politics, of all forms of essentialism and, thus, of difference feminism. Both denounced any attempt to romanticise the resistance or culture of the dominated. To recover and then celebrate the particularity of women, or any other oppressed group, from within the field of its domination is to affirm that domination. Rather, they both insist that domination is overcome by giving the dominated equal access to the universal.

Here, therefore, I wish to restore Beauvoir's originality, showing how Bourdieu's categories and arguments not only already existed, but were far better elaborated in *The Second Sex*, and, moreover, how Beauvoir goes beyond him by always gesturing to freedoms beyond domination – and all this despite her book pre-dating his by half a century.[3]

SYMBOLIC DOMINATION

Apart from the strategic importance of making an intervention in such a central trope of modern social thought, why is Bourdieu interested in masculine domination? For him, it is:

> ... the prime example of this paradoxical submission, an effect of what I call symbolic violence, a gentle violence, imperceptible and invisible even to its victims, exerted for the most part through the purely symbolic channels of communication and cognition (more precisely misrecognition), recognition, or even feeling (Bourdieu, 2001 [1998]: 1–2).

For Beauvoir, masculine domination is the supreme form of othering, of which race and class are also examples:

> [Woman] is simply what man decrees. Thus she is called 'sex', by which is meant that she appears essentially to the male as a sexual being. For him she is sex – absolute sex, no less. She is defined and differentiated with reference to man and not he with reference to her; she is the incidental, the inessential as opposed to the essential. He is the subject, he is the Absolute – she is the Other (Beauvoir, 1989 [1949]: xxii).

Already here we see that Beauvoir gives more agency to men in the constitution of women, although she will show how men are also dominated by their domination. Still, the effect is the same: 'She [woman] has no grasp even in thought, on the reality around her. It is opaque to her eyes' (Beauvoir, 1989 [1949]: 598).

Symbolic domination is not a matter of combining force and consent, but operates far more deeply through the internalisation of social structure via those 'schemes of perception and appreciation' that are constitutive of habitus:

> So the only way to understand this particular form of domination is to move beyond the forced choice between constraint (by forces) and consent (to reasons), between mechanical coercion and voluntary, free, deliberate, even calculated submission. The effect of symbolic domination (whether ethnic, gender, cultural or linguistic, etc.) is exerted not in the pure logic of knowing consciousness but through the schemes of perception, appreciation and action that are constitutive of habitus and which, below the levels of the decisions of the consciousness and the controls of the will, set up a cognitive relationship that is profoundly obscure to itself. Thus, the paradoxical logic of masculine domination and female submissiveness, which can, without contradiction, be described as both *spontaneous and extorted*, cannot be understood until one takes account of the *durable effects* that the social order exerts on women (and men), that is to say, the dispositions spontaneously attuned to that order which it imposes on them (Bourdieu, 2001 [1998]: 37–38).

A fish is so attuned to the water in which it swims and without which it could not exist that it does not recognise the water for what it is and takes it for granted as natural and eternal. It is interesting, therefore, to read how Beauvoir explains her own discovery of masculine domination.

Writing her memoirs in 1963, she reflects back on the moment of epiphany. It was 1946 and she was having a conversation with Sartre about writing her memoirs:

I realized that the first question to come up was: What has it meant to me to be a woman? At first I thought I could dispose of that pretty quickly. I had never had any feeling of inferiority, no one had ever said to me: 'You think that way because you're a woman'; my femininity had never been irksome to me in any way. 'For me,' I said to Sartre, 'you might almost say it just hasn't counted.' 'All the same, you weren't brought up in the same way as a boy would have been; you should look into it further.' I looked, and it was a revelation: this world was a masculine world, my childhood had been nourished by myths forged by men, and I hadn't reacted to them in at all the same way I should have done if I were a boy. I was so interested in this discovery that I abandoned my project for a personal confession in order to give all my attention to finding out about the condition of women in the broadest terms. I went to the Bibliothèque Nationale to do some reading, and what I studied were the myths of femininity (Beauvoir, 1964 [1963]: 94–95).

In this rendition, Beauvoir, by an act of self-conscious willpower, pursues the origins and reproduction of masculine domination, all laid out in *The Second Sex*, which reveals the architecture and archaeology of masculine domination as constituted by society. This confrontation with what had been unrecognised or misrecognised appears here as a quite conscious process – as indeed it was for Bourdieu, who claims to have discovered the structures of masculine domination through scientific observation of its elementary forms among the Kabyle. On the other hand, one might argue that Beauvoir's consciousness did not transform her practice of femininity. She does not escape the dilemma of being complicit in masculine domination, as *The Mandarins* – the novel of her two lives, the one among Parisian intellectuals and the other with her American lover, Nelson Algren – makes clear. She is far more honest about her own complicity than Bourdieu, who retreats to Virginia Woolf when he wants to talk about the concrete practices of male domination.

Like Bourdieu, Beauvoir is under no illusion about the depth of female subjugation: 'The bond that unites her [woman] to her oppressors is not comparable to any other. The division of the sexes is a biological fact, not an event of history' (Beauvoir, 1989 [1949]: xxv). So it is easily presented as natural, inevitable and eternal. 'They have no past, no history, no religion of their own; and they have no such solidarity of work and interest as that of the proletariat' (Beauvoir, 1989 [1949]: xxv). They have no awareness of themselves as an oppressed collective. 'When man makes of woman the *Other*, he may, then, expect her to manifest deep-seated tendencies toward complicity' (Beauvoir, 1989 [1949]: xxvii). Thus, Beauvoir sees masculine domination as a *special type* of domination that is stronger and deeper than class or racial domination, for the latter occupy spaces from which oppositional identities can be formed. 'Having no independent domain, she cannot oppose positive truths and values of her own to those asserted and upheld by males: she can only deny them' (Beauvoir, 1989 [1949]: 611). In one of his rare moments of comparison of different dominations, Bourdieu seems to think the opposite, namely that masculine domination is the *prototype* of symbolic domination, but that class domination is its deepest expression (Bourdieu, 1984 [1979]: 384). Yet for both – and this is the important point here – masculine domination is the most pure form of symbolic domination, i.e. domination not recognised as such, or when it is recognised, it may not affect the unconscious practical sense.

Finally, one might surmise that the revulsion that greeted *The Second Sex*, as well as its subsequent silencing, speaks to the unconscious levels it excavates and the resistance, whether among the dominators or the dominated, to recognising deeply internalised dispositions. Thus, as we shall see in detail, Beauvoir's treatment of masculine domination embraces the notion of symbolic domination, but it also seeks to transcend it. In demonstrating my claim that there is nothing in *Masculine Domination* that does not already exist in a more elaborated form in *The Second Sex*, I have organised the following sections along the thematic lines of *Masculine Domination*.

NATURALISATION, OR REVERSING CAUSE AND EFFECT

At the heart of masculine domination is its naturalisation, which gives rise to the reversal of cause and effect. If it were the case that the differences between men and women are inherent, as though these two beings were different human species, then we could indeed say that the gender division of labour merely reflects differences in natural abilities and talents. We could say, for example, that women are by their nature emotional and men by their nature rational. In reality, what is presumed to be cause – the natural differences between men and women – is actually the effect of historical forces and socialisation. Thus, Bourdieu writes:

The biological appearances and the very real effects that have been produced in bodies and minds by a long collective labour of socialization of the biological and biologicization of the social combine to reverse the relationship between causes and effects and to make a naturalized social construction ('genders' as sexually characterized habitus) appear as the grounding in nature of the arbitrary division which underlies both reality and the representation of reality and which sometimes imposes itself even on scientific research (Bourdieu, 2001 [1998]: 3; see also pp. 22–23).

Beauvoir goes into far more detail. Indeed, Part I of *The Second Sex*, entitled 'Destiny', devotes successive chapters to the biological, psychoanalytical and historical materialist foundations of masculine domination. While there are those who ground masculine domination in the biological differences between men and women, after examining biological evidence in excruciating detail, Beauvoir finds this view wanting. Biological differences there are, and the woman experiences her body very differently than the man – for the woman the body is an alien force outside her control, whereas man is at home with his body – but these experiences are not given anatomically, but are shaped by society and upbringing. In the final analysis, biological differences cannot explain the subjugation of women, which is the cumulative product of social and economic forces, most importantly the relation of production to reproduction. Biology is not destiny.

Psychoanalysis represents a major advance in that the body no longer exists in and of itself, but as lived by the subject. In a subjectivist flourish, Beauvoir writes: 'It is not nature that defines woman; it is she who defines herself by dealing with nature on her own account in her emotional life' (1989 [1949]: 38). While psychoanalysis gives the framework within which to study the dynamics of gender, it does not explain the origins of masculine domination nor its persistence, resting as it does on the assumption of the patriarchal father. Beauvoir's next chapter, therefore, turns to historical materialism and, in particular, Engels' claim that private property is at the root of masculine domination. While acknowledging the influence of economic forces, she rejects Engels' argument on the grounds that it never explains the very constitution of male and female subjects. Rejecting, therefore, both the 'sexual determinism' of Freud and the 'economic determinism' of Engels, she presents a history of male domination by integrating the biological and psychoanalytic into a materialist analysis of history:

In our attempt to discover woman we shall not reject certain contributions of biology, of psychoanalysis, and of historical materialism; but we shall hold that the body, the sexual life, and the resources of technology exist concretely for many only in so far as he grasps them in the total perspective of his existence (Beauvoir, 1989 [1949]: 60).

In this way, Beauvoir dispenses with the scientific foundations for views that regard woman as by nature destined to be man's '*Other*', showing them all to be fallacious. Yet she will also draw on these very same theories to reverse causality, showing how history and biography shape the concrete hierarchical relations through which man and woman (re)produce each other.

THE HISTORICAL LABOUR OF DEHISTORICISATION

For Bourdieu, the naturalisation of masculine domination lies with the matching of subjective and objective structures, the inculcation of a habitus by social structures, and the resulting harmonisation of the two so that domination cannot be recognised as such (2001 [1998]: 33). But this matching of the subjective and the objective is not spontaneous, but the result of a long historical labour that produces the effect of eternalisation:

It follows that, in order to escape completely from essentialism, one should not try to deny the permanences and the invariants, which are indisputably part of historical reality; but, rather, one *must reconstruct the history of the historical labour of dehistoricization*, or, to put it another way, the history of the continuous (re)creation of the objective and subjective structures of masculine domination, which has gone on permanently so long as there have been men and women, and through which the masculine order has been continually reproduced from age to age. In other words, a 'history of women' which brings to light, albeit despite itself, a large degree of constancy, permanence, must, if it wants to be consistent with itself, give a place, and no doubt the central place, to the *history of the agents and institutions which permanently contribute to the maintenance of these permanences,* the church, the state, educational system, etc., and which may vary, at different times, in their relative weights and their functions (Bourdieu, 2001 [1998]: 82–83; original emphasis).

Such a history that Bourdieu calls for in programmatic terms, Beauvoir had already attempted in Part II of *The Second Sex*, itself divided into five chapters. She knows that a history of the second sex must be a history of the social production of masculine domination and its 'naturalisation', 'eternalisation' or, as Bourdieu calls it, 'dehistoricisation'. Bourdieu's chapter 3, 'Permanence and change', does not compare to Beauvoir's ambition, scope and accomplishment – heavily influenced by Engels' flawed history, to be sure, but an enormous achievement nonetheless. Included here is an anticipation of feminist appropriation of Lévi-Strauss's idea of women as objects exchanged among men in the pursuit of masculine politics, as well as a sophisticated analysis of how the second shift will reproduce rather than undermine masculine domination. Beauvoir prefigured the work of Gayle Rubin and Arlie Hochschild, whose ideas Bourdieu subsequently takes up as though they were original to them.

In justifying his own intervention into gender studies, Bourdieu claims as his contribution the focus on the reproduction of the structure of masculine domination outside the domestic sphere in agencies such as the church, the educational system and the state (and, he might have mentioned, the economy), as if feminists have not explored these areas already. But even more to the point, *The Second Sex* itself recognised the importance of these arenas, both in the chapter 'Since the French Revolution: The job and the vote' and in Part V, where Beauvoir describes 'woman's situation'.

Having drawn up a history of masculine domination, a history in which man defines woman as other, so Beauvoir asks how men have imagined women in their dreams, 'for what-in-men's-eyes-she-seems-to-be is one of the necessary factors in her real situation' (1989 [1949]:138). Part III of *The Second Sex* is devoted to the exploration of the myths men create about women to justify their subordination. It describes the struggles of men to realise themselves with, through and against women; and the fantasies they create about women as nature, as flesh, as poetry. Woman is constituted as other, as slave and companion to man's fanciful desires for his own self-realisation, as an idol to worship, as a distraction or compensation for the anxieties of his own entrapment in the cruel or noble competition with other men. Woman serves so many functions as other to man's projection of himself, his limitations and his potentialities. Man cannot live without the mythology and reality of woman. Beauvoir discovers the most vivid expression of these imaginations in literature. There she also detects the possibility that man, seeing woman as necessary to his existence, defining himself in her mirror, also catches sight of a human being with her own needs with whom he might share a life of transcendence.

Even in his treatment of the Kabyle, there is no counterpart in Bourdieu to Beauvoir's dissection of the creative literary outpourings of men. Although Bourdieu's conception of symbolic violence is one in which the dominated apply the dominant point of view to themselves, he never explores that dominant point of view in any detail. But it is here that Beauvoir discovers not only myths that ratify and eternalise domination, but also catches glimpses of transcendence when men, caught in the grip of their dependence on women, recognise that their freedom can only be won with and through the freedom of women. The relentless pursuit of the sources of domination never blinds Beauvoir to the possibilities of liberation, so different from Bourdieu's notion of habitus as internalised social structure that pre-empts the possibility of any such vision. Important as they are in foretelling alternatives, Beauvoir is under no illusion that such imaginations can be easily sustained against woman's bondage to immanence.

PRODUCING THE GENDERED HABITUS

The history of the collective unconscious has to be supplemented, says Bourdieu, by an understanding of the personal unconscious; we need both an ontogeny and a phylogeny. Here too Bourdieu offers general formulations:

> The work of transformation of bodies which is both sexually differentiated and sexually differentiating and which is performed partly through the effects of mimetic suggestion, partly through explicit injunctions and partly through the whole symbolic construction of the view of the biological body (and in particular the sexual act, conceived as an act of domination, possession), produces systematically differentiated and differentiating habitus. The masculinization of the male body and the feminization of the female body, immense and in a sense interminable tasks which, perhaps now more than ever, always demand a considerable expenditure of time and effort, induce a somatization of the relation of domination, which is thus naturalized (Bourdieu, 2001 [1998]: 55–56).

Beauvoir devotes Part IV of *The Second Sex* to the formative years of the woman: childhood, the young girl and sexual initiation. It opens with the sentence for which she has become famous (and famously misunderstood): 'One is not born, but rather becomes, a woman.'

No biological, psychological, or economic fate determines the figure that the human female presents in society; it is civilization as a whole that produces this creature, intermediate between male and eunuch, which is described as feminine. Only the intervention of someone else can establish an individual as an *Other* (Beauvoir, 1989 [1949]: 267).

It is painful even to read the way she describes what must, after all, have been close to her own upbringing. She draws on an array of literatures to develop a psychodynamic view of the way femininity is forced upon girls, the fantasies and anxieties of compulsory segregation in adolescence, and, finally, the traumas of sexual initiation. From then on she has been made, she has been painfully disciplined, to be woman.

Well, not always. Beauvoir insists that socialisation can go awry. She points out, anticipating the work of Nancy Chodorow (1978) 29 years later, that as a result of their upbringing, specifically being mothered by women – but also in revulsion against aggressive masculinity – from early on, alongside heterosexual dispositions, women develop strong bonds with other women. This can lead to lesbian relations. She devotes an entire chapter to 'The lesbian' – a tortured chapter, perhaps reflecting her own ambivalence – in which she wavers between, on the one hand, lesbian sexuality as second best to heterosexuality, i.e. a casualty of masculine domination, and, on the other hand, lesbian sexuality as a liberated sexuality of mutual recognition. Of course, we must not forget that in the France of 1949, lesbianism was a 'forbidden' sexuality. It was an extraordinary act of courage to even broach the subject, let alone affirm its propriety.

Times have changed, so that today Bourdieu feels compelled to add what seems to be an obligatory appendix – 'Some questions on the gay and lesbian movement' – in which he too wavers between seeing the gay-lesbian movement as subversive of masculine domination and as upholding dominant classifications. But Bourdieu simply takes lesbian and gay sexuality as a given, whereas Beauvoir offers a rudimentary theory of its emergence. Bourdieu's notion of socialisation, of habitus – the bodily inscription of social structure – misses all the ambiguities, resistances and contradictions so central to Beauvoir's more open and indeterminate analysis. In *Masculine Domination*, the limitations of the notion of habitus become particularly clear.

DOMINATION AND ITS ADAPTATIONS

Once the girl becomes a woman and enters as an adult into society, she faces the strictures of marriage and motherhood, and then the transition from maturity to old age. The story is always a bleak one, a story of domestic drudgery, boredom and confinement. Isolated in a 'living tomb', woman serves only to 'assure the monotonous repetition of life in all its mindless factuality' (1989 [1949]: 604). The child becomes an obsessive focus of attention, both in resentment of and as compensation for woman's chains.[4] Working with a definite vision of the nuclear family and the male breadwinner, Beauvoir describes the woman's escape via adultery, friendship or community as unsound evasions, each road paved with falsehood. This is the picture of the American woman in the 1950s that Betty Friedan (1963) would later paint in *The Feminine Mystique*, a destiny against which the feminist movement would rebel.

Beauvoir is aware that domesticity is not necessarily woman's destiny. Although escape from confinement and entry into the labour force is a precondition for liberation, oppression actually follows her into the workplace. She is now bound in servitude to employer *and* patriarch. Nor does she think all is paradise for men. Indeed, just as Bourdieu insists that the dominators are dominated by their domination, so Beauvoir describes how men are also oppressed by their oppression, chained by their sovereignty.

Reflecting the shift that occurred over the subsequent 50 years in which women have become more mobile and less prisoners of domesticity, Bourdieu focuses more on the body in motion, the way the woman's body is a body for others, the way it is surveilled and self-surveilled, generating insecurity and anxiety. Women become objects in a market of symbolic goods. Not for nothing does he insist that masculine domination has no centre, but is diffused throughout society. Still, woman is not only object, but, even in Bourdieu's rendition, has a subjectivity and a vision of men. Here he draws on Virginia Woolf's *To the Lighthouse* to capture the many ways in which women's dependency on men leads them into a supporting role, participating vicariously in men's games, a cheerleader of their men. The wife pacifies and protects the man against other men, trying to alleviate his anxieties and to comprehend the harshness of his domestic rule as a measure of his paternal love or a response to the insecurities he faces.

Above all, women love men for the power they wield, the power denied to women:

> Because differential socialization disposes men to love the games of power and women to love the men who play them, masculine charisma is partly the charm of power, the seduction that the possession of power exerts, as such, on bodies whose drives and desires are themselves politically socialized. Masculine domination finds one of its strongest supports in

the misrecognition which results from the application to the dominant of categories engendered in the very relationship of domination and which can lead to that extreme form of *amor fati*, love of the dominant and of his domination, a *libido dominantis* (desire for the dominant) which implies renunciation of personal exercise of *libido dominandi* (the desire to dominate) (Bourdieu, 2001 [1998]: 79–80).

Here, too, Beauvoir had said it before in her extraordinary second chapter of Part VI of *The Second Sex*, 'Women in love', where she describes how women deify men, putting them on a pedestal in order to worship them. He is her representative in the outside world, his victories are her victories, his defeats her defeats. She idolises him only to drag him down into her lair, demanding his everlasting attention. She realises herself through him, but this love of the powerful man is doomed to disaster, either because man cannot sustain her expectations or because his desire is capricious and ephemeral:

> Shut up in the sphere of the relative, destined to the male from childhood, habituated to seeing in him a superb being whom she cannot possibly equal, the woman who has not repressed her claim to humanity will dream of transcending her being towards one of these superior beings, of amalgamating herself with the sovereign subject. There is no other way out for her than to lose herself, body and soul, in him who is represented to her as the absolute, as the essential. Since she is anyway doomed to dependence, she will prefer to serve a god rather than obey tyrants – parents, husband or protector. She chooses to desire her enslavement so ardently that it will seem to her the expression of her liberty; she will try to rise above her situation as inessential object by fully accepting it; through her flesh, her feelings, her behaviour, she will enthrone him as supreme value and reality; she will humble herself to nothingness before him. Love becomes for her a religion (Beauvoir, 1989 [1949]: 643).

Such are woman's attempts at salvation – idolatrous love, along with narcissism or mysticism – attempts to 'transform her prison into a heaven of glory, her servitude into sovereign liberty' (Beauvoir, 1989 [1949]: 628).

These notions of woman enclosed in domesticity sound rather antiquated, and Beauvoir herself recognises that 'Today the combat takes a different shape; instead of wishing to put man in a prison, woman endeavors to escape from one; she no longer seeks to drag him into the realms of immanence but to emerge, herself, into the light of transcendence'

(1989 [1949]: 717). She thinks it will be transcendence, but it turns out to only intensify her subjugation, the one at home intensified by the one at work (Beauvoir, 1989 [1949]: 680–81). Indeed, all these stratagems to realise herself, to become a subject, are illusory and self-defeating. They are what Beauvoir calls 'justifications' and what Bourdieu calls 'making a virtue of a necessity', adaptations of the dominated to their domination. Both paint a bleak picture in which women understand such adaptations as paths of freedom, whereas in fact they intensify subjugation.

But neither Bourdieu nor Beauvoir, but particularly Beauvoir, can leave women doubly imprisoned, objectively and subjectively. Both search for a possible escape from immanence, entrapment and symbolic domination.

LIBERATION

Once again, Bourdieu adopts a notion of liberation, surprisingly close to Beauvoir's. This is all the more astonishing as Bourdieu has generally scoffed at the attempt to formulate utopias. Yet in his postscript to *Masculine Domination*, he does just that, serving up a weak replica of Beauvoir. The postscript begins by reasserting that 'love is domination accepted, unrecognized as such and practically recognized, in happy or unhappy passions' (Bourdieu, 2001 [1998]: 109). Yet he then goes on to imagine the possibility of the suspension of domination in favour of mutual recognition:

> This is a world of non-violence, made possible by the establishment of relations based on full *reciprocity* and authorizing the abandonment and entrusting of self; a world of mutual recognition, which makes it possible, as Sartre [sic] says, to feel 'justified in existing' … the world of the disinterestedness which makes possible deinstrumentalized relations, based on the happiness of giving happiness, of finding in the wonderment of the other, especially at the wonder he or she arouses, inexhaustible reasons for wonder (Bourdieu, 2001 [1998]: 110).

This is exactly what Beauvoir had elaborated in the last chapter of *The Second Sex*:

> To emancipate woman is to refuse to confine her to the relations she bears to man, not to deny them to her; let her have her independent existence and she will continue none the less to exist for him *also*: mutually recognizing each other as subject, each will yet remain for the other an *other* (Beauvoir, 1989 [1949]: 731; original emphasis).

Even the expressions they use are the same, not only 'mutual recognition', but the idea of the 'gift of self'. Beauvoir writes of genuine love through mutual recognition as 'revelation of self by the *gift of self* and the enrichment of the world' (1989 [1949]: 667) and Bourdieu follows with the true love of mutual recognition that can be found in 'the economy of symbolic exchanges of which the supreme form is the *gift of self*, and of one's body a sacred body, excluded from commercial circulation' (2001 [1998]: 110–11).

Still, the difference is clear. For Bourdieu, liberation is thrown in as an obligatory and ill-fitting afterthought, perhaps a concession to the feminists he is trying to win over, whereas it is Beauvoir's central concern, a subterranean stream running through the entire book that springs up in a final resplendent fountain of hope – there can be no domination without the possibility of liberation. She does not imagine a dissolution of the differences between men and women, but instead imagines a plurality of such relations, 'differences in equality': 'New relations of flesh and sentiment of which we have no conception will arise between the sexes' (Beauvoir, 1989 [1949]: 730).

Whereas Bourdieu tells us nothing of the conditions for his 'pure love', 'art for art's sake of love' (2001 [1998]:111), Beauvoir insists that authentic love requires structural equality that would, in turn, require access to abortion, contraception and voting rights (remember this is France 1949), but also more radical ideas such as co-parenting (Beauvoir, 1989 [1949]: 726). Beauvoir is dismissive of that spurious 'equality in inequality' – an equality of opportunity that becomes meaningless under unequal conditions. Instead, she affirms a socialist equality that does not yet exist (Beauvoir, 1989 [1949]: 680) – a necessary (but not sufficient) condition of liberation. While she is only too mindful of the shortcomings of the Soviet Union (Beauvoir, 1989 [1949]: 724) with regard to the question of female emancipation, nevertheless she applauds its promise of equality, its imagination of equality. For Beauvoir, women's emancipation is not just an abstract utopia; it is a real utopia based on what she sees around her, what could be.

Beauvoir is clear that solitary individuals cannot successfully strive for transcendence in a capitalist society. The economically independent woman is a necessary, but certainly not sufficient, condition, as she makes amply clear in her penultimate chapter on the dilemmas of professionalism – contradictory pressures and double standards – that holds up well in the light of contemporary research. For Beauvoir, liberation can only be a collective project and under economic conditions that provide for its possibility. And yet she does not see how women can strive together, collectively, for the transformation of the conditions of their existence. Indeed, the argument of *The Second Sex* rests on distinguishing masculine domination from racial and class domination. Whereas workers or blacks can forge an organic unity among themselves in opposition to a dominant group, not so with women, who orbit around individual men, complicit in their own subjugation, seeking the best possible partnership on the matrimonial market, subjugated in body and soul to masculine domination. The only hope for women, it would seem, is for the working class to first make its revolution and then – and only then – create the conditions for women to seek emancipation. It would be hard, therefore, for Beauvoir to comprehend the feminist movement to which her own book contributed. Feminist movements that express the genuine interests of women have never existed:

> The proletarians have accomplished the revolution in Russia, the Negroes in Haiti, the Indo-Chinese are battling for it in Indo-China; but the women's effort has never been anything more than a symbolic agitation. They have gained only what men have been willing to grant; they have taken nothing, they have only received (Beauvoir, 1989 [1949]: xxv; but also p. 129).

So was the feminist movement she witnessed toward the end of her life another movement that was confined to the interests of men? Was this a movement that was conducted on the terrain of masculine domination, or did it challenge that domination?

Like Beauvoir, Bourdieu is also sensitive to the dilemmas of challenging domination from below. In writing about the gay-lesbian movement, Bourdieu analyses the possibilities, but also the dangers, of struggles that successfully articulate the interests of an alternative sexuality. Once recognised, however, gay sexuality becomes invisible again and subject to many of the same oppressions as women. Querying the extent to which the feminist movement has eroded masculine domination, he enters a polemic against consciousness raising, which cannot be what it claims to be. The very language of consciousness is inappropriate for comprehending masculine domination that is inscribed deeply in an enduring habitus. 'If it is quite illusory to believe that symbolic violence can be overcome with the weapons of consciousness and will alone, this is because the effect and conditions of its efficacy are durably and deeply embedded in the body in the form of dispositions' (Bourdieu, 2001 [1998]: 39). He continues:

Although it is true that, even when it seems to be based on the brute force of weapons or money, recognition of domination always presupposes an act of knowledge, this does not imply that one is entitled to describe it in the language of consciousness, in an intellectualist and scholastic fallacy which, as in Marx (and above all, those who, from Lukács onwards, have spoken of 'false consciousness'), leads one to expect the liberation of women to come through the immediate effect of the 'raising of consciousness', forgetting – for lack of a dispositional theory of practices – the opacity and inertia that stem from embedding of social structures in bodies (Bourdieu, 2001 [1998]: 40).

The foundations of symbolic domination, therefore, do not lie in a 'mystified consciousness', but in 'dispositions attuned to the structure of domination', so that the 'relation of complicity' that the dominated 'grant' to the dominant can only be broken through a 'radical transformation of the social conditions of production of the dispositions that lead the dominated to take the point of view of the dominant on the dominant and on themselves' (Bourdieu, 2001 [1998]: 42–43). But we have no idea what such a transformation entails or how it might occur.

Is Bourdieu's symbolic domination different from Beauvoir, who also sees women thinking in terms given to them by masculine domination when she writes of woman: 'She has no grasp, even in thought, on the reality around her. It is opaque to her eyes' (Beauvoir, 1989 [1949]: 598)? Woman's critical faculties are critically limited: 'Having no independent domain, she cannot oppose positive truths and values of her own to those asserted and upheld by males; she can only deny them' (1989 [1949]: 611). You might call this absence of a 'counter-universe' (1989 [1949]: 617) 'false consciousness', to be sure, but it is also deeply embedded, nurtured over a lifetime. Indeed, every page of *The Second Sex* is testimony to just how deep it is and the elaborate ways it is inculcated and reproduced. Moreover, let it be said that Beauvoir is no devotee of consciousness raising and is sceptical of programmes for oppressed women to assert their own standpoint. She is deeply pessimistic about any good sense emerging within common sense. Like Bourdieu, she sees an ocean of bad sense, dotted with islands of momentary liberation.

FROM FEMINIST CRITIQUE TO FEMINIST MOVEMENT

We see now just how different both Beauvoir and Bourdieu are from Frantz Fanon's writings on Algeria that advance intellectuals' engagement in revolutionary activity. That was the theme of *The Wretched of the Earth*. Fanon's earlier book, *Black Skin, White Masks* (1967 [1952]), however, is the counterpart to *The Second Sex*. There, Fanon dissects the psychic consequences of racial domination, discovered when he came to France with a view of himself as a Frenchman and not a black Martiniquan. The shock of racism, just like the shock of sexism for Beauvoir, led Fanon to a devastating account of the situation of the racially oppressed, the mythologies that support racial domination and the inauthentic responses to that domination, namely those attempts to assimilate to whiteness that were doomed to failure. The analysis closely parallels the situation, myths and justification linked to masculine domination found in *The Second Sex*.[5] More than Beauvoir does for women, Fanon emphasises the virtues of the dominated culture, specifically the Negritude movement, as necessary to give dignity to blacks, but always his goal, like Beauvoir, is to transcend racism toward a universalism where race exists, but not as an instrument of domination.

Black Skin, White Masks ends in despair, with no clear road to the universalism Fanon seeks, just as Beauvoir ends *The Second Sex* with a similar vain hope of liberation. Whereas Fanon would soon travel to Algeria, where the liberation movement becomes his key to universalism, Beauvior would have to wait many years for the feminist movement, and even then she had to overcome her scepticism before declaring her support in 1972. She had always kept her distance from feminism, thinking that the woman question was subordinate to the socialist project, but when she realised that the Left had little interest in the emancipation of women; when she saw the continuing oppression of women in France, especially around rights of abortion; and when she became more familiar with the realities of women's position in the Soviet Union, she threw her intellectual and political weight behind an autonomous and radical feminism (Schwarzer, 1984).

For Fanon, theory and practice come together in a revolutionary catharsis, whereas for Beauvoir they always remain in tension. Hers is a more contradictory position in which she dissects masculine domination, yet in her own life finds herself falling into the same traps that she denounces as inauthentic. While she is writing *The Second Sex* she is having a passionate affair with Nelson Algren that bears all the marks of her analysis of 'women in love' – knowing it to be an inauthentic and ultimately futile response to masculine domination. More successful, though never without its tensions, is the 'brotherhood' of Sartre! Throughout her life, Beauvoir lives out, reflects on, and struggles with the contradictions between her theory and her practice.

Bourdieu, on the other hand, seems far less self-conscious about the contradictions between the moral implications of his theory of masculine domination and his practice, between the logic of theory and the logic of his own practice. He acknowledges that well-intentioned men can fall victim to deeply ingrained cognitive structures and unwittingly reproduce these, even when they think they are challenging them. He suggests this is true of Kant, Sartre, Freud and Lacan, but doesn't examine his own complicity in masculine domination. We have already noted how he dismisses Beauvoir, on the grounds that she is simply an appendage of Sartre. Yet, as I have shown, his work is but a pale imitation of hers. He practices sexism in the very act of denouncing it.

Masculine domination runs deep in the unconscious of both men and women. But perhaps women, as the victims of domination, are in a better position to bring it to the surface. Even Bourdieu recognises that women's insights into the life of men are often inaccessible to men themselves. They see the games of men for what they are (Bourdieu, 2001 [1998]: 31, 75). They are more aware of the pitfalls of domination and how it leads to contradictory and inauthentic behaviour. Notwithstanding their common concern to elucidate the structures of domination, Beauvoir's analysis is incomparably more profound than Bourdieu's, addressing rather than repressing the ambiguities and contradictions of approaching freedom from within the cage of domination.

THE INSIGHT OF THE OUTSIDER

If the habitus of masculine domination runs so deep, how is it that anyone, not least Beauvoir and Bourdieu, can even recognise it for what it is? If masculine domination is opaque and beyond the grasp of men and women, how have Bourdieu and Beauvoir managed to develop their insights (and, indeed, how have we managed to recognise them as insights)? Here, too, there is some convergence, and both rely on their position as outsider.

Bourdieu argues that masculine domination is most 'magnified' in traditional societies like the Kabyle, and, while it is not recognised as such by the participants themselves, an outside ethnographer (like himself) can undertake 'a socioanalysis of the androcentric unconscious that is capable of objectifying the categories of that unconscious' (2001 [1998]: 5). He then transplanted his appreciation of the Kabyle androcentric unconscious to the more complex and differentiated unconscious structures of masculine domination found in advanced societies.

Just as Bourdieu's distance from, but connection to, Kabyle society gave him insight into its androcentric unconscious, so Beauvoir argues that it is her composite position as independent-woman-intellectual that gives her both distance from and insight into the subjugation of women – an insight denied to both intellectual men and dependent women.

> Very well, but just how shall we pose the question? And to begin with, who are we to propound it at all? Man is at once judge and party to the case; but so is woman. What we need is an angel – neither man nor woman – but where shall we find one? Still, the angel would be poorly qualified to speak, for an angel is ignorant of all the basic facts involved in the problem .... It looks to me as if there are, after all, certain women who are best qualified to elucidate the situation of woman .... Many of today's women, fortunate in the restoration of all the privileges pertaining to the estate of the human being, can afford the luxury of impartiality – we even recognize its necessity. ... Many problems appear to us to be more pressing than those which concern us in particular, and this detachment even allows us to hope that our attitude will be objective. Still, we know the feminine world more intimately than do the men because we have our roots in it, we grasp more immediately than do men what it means to a human being to be feminine; and we are more concerned with such knowledge (Beauvoir, 1989 [1949]: xxxiii–iv).

Objectivity for Beauvoir, like Bourdieu, comes from being an outsider, located in a relatively autonomous space, but, crucially, she is also an insider connected to the subjects under interrogation.[6]

While Bourdieu's 'outside from without' connection to the Kabyle is different from Beauvoir's 'outsider from within' connection to the experience of women, nonetheless they both have a notion of objectivity that is grounded in some segregated intellectual arena. For Bourdieu, it is the academy, defined by *skholè* and the competitive struggle for truth; for Beauvoir, it is the public sphere, epitomised by intellectual debate in the Parisian café or in journals like *Les Temps Modernes*. Such distance is necessary to avoid being mired in the misrecognition that accompanies symbolic domination – women seeing themselves through the eyes and with the categories of men. Thus, both are suspicious of movements based on the romanticisation of oppression, for that would be the triumph of misrecognition or bad faith. Most fundamentally, they both agree that with some exceptions (like themselves), when it comes to appreciating the foundations of masculine domination, men and women are dominated by their 'bad sense' and, specifically, women are complicit in their own subjugation.

They are, therefore, both traditional intellectuals demystifying masculine domination from on high. They are not only different from Fanon in Algeria, who is deeply engaged with revolutionary struggle, but also from Gramsci, who, like Bourdieu and Beauvoir, finds himself in what in the end proves to be a non-revolutionary context, but unlike them believes in the good sense of the oppressed, or at least the working class. Given the presumption of good sense, there is therefore a place for organic intellectuals who can elaborate that good sense (while also attacking bad sense), developing a war of position. We find analogous feminist intellectuals who see insight and good sense arising from the dominated. Patricia Hill Collins (1991), for example, argues that the most oppressed have the clearest view of the social structure and of their own position within domination and that they spontaneously generate cultures of resistance. She is specifically talking about poor black women in the United States. White women and black men, being in contradictory positions no less than white men, cannot see through the mists of domination. Collins, therefore, endorses the standpoint of an organic intellectual closely tied to communities of poor back women, elaborating their standpoints and their culture, transmitting these to wider publics. Consistent with this perspective, Collins is hostile to the traditional black intellectuals Louis Gates, Cornel West and even W. E. B. du Bois for the pretentious elitism in their representations of racial domination.

Indeed, there are strong traditions of feminism, very different from Beauvoir, that have deep roots in women's communities. Beauvoir was the traditional intellectual who gave language and vision to the movement and thereby established the very possibility of organic intellectuals. It remains to be seen whether Bourdieu's critical role as a traditional intellectual will also contribute to an organic connection between sociology and its publics – a position he himself adopted in later life, despite his oft-stated contempt for organic intellectuals.

Transforming Patriarchy?

Both Beauvoir and Bourdieu investigate the invisible domination of woman in a modern Western society – France – where modernity is layered with older orders of patriarchy going back to feudalism and before. Gender domination has been distilled over centuries and becomes for Bourdieu the prime instance of symbolic violence, which is 'a gentle violence, imperceptible and invisible even to its victims, exerted for the most part through the purely symbolic channels of communication and cognition' (Bourdieu, 2001 [1998]: 2). As Beauvoir puts it, this is an oppression where the oppressed 'has no grasp, even in thought, on the reality around her. It is opaque to her eyes' (Beauvoir, 1989 [1949]: 598).

What would Beauvoir or Bourdieu make of gender domination in South Africa, where 'gentle' and 'invisible' symbolic violence is joined by what can only be described as a campaign of private, explicit and atrocious physical violence against women? What would they make of the glaring disjunction between the new symbolic order arising out of the transition to democracy, which sets out explicitly to defend women against discrimination and empower them in all spheres – public and private – through policies, legislation and state institutions, and the competing symbolic orders that gain from society the vitality with which they continue to subjugate women?

These extraordinary disjunctions and juxtapositions between old and new, stasis and change, legislation and implementation, formal and informal, official rhetoric and daily practice, and between fractured and competing moralities, and all the contradictions, hypocrisies, clashes, enmities, alliances, polemics and fluctuations of mood – hope, anger, despair, triumph, cynicism, mirth – that accompany them, are precisely what characterise our society, providing formidable challenges to any attempt at Bourdieusian analysis of social order.

The rape trial of Jacob Zuma, at the time deputy president of the ANC, epitomised in the most public way possible the competing moralities and notions of patriarchal order in South Africa. Zuma's defence rested on a performance of himself as a traditional Zulu man deeply embedded in cultural notions of sexuality – themselves publicly contested. Outside the court, he danced and sang his trademark machine gun song before crowds of supporters, who threatened violence against the complainant. On the other side of the road, a coalition of gender activists and feminists demonstrated their support for the complainant. Inside the court, the judge dismissed all progressive arguments, criticised the women's organisations for challenging the 'conservative legal traditions of criminal law' while remaining silent about the conduct of the defendant's supporters outside the court, and brought all the most conservative assumptions of legal tradition regarding the complainant's testimony in rape trials to bear on his decisions (Vetten, 2007). Zuma was acquitted and went on to become president of the ANC and the country, and the complainant went into exile.

Much could be said about the significance of this moment for gender domination in South Africa. As Vetten remarks, two weighty traditions, that of Roman-Dutch law and that of (ostensible) Zulu culture, found common cause in their defence of patriarchy (which is not to say that, even had the court been less biased, Zuma would have been found guilty). But three points are salient in relation to Bourdieu: it cannot be said that resistance to gender domination is unthinkable; nor can it be said that domination and resistance are invisible; and the symbolism of direct physical violence (machine guns, the burning of a picture of the complainant, threats of violence) is intimately tangled with the invisible dimension of symbolic violence.

White patriarchy overlaps in many ways with black patriarchy, but it also has its own symbolic universe, related to ideas about the conquest of Africa, the significance of the farm, '*swart gevaar*', and anxieties about democracy and crime. Guns are central to this symbolic order, as an Afrikaner MP explained in an unpublished interview:

> That whole tradition and psyche and culture of 'I own a weapon. I am a man because I've got a weapon' – that was part of our culture, that was the way we grew up. I think about the days when I walked with a pellet gun, with my friends, sometimes we just shot at rocks, but I was, I was *armed* …

The vast majority of legally owned firearms belong to whites. The symbolic meaning of the gun is closely associated with white masculinity, as many submissions to parliament opposing the Firearms Control Bill made clear. 'My family sleep safe at night, secure in the knowledge that I will stand up for them', read one (Kirsten, 2008:138). It is not surprising that in the symbolic contestation over gun control legislation, Gun Free South Africa activists were subject to aggressively obscene phone calls by anonymous callers who made hostile comments about women, as well as about blacks, Jews and Muslims. But guns do not only constitute a form of symbolic violence – they also kill. South Africa has one of the highest rates of intimate femicides in the world, and many are killed with legally owned firearms (Kirsten, 2008: 8–9).

The relationship between symbolic violence and physical violence is a complex one. Some forms of symbolic violence legitimate specific repertoires of physical violence against the dominated, in which case the physical violence is girded around with tacit and explicit codes that regulate the occasions, kinds and limits of the physical violence that may be used. Part of the power of symbolic violence in this case is that it leads the dominated to accept that she deserves the 'punishment' directed against her.

In other cases, physical violence may be a response to an erosion of the efficacy of symbolic violence or a breakdown of hegemonic masculinity; physical violence then may be a strategy for restoring patriarchy or establishing the terms of a new form of patriarchy. Here, the workings of the symbolic order may be more ambiguous – it may have sufficient symbolic force to persuade the victim that she deserves punishment or, on the contrary, it may fracture further if the physical 'punishment' is seen to transgress the codes enshrined in the symbolic order – which is, after all, a kind of tacitly understood compact between men and women – and becomes thereby an injustice.

Much of the violence against women in South Africa today is a response to the breakdown or erosion of older symbolic orders of patriarchy in both black and white communities, and is an attempt to restore them or reconstitute male domination in a different way through the use of force. The older orders of patriarchy are challenged and destabilised by the anti-discriminatory provisions of the Constitution, as well as a range of policies and pieces of legislation introduced by the ANC – from the Employment Equity Act and the Domestic Violence Act to the quotas to increase the number of women holding political office.

But patriarchy was already being eroded by economic and social shifts in society, such as the growing number of unemployed men, the increasing employment of women and the breakdown of traditional households, with a growing number of women-headed households. Male 'breadwinners' who cannot bring home the bread, young men who cannot sustain their masculinity because they lack an income and cannot pay *lobola*, a growing number of women in positions of political and economic power, and the growing number of independent women who prefer to make their way outside of a relationship with a dominant male make for an explosive social mix under the sign of a destabilised symbolic order. Gender violence is one response (Mosoetsa, 2011, esp. chap. 2).

Many of these factors are visible in our research into community protests and local politics. Generally, politics and power are highly sexualised in local municipalities and women are important symbols of male power, as Beauvoir intimates. Thus, many stories and rumours circulate in political circles as well as in the community more generally about the sexual liaisons of key political figures. Men with power in the ANC, the town council or the municipal administration are said to have numerous mistresses and to have fathered numerous children with them. Mistresses and girlfriends are given jobs in the administration or, if already employed, are readily promoted, according to these stories. In the symbolic order crystallising around the new elite, politics and power are highly sexualised, and sexual liaisons with mistresses and girlfriends signal status (Langa, Dlamini & Von Holdt, 2011).

For women in the elite, however, the symbolic terms are reversed. Here the rumours are about the powerful man with whom the woman is involved in a sexual liaison, and her access to power is explained by his patronage. So, the woman mayor in one of the towns we studied was said to have got her position only because she was having an affair with a provincial MEC who 'forced her down the throat of the community'. In this way, the leadership of women who are appointed because of the ANC's official policy of increasing the number of women in political office is subverted by rumours that they owe their positions to their sexual subjugation to powerful men (Langa, Dlamini & Von Holdt, 2011). This goes along with the sense, articulated by these women, that they are generally disempowered and disregarded within ANC structures.

For young men who have little prospect of work or income, as for women in the elite, the symbolic terms of male power are reversed. To have a girlfriend, a young man needs money. Even more seriously, a young man without money cannot pay *lobola* to the parents of the woman he hopes to marry and so is unable to start a family. Young unemployed men in our research sites constantly compared themselves to men in the elite, expressing envy, anger and powerlessness, and criticising women for their materialism and a willingness to trade jobs for sex: 'I hate that M– guy [a councillor], he took my girlfriend. He has money and I don't have money. You can't find a girlfriend if you don't have money.'

In contrast to those who display their status, wealth, and power through mistresses and girlfriends, these young men are excluded from expressing their masculinity. Violent protest provides an alternative avenue for asserting their masculinity, whether in street battles with the police or in demanding and bringing about the downfall of a councillor or mayor. In two of our research towns, the mayors who were under attack by the protest movements were women. Some of the young male protesters, their masculinity deeply troubled and insecure, were adamant that they would not be ruled by a woman, because woman made poor leaders, being incapable and 'stubborn' (Langa, Dlamini & Von Holdt, 2011; Dlamini, 2011; Von Holdt, 2011a).

This instability in, or destabilisation of, the symbolic order that gives meaning to patriarchy generates multiple fissure lines through which violence may erupt. Such violence has a complex relationship with symbolic violence, as new symbolic orders are elaborated or resisted. Thus, the young male protesters in one focus group told us that young women like to be beaten, so that they can display the marks of assault as a sign of how much their men love them. If young women do indeed react like this, then they are subject to a symbolic violence that predisposes them to accept – and, indeed, treasure – the physical violence of their men against them. This may, on the other hand, be a fantasy of power on the part of disempowered young men – a symbolic violence they wish to exist, but does not – and nonetheless may predispose them to behaving violently. Young men who gang-rape lesbians, who also have benefitted from the expansion of anti-discriminatory legislation and litigation, in an effort to 'discipline' them are no doubt also resorting to violence in an attempt to shore up patriarchy and fragile masculinity (Toyana, 2011).

What we have in South Africa, then, is a picture of a destabilised patriarchal symbolic order and contending projects to reconstitute symbolic order. This applies as much to patriarchy as it does to class and racial hierarchies, and, indeed, the destabilisation of one has repercussions in the others, since different hierarchies in society do not exist in parallel, but mesh with each other, each hierarchy modifying or reinforcing the others. Bourdieu's concept of symbolic order and the symbolic violence it perpetrates provides powerful analytical tools for understanding society, but only if we push it to expand and take in the possibilities for destabilising and contesting symbolic order, and if we explore a much closer relationship between the gentle violence of symbolic domination and the brutality of direct physical violence.

Moreover, the South African case demonstrates that symbolic violence can be rendered visible and challenged. The numerous women's organisations and movements that have championed women's rights and contributed to progressive legislation and policies, and the difficult battles they take on in their communities are evidence of this. Even when the impact is limited, new rhetoric and new formal rights bolster discourses through which oppressed women may see their world afresh, its opacity becoming transparent, and find ways to challenge their domination. Indeed, in the same focus group described above, a feisty young woman drew on such discourses to challenge the men's views and made it clear that she would never tolerate such abuse.

It may indeed be that stripping away or rooting out one layer of symbolic violence simply reveals other, deeper and more intractable layers. But this is no reason to abandon the idea of freedom that is enshrined in our constitution and in much of the legislation enacted by the post-apartheid democratic parliament.

NOTES

1   An obvious reference to *Memoirs of a Dutiful Daughter,* the first volume of Beauvoir's autobiography.

2   I will rely on the original English translation of *The Second Sex*, despite its known problems; see Moi (2002).

3   Toril Moi says as much herself in her essay, 'Appropriating Bourdieu: Feminist theory and Pierre Bourdieu's sociology of culture' (Moi, 1999; see p. 283, footnote 21). There is nothing original in his gender analysis, but, so she argues, his concepts are nonetheless very useful for feminism. This is also the general tenor of the collection *Feminism after Bourdieu* (Adkins & Skeggs, 2004).

4   Beauvoir devotes a whole chapter to prostitution as an alternative to marriage. Just as lesbianism is a departure from normal sexualisation, so prostitution is a similarly alternative road to marriage whose significance and evaluation differs from society to society.

5   The same structure can also be found in Sartre's *Anti-Semite and Jew* (1948 [1946]), which appeared, probably not coincidentally, just as Beauvoir began work on *The Second Sex*.

6   This is what Patricia Collins 40 years later (1991) will call the perspective of 'the outsider within', although she will trace its genealogy not to Beauvoir, but to George Simmel.

CONVERSATION 7

INTELLECTUALS AND THEIR PUBLICS

MICHAEL BURAWOY

Mills Meets Bourdieu

*It is the political task of the social scientist – as of any liberal educa-
tor – continually to translate personal troubles into public issues,
and public issues into the terms of their human meaning for a variety of individuals. It is his task to display in his work – and, as an
educator, in his life as well – this kind of sociological imagination.*
Mills (1959: 187)

*Political competence, inasmuch as there can be a universal defini-
tion of it, undoubtedly consists in the ability to speak in universal
terms about particular problems – how to survive dismissal or
redundancy, an injustice or an accident at work, not as individual
accident, a personal mishap, but as something collective, common to a class. This universalization is possible only by way of language, by access to a general discourse on the social world. This
is why politics is in part bound up with language. And here again,
if you like, we can introduce a bit of utopia to attenuate the sad-
ness of sociological discourse, and convince ourselves that it is not
too naive to believe that it can be useful to fight over words, over
their honesty and proper sense, to be outspoken and to speak out.*
Bourdieu (2008 [1977]: 76–77)

*All this means that the ethno-sociologist is a kind of organic intel-
lectual of humanity, and as a collective agent, can contribute to
de-naturalizing and de-fatalizing human existence by placing his
skill at the service of a universalism rooted in the comprehension
of different particularisms.*

Bourdieu (2008 [2000]: 24)

So far, I have created imaginary conversations between Bourdieu and
Marxism: how Bourdieu appropriated so much of Marx, but took it in
a direction unimagined by Marx, namely the political economy of symbolic goods; how in many ways Gramsci and Bourdieu are at logger-
heads over the sources of the durability and depth of domination; how,
despite their common views of colonialism, Bourdieu and Fanon clash
over the means of its transcendence; and, finally, how Bourdieu's understanding of masculine domination as symbolic power was a pale replica
of Beauvoir's feminism. We turn now to another conversation, between
Bourdieu and Mills. Both deeply ambivalent about Marxism, they shared
similar sociological and political projects, despite living half a century
apart and on different continents.

The quotes from Bourdieu and Mills above are chosen to underscore
their convergent views on the relations between sociologists and their
publics, a notion of the traditional intellectual who can potentially challenge domination by denaturalising and defatalising what exists, demonstrating the links between the taken-for-granted lived experience (the
particular) and the social forces that constitute it (the universal). They
differ, however, in that Bourdieu recognises and lives out the contradictions between 'science as a vocation' and 'politics as a vocation', to use
Max Weber's terms, since science rests on a *break* with common sense
and politics on an *engagement* with common sense. Mills, on the other
hand, would probably have as little tolerance for Bourdieu's scientific
'jargon' as he did for Parsons's, since he doesn't see a fundamental break
between science and common sense, identifying the sociological imagination (linking micro and macro) with the political imagination (turning
personal troubles into public issues). We will return to this question in
the conclusion to this conversation, but first we must build up the case
that, despite their obvious differences, Mills is Bourdieu draped in 1950s
American colours.

STRIKING CONVERGENCES

Bourdieu's major methodological text, *The Craft of Sociology* (written with Jean-Claude Chamboredon and Jean-Claude Passeron in 1968), exhibits uncanny parallels with C. Wright Mills's famous elaboration of the sociological imagination in 1959. Indeed, one cannot but notice that the title of Bourdieu's book is borrowed from Mills's famous appendix, 'On intellectual craftsmanship'. Both books are critical of the divorce of theory from empirical research; both emphasise social science research as process – a *modus operandi* rather than an *opus operatum*, as Bourdieu would say. Bourdieu follows Mills in attacking US sociology for its professionalism, its formalism, its empiricism and its provincialism. Yet there is not a single reference to Mills in Bourdieu's writings, except the inclusion of a short extract – one of 44 'illustrative texts' – from *The Sociological Imagination* (1959), in which Mills criticises public opinion research for creating its own spurious object, an argument also found in *The Craft of Sociology* and one that Bourdieu will elaborate later in his career.

Given their similar methodological outlooks and empirical foci, the comparison of Bourdieu and Mills underlines how the world has changed since the 1950s (while in some ways reverting back to that era), as well as the abiding differences between the United States and France. Still, there are parallels in the political context that shaped their writing. In the United States, the years immediately after the Second World War witnessed the continuity of the radicalism that had begun in the 1930s, but it wasn't long before reaction asserted itself in the form of McCarthyite witch hunts, a broad anti-communism, American triumphalism and the 'end of ideology'. Just as Mills confronted the swing away from the political configuration of the New Deal, much of Bourdieu's writings can be seen as coming to terms with the dénouement of the 1960s and the rightward turn in the 1980s and 1990s. Both sustained a critique of the present at a time when progressive alternatives were in retreat.

Biographically, Mills and Bourdieu came from very different backgrounds – the one grew up the son of a postman in a village in the French Pyrenees, the other from middle-class stock in Texas. More interesting, however, they both began as philosophy students, but quickly turned from abstract and abstruse intellectual preoccupations to a more direct engagement with the world. For Mills, his interest in pragmatism gave him a particular stance on sociology that was opposed to structural functionalism and survey research, just as Bourdieu reacted against the pretensions of Sartre and his circle, as well as against social reform sociology.

Like Bourdieu, who developed a knee-jerk reaction against the Marxism of the communist intellectuals who surrounded him at the École Normale Supérieure, Mills had his Marxism refracted through the milieu of New York leftism. Only very late in his life would Mills take up a serious engagement with the history of Marxism. Like Bourdieu, he borrowed many ideas from Marxism, but, also like Bourdieu, he never quite identified with its political project. Thus, both were hostile to the Communist Party and were never members, although – again – both exhibited sometimes overt and sometimes covert sympathies for democratic variants of socialism.

Both openly recognised the influence of Weber, with whom they shared a pre-eminent concern with domination, its reproduction and its repercussions. Like Weber, they never spelled out any future utopia. Both had only a weakly developed theory of history: Mills focused on the shift from a 19th-century aristocratic order (alongside putative democratic publics) to the new regime of power elite and mass society, while Bourdieu subscribed to modernisation theory based on the differentiation of relatively autonomous fields, analogous to what Weber called value spheres.

Mills and Bourdieu were reflexive sociologists inasmuch as they dissected the academic and political fields in which they operated – although they were more adept at applying that reflexivity to others than to themselves. Both were invested in the sociology of knowledge, both a sociology of sociology and a sociology of the academy. Mills's dissertation was a study of the history of pragmatism – the secularisation and professionalisation of philosophy. Following in the footsteps of Veblen, Mills was always critical of the American system of higher education, but, again like Bourdieu, had a fondness for its elitist aspects that gave them the space and autonomy to develop their distinctive sociologies. Still, both felt themselves to be outsiders in the academy and from this vantage point wrote their savage criticisms, lambasting the establishment and generating the hostility of their colleagues and the adoration of new generations of students.

Both were public sociologists, but also major public intellectuals, and not just in their own countries, but across the world. Both served their scholarly apprenticeships as professionals, but soon sought out wider audiences. Neither hesitated to enter the political arena as an intellectual, and their careers displayed a steady movement from the academy into the public sphere. Mills was writing in an era of passivity, and his notions of mass society reflect this. Like Beauvoir, he inspired a movement he never anticipated – the New Left of the 1960s. It remains to be seen whether Bourdieu will inspire such a movement – certainly his political writings and addresses played an important role in public debate in France. Both held out hope for intellectuals as a 'third force', as Mills once called it, that would pioneer progressive politics in the name of reason and freedom.

CLASSES AND DOMINATION

Bourdieu has come to be known for his meta-theoretical framework – centring on fields, habitus and capital, and above all on symbolic violence – that transcended his own empirical projects, a theoretical framework that has been taken up by others. Mills's only venture into broader theoretical issues, *Character and Social Structure*, written with Hans Gerth (Gerth & Mills, 1954), was never taken up by sociologists. Nonetheless, Mills's critical evaluation of the social structures of his time and his invitation to the sociological imagination have inspired successive generations of students. There are definite parallels in Bourdieu's corpus, since, like Mills, he rarely made sorties into pure theory, even though his empirical research was always more theoretically self-conscious than Mills's. Its impact transcends sociology not just in reaching the public realm, but it has also spread into many disciplines, beyond sociology and beyond the social sciences into the humanities.

The three major works of Mills to address US society in the 1950s dealt sequentially with labour and its leaders (*The New Men of Power*, 1948), the new middle classes (*White Collar*, 1951) and the dominant class (*The Power Elite*, 1956). Mills's framework for studying US society does develop over the decade of his writing, but there is also a clear continuity in his approach to that society: ever-greater concentration of power in a cohesive economic-political-military elite; a passive, but burgeoning new middle class of professionals, managers, sales workers and bureaucrats; and, finally, a working class betrayed by its leaders. These are also the three classes treated in Bourdieu's monumental *Distinction*. Whereas Mills works his way up the social hierarchy, Bourdieu works his way down, from the dominant classes to the petty bourgeoisie, and finally to the working class. Both study the way the dominant classes impose their will on society, but where Mills focuses on the concentration of resources and decision making in the power elite, Bourdieu takes this concentration of power and wealth for granted, instead focusing on how domination is hidden or legitimated by the categories that the dominant classes use to secure their domination.

Bourdieu, therefore, aims his analysis at symbolic domination – the exercise of domination through its misrecognition. Simply put, the dominant class distinguishes itself by its cultural taste. Whether this be in art, architecture, music or literature, the dominant class presents itself as more refined and more at ease with its cultural consumption than the petite bourgeoisie, whose taste is driven by emulation, and the working class, whose lifestyle is driven by economic necessity. The distinction of the dominant class actually derives from its privileged access to wealth and education, but it appears to be innate, thereby justifying its domination in all spheres of life. According to Bourdieu, the popular aesthetic of the working class – its concern with function rather than form, with the represented rather than the representation – is a dominated aesthetic, bereft of genuine critical impulse. Bourdieu's innovation, therefore, turns on viewing class not just as an economic-political-social formation, but also as a cultural formation. Class members possess not just economic capital, but also cultural capital, so that a class structure is a two-dimensional space defined hierarchically by the total volume of capital, but also horizontally (within class) by the composition of capital (i.e. the specific combination of economic and cultural capital). He shows how this class structure is mirrored in the distribution of cultural practices and patterns of consumption.

It is interesting to compare this vision of class structure with Mills's *Power Elite*, where he describes the dominant class as three interlocking sets of institutions – economic, political and military. He calls them 'domains', but he might as well have called them fields. He also writes about their distinction and their ruling-class lifestyle, inherited through families, acquired in elite schools and colleges, and developed through networks of self-assurance. Mills even devotes a chapter to 'celebrities' who distract attention from the concentration of power. Symbols of prestige hide the power elite from public view. This is all quite parallel to Bourdieu, but ultimately the emphasis is very different. Mills is not interested in the relation between cultural and economic-political elites – between the dominant and dominated fractions of the dominant class, as Bourdieu puts it – but in the changing relations among the three pillars of the power elite, and in particular the ascendancy of the military (the warlords). This different emphasis reflects the very different place of the United States and France within the world order – the one a dominant military power, the other a cultural nobility.

If there is divergence in the conceptualisation of the dominant class, there is more convergence in their respective discussions of the middle classes. A theme that threads through both discussions is the insecurity of the middle class, trying to maintain its position within the stratification system. As the gap between the middle classes – especially the old middle classes subject to deskilling, but also the new middle classes subject to bureaucratisation – and the working class closes, so the status panic of the former intensifies. As a form of capital, education becomes more important than property in asserting middle-class distinction. *White Collar* makes much of the rising importance of education, but also the role of the mass media and the illusory world it creates. Mills devotes considerable space to the fate of the intellectuals and their loss of independence through bureaucratisation, becoming a technocracy-serving power that is unresponsive to publics. Mills describes, in terms directly analogous to those of Bourdieu, how the academic field is looking more and more like an economic market, invaded by the logic of corporate capital.

On the subject of the working class, both Bourdieu and Mills have much less to say. Bourdieu's more ethnographic *The Weight of the World* has a richer, if untheorised, exploration of working-class life than *Distinction*, which is reliant on survey research. The culture of the working class is a dominated culture, responsive to the pressing needs of economic necessity and the prestige of the dominant culture. Mills's analysis of the working class is thinner, since *The New Men of Power* is devoted more to labour leaders than to the led. The argument is very similar to the one Bourdieu makes in *Language and Symbolic Power* (1991) – the representatives of subordinate classes enter the field of power, where they engage in a competitive game among themselves and the logic of the field of power trumps their accountability to the dominated. Mills describes how labour leaders, through their negotiations, are co-opted onto the terrain of the business class. They seek to attach themselves to the lower levels of the power elite. Both Mills and Bourdieu, therefore, see leaders manipulating the led – representation becomes rhetoric used to simultaneously pursue and hide games within the higher reaches of society. Bourdieu's (1990 [1982]; 1993 [1984]) essays on public opinion follow Mills's contempt for mass society.

Yet alongside Mills's cynicism is an alternative political vision, albeit a political vision that becomes more utopian over time. *The New Men of Power* describes the absorption of labour leaders into the power elite, accomplices of the 'main drift', but it also maps out the political field of the immediate post-war period as an array of publics that includes the Far Left (Leninist Left), the Independent Left (more critical than interventionist), the Liberal Centre (which might include support for trade unions), the Communists (which he sees as anti-democratic fifth columnists), the Practical Right (which supports class war against unions and leftists), and Sophisticated Conservatives (corporate liberals tied to the military-industrial complex who see unions as a stabilising force that manages discontent). Like so many commentators of his time, Mills expected capitalism to undergo another 'slump' that would force the hand of the Sophisticated Conservatives, but also attract popular support to a true Labour Party (Mills supported Norman Thomas's 1948 presidential bid as a candidate of the Socialist Party) that would organise worker control and democratic planning. Socialism, he asserted, had been derailed by social democracy, petty trade unionism and communism. In line with this programme, Mills hoped for a new type of intellectual, a 'labour intellectual', independent of, but also committed to the working class, capable of forging a new vision and a new collective will.

Mills's political optimism did not last long. Reaction swept across the country, so that when he turned to *White Collar* (1951) he came up with a much bleaker scenario. There he refers to the middle classes as a rearguard, without a will of their own, siding with the prevailing forces in society, and, pending a slump, the prevailing forces lay with the power elite. When it comes to *The Power Elite* (1956), Mills is consumed by despair. Denouncing the 'higher immorality' and 'organized irresponsibility' of the dominant classes, his political imagination turns from the bleak future to the radiant past. He contrasts the mass society he sees around him with a democracy of publics – the founding dream and early practice of American society. Mills never reconciles himself to the present, never withdraws from the intellectual battle for another world.

If there was always a strong utopian element in Mills's writings – at first projected onto leftist political forces and then as emancipatory projects buried in history – one is hard pressed to find any equivalent in the writings of Bourdieu, who saw his public jeremiads as being adequately political in their own right. They would be less effective if connected to utopian thinking. In part, this was because of the historic role of French intellectuals, starting with Zola, and the openness of the public sphere to such intellectuals – so different from their more marginal place in US politics. No less important, Bourdieu was always opposed to conjuring up false hopes in the transformative potential of the dominated classes. His political engagement around issues of human rights, labour rights, education and so forth was firmly rooted in the concrete present. Bourdieu mobilised his analysis of the subjective experience of domination, so absent in Mills's writings, against what he regarded as the illusions of leftist intellectuals. Bourdieu refused speculative connections across the yawning gap between hope and reality, the yawning gap that separated Mills's utopian schemes and his sociological analysis, political imagination and sociological imagination.

THE SOCIOLOGICAL IMAGINATION

The refusal to confront the gap between sociological imagination and political imagination – indeed, the confusion of the two – can be found in *The Sociological Imagination,* one of the most widely read and inspiring introductions to sociology. *The Sociological Imagination,* published in 1959 just three years before Mills died, looks two ways – back to sociology and forward to politics. When looking back to sociology, it is a devastating and memorable indictment of professional sociology for the sins of abstracted empiricism and grand theorising. Abstracted empiricism refers to survey research divorced from any historical or theoretical context, typified in Mills's mind by the work of his titular boss, Paul Lazarsfeld, with whom he had a most rocky relationship. Abstracted empiricism approximates to market research and exemplifies the bureaucratisation of sociology, and more generally to how intellectuals were increasingly serving the corporate world as consultants and experts, and as orchestrators of public opinion. Grand theory, on the other hand, refers to the hegemony of structural functionalism within the world of theory – formal theory, arcane and inaccessible except to the initiated elite around Talcott Parsons. Grand theory builds an elaborate, but empty architecture of the most mundane, yet unsubstantiated claims.

Against abstracted empiricism and grand theory, Mills celebrated the sociologist as craft worker, uniting in one person the development of sociological theory through engagement with empirical data. He paints a romantic image of the lone sociologist uncorrupted by the academic environment – a self-portrait of his isolation in and alienation from the academic world. This image is an absurdly unsociological vision of professional sociology – a Manichean struggle between God and the Devil – but one that justified his own abandonment of that world.

If the first romance in *The Sociological Imagination* is with the sociologist as craft worker, the second is with the sociologist as 'independent intellectual', looking outwards into politics rather than inwards into academia. Here too there are two positions to avoid: on the one hand, the sociologist as adviser to the prince – the technician, the consultant – and, on the other hand, the philosopher king who aspires to rule the world. In the political realm, the adviser to the prince and the philosopher king are the counterparts to the abstracted empiricist and the grand theorist in the academic realm, while the independent intellectual is the counterpart of the craft worker. The independent intellectual speaks *to* publics and *at* rulers, maintaining a distance from both. Here indeed is Mills's notion of the public sociologist – a concept he describes, but does not name – for him a traditional rather than an organic intellectual.

The connection between the craft worker and the independent intellectual is made through the idea of the sociological imagination that famously turns private problems into public issues. But here the slippage begins: between, on the one hand, the *sociological imagination* – i.e. the connection between social milieu and social structure, micro and macro – and, on the other hand, the never-specified *political imagination* that connects private troubles to public issues. It is one thing to demonstrate that unemployment is not a problem of individual indolence, but one of the capitalist economy; it is another matter to turn that sociological understanding into a public demand or a social movement for security of employment. Indeed, appreciating the broad structural determinants of one's personal troubles is as likely to lead to apathy and withdrawal as to engagement. *The New Men of Power, White Collar* and *The Power Elite* each attempts to bridge the divide between sociology and politics, but in an abstract way as though sociological imagination inevitably leads to political engagement. Political imagination cannot be reduced to sociological imagination, as Bourdieu knows only too well.

The first problem concerns the very existence of publics for Mills's public sociologist to address. His books all point to the disappearance of publics and the rise of mass society, so with whom, then, will the public sociologist converse? Bourdieu recognises the dilemma quite explicitly, albeit in a specific way. The argument is laid out in *The Craft of Sociology*, which speaks directly to Mills's sociologist as craft worker. It criticises both existentialism (the counterpart to Parsons's structural functionalism) and the reaction to it in the form of imported American empiricism. Like Mills, Bourdieu's work is a continual dialogue of theory and empirical research: the one cannot exist without the other. Bourdieu rarely indulges in flights of political fancy;[1] his claims are always empirically grounded. On the other hand, he closely follows Bachelard, the French philosopher of science, by insisting on the break between science and common sense, or what Bourdieu calls *spontaneous sociology*. For sociology, such a break with common sense is especially important, because its subject matter deals with familiar problems about which everyone has an opinion. Throughout his academic life, Bourdieu will be fighting against what he regards as amateurish commentators – so-called 'doxosophers' – who claim to know better than sociologists.

Although the home of sociology, France has always had difficulty developing an autonomous professional sociology and separating itself from social reform and public discourse. In this sense, the academic context of Bourdieu is very different from that of Mills. The one faces the struggle to create a science against common sense, while the other is suffocated by professionalism and struggles to reconnect science to common sense. This accounts, at least in part, for their opposed genres of writing, the one always simple and accessible, the other dominated by complex linguistic constructions and the coining of esoteric concepts.[2] For a renewal of sociology to be accepted by the French academic pantheon, it was necessary to adopt the style of writing of the discipline with the highest distinction, namely philosophy. While denouncing the detachment of philosophy from everyday reality, Bourdieu nevertheless replicates a philosophical rhetorical style to establish sociology's distinction, but the result can be separation from the wider publics he seeks to reach. He is only too aware of the gap between sociology and politics, even as he tries to overcome the gap in his later years. Mills suffers from the opposite problem – by making his books accessible and by resisting the idiom of science and high theory, he loses credibility within the world of sociology, and mistakes his sociological imagination for political imagination.

Still, reacting to opposite challenges – Bourdieu embracing science against common sense; Mills embracing common sense against hyperscience – they converge on a common understanding of methodology, represented in the idea of craftwork as the interactive unity of theory and research. Likewise, Bourdieu, no less than Mills, is committed to the idea of the independent intellectual. Moreover, his targets are the same as Mills's. On the one hand, he denounces the philosopher king, or what he calls the 'total intellectual' epitomised by Jean-Paul Sartre and, on the other hand, he denounces the advisers to the king – the technocrats, experts, consultants to the state and servants of power. The philosopher king – the public intellectual as total intellectual – has a certain reality in France that it does not have in the United States. Notwithstanding the higher appreciation of the intellectual in France, Bourdieu nonetheless faces the same dilemma as Mills. Neither sees a public out there that he can address. Mills talks of a mass society, atomised, withdrawn, and alienated from politics and public discussion, whereas for Bourdieu the problem is, if anything, even more serious. The habitus is so deeply inculcated that the dominated are unreceptive to criticism of domination.

Furthermore, the independent intellectual faces the power of the media and their own mediators. Bourdieu lost no opportunity to attack the media's power to determine the message, to even shape the research that becomes the message. Although Mills was also aware of the power of the media, he never wrote such a broad assault on the media as Bourdieu carries out in *On Television* (1999 [1996]).

Whether they sought it or not, both – but Bourdieu more than Mills – became celebrities in their own time for their angry oppositional views. They became media events in their own right, and the more they railed against the establishment, the more celebrated they became! Yet both were opposed to the idea of the organic intellectual who would circumvent the media and engage directly with publics. In theory, both opposed the organic intellectual on the grounds that it compromised their independence, yet their actual practices were quite different.

C. Wright Mills rarely so much as participated in any collective demonstration, protest, refused to sign petitions and generally avoided the people he somewhat contemptuously dismissed as the masses. He was a pure intellectual, speaking down to the people from his pulpit. Bourdieu, however, was very different. He was always ready to initiate or sign a petition, he was ready to talk to all sorts of publics and he could be found addressing workers on picket lines. He had no allergy to the people in whose name he spoke. Quite the contrary, he had enormous sympathy for those at the bottom of social hierarchies, vividly expressed in *The Weight of the World*, which describes the plight of the lower classes and immigrants under modern capitalism. Here lies the paradox – according to his theory, such unmediated engagement is not only a futile, but a dangerous activity. Yet he also saw this practice of public sociology as developing a political imagination out of his sociological imagination. Mills was always truer to the idea of the traditional intellectual, standing aloof from the individual and collective struggles below, but even he, in the last three years of his life, compromised his independence in a desperate political partisanship.

FROM SOCIOLOGY TO POLITICS

The Sociological Imagination (1959) was Mills's farewell to sociology. In the remaining three years of his life he became a public intellectual, writing two short polemical books intended to capture the public imagination. The first was *The Causes of World War Three* (1958), a continuation of the arguments of *The Power Elite*, but written for an even broader public.

It condemned 'crackpot realism' and 'organized irresponsibility' not just in the United States, but in the Soviet Union too. Together, these power elites were ushering in World War Three. He ends the book with an appeal to intellectuals to fight against the insanity of 'rationality without reason', calling instead, you might say, for Bourdieu's 'Realpolitik of reason'.

The second book was of a very different character. If *The Causes of World War Three* diagnosed the way the power elites of the two superpowers were heading toward the annihilation of the human race, *Listen, Yankee*, written in 1960, pointed to an alternative scenario – a socialism that was neither capitalist nor communist. The Cuban Revolution served to make the alternative real – as a 'concrete fantasy' intended to galvanise a collective political imagination. *Listen, Yankee* is based on Mills's short, but intense visit to Cuba in 1960. He spent three-and-a-half long days with Fidel Castro and nearly a week with the head of the Institute for Agrarian Reform. In his account of the Cuban Revolution through the eyes of its leaders, Mills points to the already ongoing and remarkable experiments in economic planning, education expansion, welfare provision and land reforms – experiments that would be institutionalised as the mark of Cuban socialism. He undertakes a class analysis of the social forces that are driving the social transformations and the counter-revolutionary forces opposing it, not least the support being given to the counter-revolution by the United States. He describes the challenges Cuba faced both domestically and internationally. The open hostility of the United States, Mills says, was driving Cuba into the arms of the Soviet Union, which thereby intensified US military threats. *Listen, Yankee* addresses the US public, befuddled by the jingoist media and ignorant of the destructive path of US imperialism throughout Latin America, but particularly in Cuba – imperialism justified under the Monroe Doctrine. The Cuban Revolution should be seen, he argued, as a reaction to Yankee supremacy, an experiment in true democracy, an experiment that all people of conscience can learn from, an experiment they must defend.

It was only two years before the end of his 46-year life that Mills discovered the potential of Third World revolutions. He was ahead of his time. In its class analysis, in its understanding of colonialism and imperialism, in its vision of socialism, *Listen, Yankee* is a precursor to Fanon's *The Wretched of the Earth*, which appeared in the following year – the same year that its author died at the age of 35. These two sadly curtailed lives – Mills's and Fanon's – ended within three months of each other, inspiring in their different ways social movements across the world. Both saw the key role of intellectuals in forging revolution, but Mills developed this idea very late in life, only when he began travelling abroad, especially to Latin America, where he discovered first hand the significance of revolutionary theory, which he had previously dismissed as a Marxist ruse.

Just as Mills became ever more outspoken and radical during the last three years of his life, so in the last decade of his life Bourdieu also became more angry, more public, more accusatory. He had always seen sociology – or, at least, his sociology – as having political consequences in the sense that it revealed the hidden bases of domination; nonetheless, his denunciations took on polemical force when faced with the conservative turn of politics in France and elsewhere. His book *On Television* (1999 [1996]) and then the two short collections of essays *Acts of Resistance* (1998 [1998]) and *Firing Back* (2003 [2001]) spoke out against neoliberalism and the tyranny of the market. He established his own press, Liber-Raisons d'Agir, to publish such politically motivated and publicly accessible books. His magazine *Actes de la Recherche de Science Sociales* had always had a broad intellectual audience. He became a major intellectual spokesman of a broad left front in France, but also worked to develop what he called an 'International of intellectuals'. He could be found on picket lines with workers, as well as writing open letters to prominent leaders protesting against violations of human rights. He was committed to intellectuals as an independent collective force, to the intellectual as an 'organic intellectual of humanity', as he once called it. C. Wright Mills had a similar vision of intellectuals as a 'third force', an idea he had formulated as early as the Second World War when he taught at the University of Maryland, a view that stuck with him until his dying days. In *Listen, Yankee* he wrote of Cuba as a cultural centre of the world, proposing to establish a 'world university' and with it create an international community of progressive intellectuals. The parallels between Mills and Bourdieu are perhaps astonishing, but then they are also expressing the unconscious desires of intellectuals as a class.

Yet here is the paradox: Bourdieu recognises that ideas can have only limited effect on social change. The dominated, who have an interest in a critical sociology, cannot grasp their meaning, because their submissive habitus is so deeply inscribed, whereas those who can grasp their meaning have no interest in the message. There is a mismatch, as I have said before, between Bourdieu's logic of theory and his logic of practice. His theory says such interventions are futile, yet his actions imply that such interventions might dislodge public discourse and thus destabilise symbolic violence. In the final analysis, his own political engagement contradicts his attacks on ideology and consciousness as too thin to grasp the depth of domination. In the end, despite his theory, Bourdieu cannot but subscribe to the idea of the organic intellectual engaged directly with publics, as well as the traditional intellectual speaking from the tribune, addressing humanity. He feels compelled to supplement his sociological analysis with political engagement. We need to make sense of this by turning Bourdieu on Bourdieu.

INTELLECTUALS AND THEIR PUBLICS

One of the curious features of Bourdieu's writings, as we have seen time and again, is his simultaneous insistence on reflexivity and his failure to apply this to himself. To do so would have meant placing himself inside various academic fields, relativising his knowledge and thereby weakening his position in the combat sport that is sociology. To wrestle with the question of science and politics it is necessary to restore the idea of sociology as a field of contradictions and antagonisms. Bourdieu provides us with the ammunition to do precisely this. We can turn, for example, to his analysis of the scientific field in which established players compete to accumulate academic capital in the face of challenges from the new generation, but it is more fruitful to go further afield and appropriate his analysis of the literary field in *Rules of Art* (1996 [1992]) as a framework for examining the sociological field.

The literary field begins with an account of 'bourgeois art', i.e. art sponsored by the dominant classes. In the context of sociology, this is what I call the *policy moment* in which sociology enters the service of various clients. The first rebellion against bourgeois literature comes from writers attentive to an audience of subaltern classes – what Bourdieu calls 'social art'. Within sociology, this corresponds to *public sociology*, i.e. a sociology that is accessible and accountable to diverse publics, and entering into a dialogue with such publics. The literary field, however, is only really constituted when writers separate themselves both from the patronage of bourgeois art and the affiliations of social art to constitute 'art for art's sake', i.e. 'pure art' following its own autonomous principles. For sociology, too, this is the moment of its true birth. It comes with the constitution of what I call *professional sociology* – a sociology that is accountable to itself – i.e. to the community of scholars who develop their own research programmes. Finally, the dynamism of the literary field comes from challenges to the consecrated artists, i.e. challenges from the avant-garde who seek to further the autonomy of art, but also shift the principles upon which its autonomy rests. Today's consecrated art can be found in yesterday's avant-garde. Within sociology, this is the *critical moment* in which the assumptions of professional sociology are interrogated and transformed. New research programmes emerge – at least in part – from the critical theorists of yesterday.

Table 1. Division of academic labour

	SCIENCE Academic audience	POLITICS Extra-academic audience
DOMINANT Instrumental knowledge	PROFESSIONAL	POLICY
SUBORDINATE Reflexive knowledge	CRITICAL	PUBLIC

We can now look upon the field of sociology – or, indeed, any other academic discipline – in terms of the relations among these four types of knowledge: what we might call the division of sociological labour. The four types can be arranged along two dimensions, as in table 1. On the one hand, there is the distinction between, on the one side, science with its academic audience (Bourdieu's autonomous pole) that includes professional and critical knowledge, and, on the other side, politics with its extra-academic audience (Bourdieu's heteronomous pole) that includes policy and public knowledge. The other dimension is defined by the distinction between dominant or consecrated knowledges (professional and policy), as opposed to the subordinated or subversive knowledges (critical and public). The dominant knowledges involve an *instrumental rationality* – solving puzzles defined by research programmes (professional sociology) or problems defined by clients (policy sociology) – whereas subordinate knowledges involve value rationality, or what I call *reflexive knowledge*, i.e. dialogue either among sociologists themselves about the foundations of their discipline (critical sociology) or between sociologists and their publics (public sociology).

Any disciplinary field consists of these four interdependent and antagonistic knowledges. Without professional knowledge of the sort that Bourdieu created in most of his classic works, there cannot be a public sociology, whose intensity rose in his later life. Public sociology requires the translation of professional sociology into an accessible language, but it also requires an accountability to publics achieved through dialogue. This is what Bourdieu tries to conjure up in *The Weight of the World*, but the dialogue is at odds with his theoretical claims about the deep misrecognition of the dominated. His more polemical tracts, such as *On Television*, are widely read and discussed, and thus generate dialogue, but it is a dialogue conducted, in a sense, at arm's length.

Just as one can study the history of a field by studying the shifting patterns of relations among the four knowledges, so one can trace an individual's career through these knowledges. Looking at Bourdieu's academic trajectory, one might argue that he sets out as a critical sociologist, but over time his critique becomes absorbed as a reigning orthodoxy, at which point he turns to public engagement. Although he is critical of policy science and its army of consultants, media celebrities and experts of one form or another, all servants of power, he nonetheless sits on government-sponsored commissions for educational reform. The policy world cannot be excised from the discipline, although, like the other knowledges, it must not come to dominate the discipline – the heteronomous pole must be kept in check. Likewise, instrumental knowledge can prevail, but not to the exclusion of reflexive knowledge.

We can now better appreciate the problems with Mills's view of sociology. By celebrating the sociologist as a romanticised craft worker and independent intellectual, and by reducing policy sociology and professional sociologies to their pathological types (abstracted empiricism and grand theory), he is denying the existence of a viable division of academic labour. He collapses all four types of knowledge into a single type of public sociology defined as the sociological imagination. Table 1 situates his early career as a professional sociologist in Wisconsin and Maryland, and his early years at Columbia. But as he writes his famous trilogy, he cuts himself off from professional sociology to become a public sociologist, from which vantage point he writes *The Sociological Imagination* – critical sociology par excellence – before leaving the field of sociology altogether.

Mills's critique of professional and policy sociology underscores the ever-present danger of professional sociology becoming irrelevant through self-referentiality and of policy sociology being captured by the client. These warnings are especially relevant today when regulation of the profession and the commodification of knowledge threaten to cut off instrumental knowledge from its lifeblood – reflexive knowledge. We have, therefore, to apply the sociological imagination to the field that is sociology, recognising the broader forces at work in shaping its contours. Indeed, each type of knowledge can be divided into two zones, one looking inward and the other outward. Thus, policy sociology can be of the sponsored type, but it can also be more independent and assume an advocacy role. Professional sociology can take the form of ritualised processes of regulation and control, but it can also advance exciting research programmes, especially when open to critical sociologists. Critical sociologists also suffer from a dogmatism often rooted in subservience to other disciplines rather than a carefully trained critique of professional sociology as it is practised.

Finally, we come to the two faces of public sociology. Mills's public sociology sustained the independence of the sociologist through the dissemination of widely read exposés of domination and its ideological justification. It was a traditional form of public sociology addressed to publics without direct conversation with them, although his writings did, and still do, generate much debate. He stood aloof from the organic public sociology that would have brought him into dialogue with the very people he was writing about. Mills kept his distance from the 'cheerful robots' – the duped and manipulated citizens of mass society – as though any engagement with them would contaminate his intellectual endeavours.

Similar sentiments can be found in Bourdieu, but his venom was more usually aimed at the 'organic intellectuals' who misguidedly think they can overcome the hiatus of habitus – intellectuals who do not appreciate that the dominated adjust to the conditions of domination in ways that are difficult for intellectuals to comprehend. Yet Bourdieu violates his own admonitions and crosses over from traditional to organic public sociology when representing the voices of the dominated in *The Weight of the World*. He can no longer remain aloof from the plight of the subaltern. Although it requires a move outside the United States, even Mills discovers organic intellectuals in the Cuban Revolution and, indeed, becomes their spokesperson to the American people. In the end, both Mills and Bourdieu joined Marx, Gramsci, Freire and Fanon in recognising organic intellectuals as playing a crucial role in ideological warfare against the dominant classes. As Gramsci might say, by themselves, intellectuals cannot fight a war of position; they need allies from the popular classes.

The Symbolic World of Politics

Bourdieu writes about the 'Realpolitik of reason' or the 'Realpolitik of the universal' as the form of politics engaged in by the public sociologist – in other words, the struggle to defend the social conditions of the exercise of reason and expand access to its fruits. What might this mean in a country such as South Africa, emerging from a long history of colonialism and apartheid into a world order still dominated by the West?

As we noted in Conversation 5 (p121), Bourdieu understands the 'ambiguity of reason': on the one hand, it is a form of symbolic capital that serves 'as an instrument of domination and legitimation' for injustice and inequality; on the other, it is the basis of emancipation, democracy and human rights. Bourdieu argues for mobilisation and struggle through which those who are denied access to the universal can claim and realise such access (2000 [1997]: 70–72, 77–80), but his formulations are elliptical. What might they mean in practice? And what might they mean in a country of the Global South?

Bourdieu's text conveys a sense of the social scientist whose scholarship provides a unique access to the truth, which, as public intellectual, he conveys to society from his lectern – but at the same time the symbolic weight of the lectern and of his professorial knowledge serves to legitimate the existing authorities and hierarchies of society. There is little sense here of knowledge gained through concrete practice, which is consistent with Bourdieu's distinction between the logic of theory and the logic of practice. The impression is reinforced by the closing scenes of the documentary film on his life and work, *La sociologie est un sport de combat*, in which he attempts to persuade a militant meeting of immigrant community members in France that they cannot understand their own situation and should therefore read works of sociology – which they angrily reject, asserting the clarity of their own understanding of their oppression as they do so.

This is almost the public sociologist as parody. Any sociologist in South Africa who in the times of struggle against apartheid attempted such a role would have been met with a similar response. The inability of either side in this interchange to hear the other illustrates the breakdown of language that occurs at the interface of sociology and the public or political sphere, and the profound challenges confronting any project for the Realpolitik of reason. The discourse of reason encounters in the public sphere a symbolic order, or a symbolic contest, which demands a distinctive discourse of its own, and the sociologist who fails to translate his/her thought into this symbolic contest and its discourse literally cannot be heard.

While both Bourdieu and Mills wrote in the context of right-wing ascendancy and the demobilisation of mass society – a context that posed the question 'what public?' to the would-be public sociologist – in South Africa in the 1980s we lived and worked in the context of an increasingly polarised and mobilised public. Apartheid, on the one hand, and the democratic movement, on the other, posed intellectuals and social scientists with stark choices: whose side were we on? Which power would reason serve – that of the apartheid regime or that of the emerging popular movement?

While many progressive white scholars desisted from entering this terrain, and concentrated on their research and teaching – through which generations of white and black students did indeed gain access to historical and political knowledge, which constituted an important resource for those who went on to participate in student and popular struggle – others chose to engage in a more organic relation with popular politics, working with trade unions or the United Democratic Front (UDF), often through non-governmental organisations. A handful straddled both roles.[3] Here we found sharp clashes over 'truth' and the meaning of reason, both within the popular movement and, often, between 'organic' intellectuals and the more 'traditional' intellectuals in the academy.

Take, for example, the case of the re-emergent trade union movement. In the early 1970s radical white students, rebuffed by the Black Consciousness movement, turned towards the working class and played a significant role in the formation of the new black trade unions. They did this as Marxists, many of them with a strong critique of previous periods of black trade unionism in South Africa, in particular the history of alliances between trade unions and the African nationalist political movement. There were different currents within the new trade unions, but the biggest and strongest formation, the Federation of South African Trade Unions (FOSATU), was characterised by an aversion to such alliances and an allegiance to 'working-class politics' – and, many suspected, to the formation of an independent workers' party. When, in the early 1980s, the question of trade union unity rose to the top of the labour agenda, fierce struggles broke out between the different factions.

On the one side were the 'workerists', strongly influenced by the perspective of the white Marxists described above, who rejected the ANC and UDF, and their guiding document, the Freedom Charter, as a petty bourgeois, populist movement that was bound to sell out the working class, and on the other were the 'populists', who supported the liberation movement, advocated a multiclass popular alliance against apartheid, and argued that workers were being misled by white agents of liberalism and imperialism. Both sides imagined that reason was on their side; both were economical with the truth. FOSATU newspapers avoided naming or referring to the UDF, at the time a massively growing movement with hundreds of affiliated organisations and hundreds of thousands of supporters. On the other side, I remember a seminar in one of the populist unions where the leading white intellectuals of a rival workerist union were denounced as agents of the Central Intelligence Agency. In the end, the popular insurgency in the townships drew in entire working-class constituencies, and the trade union movement swung into alliance with the UDF and the ANC, albeit with a strongly independent stance.

This is a schematic representation of a complex series of political contestations and shifts in the politics of the trade union movement, but the point is to consider its implications for Bourdieu's idea of the Realpolitik of reason and the role of the public sociologist. Firstly, oppression was not opaque to workers, and it was not social science that opened their eyes, but rather the interaction between the daily logic of practice and the symbolic world of politics. Social science (knowledge of history, economics, corporate analysis, etc.) could of course play an adjunct role, but what workers needed most was organisation, and in those early days white intellectuals brought important organisational, legal and negotiating skills to the fledgling movement. Education programmes were important, but many of them were technical and organisational. When education became more political as the movement grew, it was precisely the critical line on alliances and the Freedom Charter introduced by white intellectuals that aroused resistance.

Which brings us to the second point: workers' consciousness was not a tabula rasa on which intellectuals could inscribe the truths discovered by reason. Workers already had ideas and allegiances and the language that went with this – precisely, symbolic power, or what Bourdieu would call symbolic capital (1994) – influenced as well by the long history of

Communist Party involvement in the national liberation struggle. Indeed, the new white intellectuals from the universities were frequently unaware of this history, and unaware too that black working-class activists with roots in communist and national liberation histories were quietly active in the new trade unions as well – showing a caution fashioned by long histories of state and employer repression against the Communist Party and black trade unions. In both the trade unions and community organisations, white students and intellectuals, inspired by the New Left Marxism of the 1960s, came up against the orthodox communism of the South African Communist Party (SACP).

In other words, the public sociologist does not address a public sphere founded on reasoned debate – a point Bourdieu makes in his criticism of Habermas. Rather, in a situation such as that presented by South Africa in the 1980s, the public sociologist is confronted with an already existing politics, a terrain of contending movements, organisations and publics in which his/her voice may be drowned or denounced or, worse, fail to find any audience at all. What we became in the 1980s were *activist* intellectuals, deeply involved, partisan, passionate. We engaged in continuous dialogue and negotiation with our chosen, partisan publics. We negotiated truth and we negotiated reason. Scholars who preferred not to dirty their hands or compromise their views remained in the academy – but at the cost of choosing silence in the symbolic world of politics (Muller & Cloete, cited in Morphet, 1990: 97).

Did intellectual practice of the activist kind approximate what Bourdieu meant by the Realpolitik of reason, or were we mere fellow travellers, as Bourdieu called Gramsci's organic intellectuals, who had abandoned the path of reason? Of course, there were many variants to this practice, and some behaved merely as cheerleaders for the movement, while others pursued a role of critical engagement. In a profound way, though, despite the many sordid events in its history and despite untruths it may have uttered, the popular movement did represent truth in our world – the truth that denounced apartheid and spoke for freedom, democracy and human rights. I well remember Dullah Omar, an intelligent, principled, steely and gentle UDF leader, telling a mass rally in the early 1980s that the liberation movement was the only beautiful thing in a land made ugly by oppression and exploitation.[4] The kind of truth and beauty we are discussing here belongs to the symbolic world of politics, where it wields an immense power to move people to struggle and sacrifice – but it is nonetheless true: true to a vision of how people can live their lives differently. Beside them, the truth of the scholar may appear paltry and threadbare. It is this interface that the Realpolitik of reason has to negotiate.

Where does this leave us now? The public sphere is still undergoing a series of transformations. Processes of class formation; growing divergences within the Tripartite Alliance among the ANC, COSATU and the SACP; and the many failings of the post-apartheid state are the source of increasing contention in the public sphere. These trends, perhaps, create a greater scope for a more independent public sociology. However, the public is still sharply divided into deeply racialised partisan blocs, into those who owe a broad allegiance to transformation and therefore to the ANC alliance, and those, mostly white, who are resistant (and who have a less automatic allegiance to the political party that most represents this camp, the Democratic Alliance or DA, than do their counterparts in the opposite camp).

In such a context, public criticism of the government or the ANC plays easily into the symbolism of the racial colonial gaze discussed by Frantz Fanon, can thereby be construed as pro-DA rhetoric, and is dismissed or simply not heard by the majority bloc. Once again, the Realpolitik of reason encounters the symbolic power of the political world and finds itself translated or appropriated into meanings that it cannot recognise. The political world itself is divided into two worlds, the product of the colonial and apartheid experience, each of which is characterised by mutually unintelligible understandings and meanings. It is as if there are two musics composed of mutually incompatible harmonic schemas, which, played at the same time, produce only a cacophony.

It is also true, as Bourdieu points out, that in this world, reason is yoked to the order of capital and the order of the imperialism, and the full weight of its authority is invoked to justify the current order of things and people, and to explain why economic orthodoxy defines the outer limits of what it is possible to do – that is, what problems can be admitted as problems and what may be done about them. Yesterday's revolutionaries become today's paragons of fiscal prudence, and freedom has become the right of a few to celebrate their sudden access to wealth by eating sushi off the bodies of naked women. It should no longer be possible for the liberation movement to claim it is the only beautiful thing in an ugly landscape, but old truths die hard. The Realpolitik of reason, if it wishes to make its mark on this world, will be forced as before to find a language with which to negotiate its way in the symbolic world of politics.

If the situation in South Africa reveals the limits of public sociology and the Realpolitik of reason, on the one hand, on the other, it makes it all the more necessary. Bourdieu's vigorous defence of reason, scholarship and the logic of theory is attractive in a society rapidly losing its way, and where an increasingly divided and paralysed ANC becomes susceptible to defensiveness and the seductions of control and repression. Indeed, it may evoke a longing to abandon the compromised truth that seems so much part of the symbolic negotiation with the world of politics, for an uncompromised and denunciatory truth freed from politics. The transformation of our society requires the defence of reason and poses the obligation to speak truth to power, nothing less.

But what our history of practice suggests is that such truth does not emerge only from the practice of theory in scholarly fields, but also from the actions and thoughts of the people, that is, from the logic of practice, from the truth of ordinary lives. Moreover, and necessarily, it has to find an existence in the form of a symbolic power that can enter into symbolic contestation in the political field. Once again, we return to the necessity for negotiation. Only from a dialogue between these two truths may emerge a combined truth that has the symbolic force to truly remake authority.

NOTES

1   Thus, one is surprised by the way he treats 'love' and gay-lesbian movements in Masculine Domination.
2   Obviously, Mills and Bourdieu are also affected by the styles of thinking and writing that prevail in their own national intellectual fields, manifested in the opposed styles of Continental and Anglo-American philosophy.
3   Those who did had, perforce, to engage the political, developing what Burawoy in his study of Eddie Webster's sociological life calls a 'political imagination', in contrast to Mills's idea of a 'sociological imagination' (Burawoy, 2010).
4   Omar was a leading figure in the Unity Movement, a Trotskyist grouping in the Cape, shifted allegiance to the Congress movement in the early 1980s, and served as justice minister and transport minister in post-apartheid governments.

MANUFACTURING DISSENT

MICHAEL BURAWOY

Burawoy Meets Bourdieu[1]

.

Like the gift, labour can be understood in its objectively twofold truth only if one performs the second reversal *needed in order to break with the scholastic error of failing to include in the theory the 'subjective' truth with which it was necessary to break, in a first para-doxal reversal, in order to construct the object of analysis. The objectification that was necessary to constitute wage labour in its objective truth has masked the fact which, as Marx himself indicates, only becomes the objective truth in certain exceptional labour situations: the investment in labour, and therefore miscognition of the objective truth of labour as exploitation, which leads people to find an extrinsic profit in labour, irreducible to simple monetary income, is part of the real conditions of the performance of labour, and of exploitation.*

Bourdieu (2000 [1997]: 202)

The defining essence of the capitalist labor process is the simultaneous obscuring and securing of surplus value. How does the capitalist assure himself of surplus value when its production is invisible?

Burawoy (1979: 30)

Tucked away toward the end of Bourdieu's masterpiece, *Pascalian Meditations*, are four startling pages under the heading 'The twofold truth of labour' (Bourdieu, 2000 [1997]: 202–5). They are startling, firstly, because they deal with the labour process, a topic Bourdieu rarely broached, and, secondly, because his interpretive framework follows Marxist orthodoxy, a framework he generally dismissed as anachronistic and misguided.

His argument is presented in typically intricate form in the quotation above. Let me translate. In constituting the object of knowledge – i.e. the notion of wage labour – Marx breaks with the subjective (lived) experience of workers that they are paid for a full day's work, for eight hours in an eight-hour day. In reality, workers are exploited and only receive wages that are equivalent to a portion of the working day, say five hours, leaving three hours as surplus labour, which is the basis of profit. So far, this is straightforward Marx. But, says Bourdieu, it is not enough to make this first break – first reversal – with lived experience to produce the objective truth of exploitation, it is further necessary for theory to make a second break, a second reversal, this time *against* the 'objective truth' in order to reincorporate the 'subjective truth' – the lived experience of workers. It is one thing to discover the objective truth of labour, i.e. exploitation; it is another to show how exploitation is sustained by workers themselves.

More concretely, how is it that workers work sufficiently hard so as to produce surplus value and thus make exploitation possible, even while it is invisible? The answer, Bourdieu claims, lies in the workers' 'investment in labour', through which they find an 'extrinsic profit in labour, irreducible to simple monetary income', with the result that exploitation is assured even as it is not experienced as such. In other words, in the organisation of work there is 'a miscognition of the objective truth of labour as exploitation', which induces the hard work that is the foundation of exploitation. Further – and here too Bourdieu follows Marxist orthodoxy – the less autonomy a worker has, the less room for meaningful investment in labour and the more likely workers will see themselves as exploited, i.e. the more likely there is a convergence of objective and subjective truths.

I find these pages startling not only for their focus on labour and their unqualified embrace of the Marxist theory of exploitation, but for their convergence with the argument I made 20 years earlier in *Manufacturing Consent* – an ethnography of an industrial plant in south Chicago where I worked as a machine operator for ten months between 1974 and 1975. In *Manufacturing Consent* I formulated the twofold truth of labour as follows: if surplus labour is *obscured* (the objective truth of capitalist work, first break), then the question becomes how it is *secured* (the subjective truth of capitalist work, second break). Marx assumed it was secured through coercion, the fear of loss of the job, but under advanced capitalism, I argued, there were employment guarantees and legal constraints on managerial despotism that made the arbitrary application of coercion impossible. This gave workers a certain autonomy on the shop floor that allowed them to 'invest in labour' through constituting work as a 'game'. In my case it was a piece-rate game that we called 'making out'. The game compensates workers for their intrinsically boring work, by giving them 'extrinsic profits' – emotional satisfaction and symbolic rewards. Taking Gramsci's ideas to the workplace, I argue that consent rather than fear ruled the shop floor. We were subject to what I call a hegemonic rather than a despotic regime of production.

I used the game metaphor as Bourdieu sometimes used it – as a way of understanding the reproduction of social structure and its patterns of domination. Games obscure the conditions of their own playing through the very process of securing participation. Just as one cannot play chess and at the same time question its rules, so one cannot play the game of 'making out' on the shop floor and at the same time question its rules – rules that are socially sanctioned by workers and shop floor management alike. This is the twofold truth of the game – the truth of the outsider studying the game and the truth of the insider playing the game – with each truth hidden from the other and thereby reproducing the other. As I worked on the shop floor I operated with the truth of the machine operator; as a sociologist I interrogated those experiences for the objective truth underlying the game of making out. My sociology, however, did not affect the way I worked on the shop floor.

How had Bourdieu arrived at a seemingly identical formulation to my own? How could I be using the language of hegemony and consent to describe what, indeed, looked more like symbolic domination and misrecognition? Thus began five years of field work into the complex and fascinating texts of Bourdieu involving a reassessment of my own understanding of the nature of advanced capitalism and its durability, as well as of the nature of state socialism and its fragility. On the one hand, it compelled a critique of Gramsci for overlooking the *mystification* that characterises advanced capitalism. On the other hand, it led to a critique of Bourdieu for projecting *misrecognition* as a universal – the result of the incorporated and embodied habitus – rather than seeing it as mystification, i.e. something socially produced and historically contingent.

These investigations, therefore, examine the question: how durable is domination? – which divides into three related questions. If the habitus of subjugation is universal and deep, how can domination be challenged? If, on the other hand, mystification is historical and contingent, when does domination become transparent? And under what conditions, if any, does the objective truth of the sociologist converge with the subjective truth of the worker? Here I address these questions through an examination of the stability of workplace regimes in advanced capitalism and state socialism.

HOMO LUDENS VS. HOMO HABITUS

Bourdieu is always seeking to transcend antinomies, subject and object, micro and macro, voluntarism and determinism. All too often, however, he does not so much transcend the antinomy as combine the two opposed perspectives. Such is the case, I believe, for his conception of structure and agency, where he fuses *homo ludens* and *homo habitus*.

Sometimes, Bourdieu starts with *homo habitus* – with habitus, as we have seen, being the notion that the human psyche is composed of 'durably installed generative principle of regulated improvisations', producing 'practices which tend to reproduce the regularities immanent in the objective conditions of the production of their generative principle' (Bourdieu, 1977 [1972]: 78). Here the emphasis is on doxic submission, but one that allows for improvisation within limits. We might call this a deep notion of social reproduction.

On other occasions, Bourdieu starts with *homo ludens* – the individual whose character is given by the games he/she plays, giving rise to a notion of social structure as rules that guide individual strategies. Human beings are players motivated by the stakes and constrained by the rules that define the game. This is a contingent notion of social reproduction that depends on the continuity of a particular game embedded in a particular institution. The only assumption it makes about human brings is that they are game players seeking control of their environment.

Bourdieu has both a contingent notion and a deep notion of social action, alternating between the two and often fusing them – *homo ludens* and *homo habitus*. Game playing accompanies deeply inculcated, almost irremovable dispositions, which vary from individual to individual, depending on their biographies. Here, however, I want to oppose rather than merge these two notions of human action: on the one hand, *homo habitus*, for whom social structure is internalised, and, on the other hand, *homo ludens*, for whom social structure is a set of external constraints to be negotiated. Is submission deeply engraved in the psyche or the product of institutionally ordered practices? Bourdieu wants it both ways, but the result is a notion of social structure that can never change and a pseudo-science that is unfalsifiable.

In adopting *homo ludens* rather than *homo habitus*, I show how social structures are more malleable and unstable than Bourdieu admits, although some more so than others. Thus, I argue that capitalist hegemony requires and obtains mystification as its precondition, which makes it relatively stable, whereas state socialism, unable to produce such a mystification, could not sustain hegemony and instead alternated historically between coercion and legitimation – an unstable arrangement that, in the final analysis, proved to be its undoing. The comparative analysis of advanced capitalism and state socialism shows the limits of both Bourdieu and Gramsci – the first too pessimistic about the possibilities of social change, the second too optimistic about such change.

MYSTIFICATION VS. MISRECOGNITION

My disagreement with Bourdieu turns on the crucial distinction between *mystification* and *misrecognition*. When Karl Marx writes about the mechanism through which exploitation is hidden in the form of wage labour or when he writes about commodity fetishism and the way the market obscures the human labour that goes into the commodity, he insists that this happens automatically and independently of the particular characteristics of any individual who experiences it – male or female, black or white. Thus, Marx and Engels famously write in *The German Ideology* (1978 [1845–46]: 154): 'If in all ideology men and their circumstances appear upside-down as in a *camera obscura*, this phenomenon arises just as much from their historical life-process as the inversion of objects on the retina does from their physical life-process.' There is no psychology here – there is only the 'historical life-process'. Individuals are both the carriers and the effects of social relations, so if they experience things upside down, then this is the consequence of the social relations into which they enter. *Mystification* is the term we use to describe the social process that produces the gap between experience and reality *for all who enter a specific set of social relations.*

We can find examples of mystification in Bourdieu, most notably his repeated analysis of the gift economy in which the gift is experienced by givers and receivers as an act of generosity, while to the outside 'scientist' it is viewed as an act of self-interested economic behaviour – an act that will reap its rewards – or as the collective creation of social bonds of interdependence. Bourdieu says that the scientists who impose their views on the agents misunderstand the nature of the gift exchange, which depends on the coexistence and separation of the subjective truth (an act of generosity) and the objective truth (building symbolic domination or social solidarity). But how are the two truths sustained? In *Outline of a Theory of Practice*, Bourdieu (1977 [1972]: 1–9) focuses on the separation in time of successive gift giving, so that the gift appears to be an isolated act of generosity. Thus, any attempt at immediate reciprocity is regarded as a crude violation of the basic norms. So here the structuring of exchange as a process evolving over time explains the misrecognition or, more precisely, the mystification.

When he turns to the gift exchange in *Pascalian Meditations*, however, the emphasis is more on the inculcation of perceptions and appreciations (habitus) that is shared by gift giver and receiver. This habitus of generosity is at the foundation of the gift economy, a habitus that is being replaced by the calculative disposition, making gift exchange rarer and more difficult to sustain. Insofar as the gift economy depends on the prior inculcation of a certain habitus, so we are shifting from mystification that is the product of social processes to misrecognition that is the result of an individual's internalised habitus (which in turn mediates and reflects social processes).

Reading *Pascalian Meditations*, Bourdieu's climactic theoretical work, I was struck by how much it sounded like Talcott Parsons's sealing of the social order. Individuals internalise the norms of the social order: 'incorporated cognitive structures attuned to the objective structures' secure 'doxic submission to the established order' (Bourdieu, 2000 [1997]: 178); or, in other words, there is a mutual adjustment of position and disposition, or expectations and possibilities, of habitus and habitat. 'The schemes applied to the world are the product of the world to which they are applied' (2000 [1997]: 147), which guarantees the unknowing, unconscious adaptation to the world:

> The agent engaged in practice knows the world but with a knowledge which, as Merleau-Ponty showed, is not set up in the relation of externality of a knowing consciousness. He knows it, in a sense, too well, without objectifying distance, takes it for granted, precisely because he is caught up with it; he inhabits it like a garment [*un habit*] or a familiar habitat. He feels at home in the world because the world is also in him, in the form of habitus, a virtue made of necessity which implies a form of love of necessity, *amor fati* (Bourdieu, 2000 [1997]: 141–42).

Just as Parsons acknowledges the existence of 'deviance' when role expectations are not complementary, so Bourdieu acknowledges that there can be mismatches between habitus and field – misfirings – that may or may not lead to new adaptations. But just as deviance is a residual category for Parsons, mismatches and misfirings are residual categories for Bourdieu. In both cases, the weight of the argument is to show the impossibility of contesting a social order, which means in Bourdieu's case bending the stick against Marxism, feminism, populism and any other 'ism' that celebrates transformation from below. It is not that some social orders lead to mystification and others to transparency, but that all social orders reproduce themselves through the inculcation of habitus and necessary misrecognition. We are all fish in water, unable to comprehend the environment in which we swim – except, of course, Bourdieu and his fellow sociologists.

The question we have to ask is whether social orders are held together by mystification, with the emphasis on *social relations independent of the particular individual*, or by misrecognition constituted through a *deeply implanted habitus at least partially independent of the particular social relations into which an individual is inserted*. How can one discriminate between these alternative explanations for social order: a contingent domination dependent on social relations producing an *ideology as mystification* versus an internalised deep *symbolic domination that works through misrecognition*? To adjudicate between these rival notions requires a comparative study that compares submission in different societies. In what follows, I undertake such a comparative analysis by reconstructing my studies of the subjectivities that arise from work organisation and its regulation in advanced capitalist and state socialist workplaces. I show that mystification of domination is present in advanced capitalism, but not in state socialism, explaining the durability of the one and the instability of the other. Symbolic domination through misrecognition, however, being universal, cannot discriminate between societies. Bourdieu falsely generalises from his conception of contemporary France and pre-capitalist Kabyle society to all social orders. He cannot – and, indeed, makes no attempt to – explain how it is that state socialism collapses while advanced capitalism endures. That is what I attempt to do in the following pages through a reconstruction of arguments I have been making over the last 30 years.

THE GRAMSCIAN MOMENT: MANUFACTURING CONSENT

I begin again with Antonio Gramsci, whose originality lay in a periodisation of capitalism not on the basis of the economy, but on the basis of its superstructures, and in particular on the rise of the state–civil society nexus that organised consent and absorbed challenges to capitalism. This was the story of the rise of capitalist hegemony in Europe. In the United States, by contrast, without parasitic feudal residues, Gramsci writes that 'hegemony was born in the factory' and not in civil society – a streamlining of domination that allows the forces of production to expand more rapidly than elsewhere – what he calls Fordism.

Manufacturing Consent (Burawoy, 1979) endeavoured to elaborate on what Gramsci might have meant when he spoke of hegemony being born in the factory. The study was based on participant observation in a south Chicago factory where I was a machine operator for ten months, from July 1974 to May 1975. I was a wage labourer like everyone else, although it was apparent that I was from a different background, not least because of my limited skills and my strange English accent. I made no secret of my reason for being there, i.e. to gather material for my dissertation.

Influenced by the French structuralist Marxism of the 1970s and its appropriations of Gramsci, I argued that the theories of the state developed by Althusser, Poulantzas and Gramsci could be applied to the internal workings of the factory. In my Chicago plant, an *internal state*[2] constituted workers as industrial citizens, individuals with rights and obligations, recognised in grievance machinery and in the details of the labour contract. Here I could see in miniature Poulantzas's 'national popular state'. At the same time, the internal state orchestrated what Gramsci called the concrete coordination of the interests of capital and labour through collective bargaining, which provided the material basis of hegemony. Capital granted labour concessions that were necessary for the latter's consent – concessions, as Gramsci would say, that do not touch the essential. Finally, following Gramsci, but also Poulantzas's analysis of the dominant classes and their relation to the state, I saw factory management as a power bloc, made up of different divisions (fractions) under the hegemony of its manufacturing division.

As well as an internal state, there was also an *internal labour market* that reinforced the individualising effects of the internal state. It gave workers the opportunity to bid on other jobs within the factory, which were then allocated on the basis of seniority and experience. This internal labour market gave individual workers power and leverage against management. If workers did not like their job or their supervisor, they could bid on and then move to an alternative job. Workers who somehow made themselves indispensable to their foremen could wield considerable power. Like the internal state, the internal labour market constituted workers as individuals and, through rewards based on seniority, tied their interest to capital. If it gave workers some power on the shop floor, it also cultivated their loyalty, since moving to another firm would put them at the bottom of the seniority ladder. Workers had another interest, therefore, in the success – profitability – of their enterprise, even at their own expense, as happened when in the 1980s workers entered into concession bargaining just to keep their jobs.

The internal state and internal labour market were the conditions for a third source of consent, the constitution of *work as a game* – in my case, the game of making out, whose rules were understood and accepted by operators, auxiliary workers and shop-floor supervisors alike. It was a piecework game and the goal was to 'make out', i.e. make an acceptable percentage output, one that was not higher than 140% and not lower than 125%. The details need not detain us here; suffice to say that constituting work as a game is common in many workplaces because it counters ennui and arduousness, and it makes time pass quickly, enabling workers to endure otherwise meaningless work. There were good psychological reasons to participate in such a game, but, just as important, the social order pressured everyone into playing the same game with more or less the same rules. We continually evaluated each other as to how well we were playing the game. It was also difficult to opt out without being ostracised.

Playing the game had two important consequences. First, the game certainly limited output through goldbricking (going slow on difficult piece rates in the hope that they would be loosened) and quota restriction (limiting output to 140% so as to avoid rate increases), but it also got operators to work much harder, and often with ingenious improvisation. It was a game that favoured the application of effort and thus increased profits for management, and with only small monetary concessions. Second, it not only contributed to profit, but also to hegemony. The very act of playing the game simultaneously produced consent to its rules. As we've seen, you can't be serious about playing a game – and this was a very serious game for those who played it – if at the same time you question its rules and goals.[3]

If the organisation of work as a game was the third prong of hegemony, it was effective in generating consent only because it was protected from the *arbitrary* application of coercion (punitive sanctions that ranged from disciplinary procedures to firing) – a protection that was made possible by the constraints imposed on management by the internal labour market and internal state. This three-pronged hegemony was a distinctive feature of advanced capitalism in which management could no longer hire and fire at will. No longer able to rely on the arbitrary rule of the despotic regime of production of early capitalism, management had to *persuade* workers to deliver surplus; i.e. management had to manufacture consent. Thus, the internal state and the internal labour market were the apparatuses of hegemony, constituting workers as individuals and coordinating their interests with those of management, applying coercion only under well-defined and restricted conditions. Management could not arbitrarily close down the game or violate its rules – at least, if it wanted to uphold its hegemony.

A game has to have sufficient uncertainty to draw in players, but it also has to provide players with sufficient control over outcomes. A despotic regime, in which management applies sanctions in an arbitrary fashion, creates too much uncertainty for a game to produce consent. In short, the hegemonic regime creates a relatively autonomous arena of work with an appropriate balance of certainty and uncertainty, so that a game can be constituted and consent produced. In a hegemonic regime, the application of force (ultimately being fired), whether it occurs as a result of a worker's violation of the rules or as a result of the demise of the enterprise, must itself be the object of consent. Thus, we have Gramsci's 'hegemony protected by the armour of coercion' (1971: 263).

In short, the *economic* process of producing things constituted as a game is simultaneously a *political* process of reproducing social relations and an *ideological* process of producing consent to these relations, made possible by the relatively autonomous internal state and internal labour market. I had advanced Gramsci's analysis by taking his analysis of the state and civil society into the factory, applying it to the micro-physics of power and, further, adding a new dimension to organising consent – the idea of social structure as a game.[4]

THE BOURDIEUSIAN MOMENT: THE TWOFOLD TRUTH OF LABOUR

The preceding account of manufacturing consent derives from Gramsci, but it misses the fundamental dilemma capitalists face: to secure surplus (unpaid) labour at the same time as its existence is obscured. The organisation of consent is concerned only with the securing of surplus, but it coexists with the mystification of exploitation. This is none other than Bourdieu's twofold truth of labour: (1) the objective existence of exploitation, and (2) the subjective conditions of its simultaneous concealment and realisation. It took my engagement with Bourdieu to realise that mystification is simply not part of Gramsci's theoretical toolkit. His idea of hegemony is not about mystification or misrecognition, but largely about the rational and conscious basis of consent. At most, it is an account of the naturalisation of domination, not the concealment of exploitation.

A Bourdieusian moment, therefore, is powerfully at work in my analysis of games. The peculiarities of the game of making out – and, indeed, all workplace games – lie in the way playing the game enlists workers not only in defending its rules and thereby producing surplus, but also in mystifying the conditions of its existence, i.e. the relations of production between capital and labour. This is how Bourdieu presents the same point:

> Social games are in any case very difficult to describe in their twofold truth. Those who are caught up in them have little interest in seeing the game objectified, and those who are not are often ill-placed to experience and feel everything that can only be learned and understood when one takes part in the game – so that their descriptions, which fail to evoke the enchanted experience of the believer, are likely to strike the participants as both trivial and sacrilegious. The 'half-learned', eager to demystify and denounce, do not realize that those they seek to disabuse, or unmask, both know and resist the truth they claim to reveal. They cannot understand, or take into account, the games of self-deception which make it possible to perpetuate an illusion for oneself and to safeguard a bearable form of 'subjective truth' in the face of calls to reality and to realism, and often with the complicity of the institution (the latter – the university, for example, for all its love of classifications and hierarchies – always offers compensatory satisfactions and consolation prizes that tend to blur the perception and evaluation of self and others) (Bourdieu, 2000 [1997]: 189–90).

In 'making out', workers secure 'compensatory satisfactions and consolation prizes', winning freedoms at the margin that become the centre of their lives on the shop floor. To the outsider, 'making out' appears as absurd; to the insider, it is what gives meaning to life. Through their small gains and the relative satisfactions these gains bring – 'I'm so excited; today I made 129% on that lousy drilling job' – alienating work not only becomes enchanting, but workers think they are outwitting management even as they are unwittingly contributing to their own exploitation. Management succeeds in securing surplus labour through the rebellion of workers against management. Bourdieu follows suit: 'Workers may contribute to their own exploitation through the very effort they make to appropriate their work, which binds them to it through the freedoms – often minute and almost always 'functional' – that are left to them' (2000 [1997]: 203).

If both I and Bourdieu emphasise the concealing of the underlying social relations – and here we are continuous with the Marxist tradition from Marx through Lukács and the Frankfurt School, although, unlike them, Bourdieu considers the mystification to involve an almost unalterable misrecognition – how is it that it plays no role in Gramsci, who instead develops a theory of conscious consent to domination? The most general answer must be that he participated in revolutionary struggles at a time when socialist transformation was on the political agenda, when capitalism did appear to be in some deep organic crisis – although, in the end, it gave rise to fascism rather than socialism. Capitalism was not the stable and enduring order it appeared to Bourdieu. For Gramsci, we can say, capitalism was more durable than it appeared to classical Marxism, but it appeared less durable than it appears to us today in our post-socialist pathos.

A more specific answer has to do with his participation in the factory council movement and the occupation of the factories in Turin in 1919–20. As skilled workers, many of them craft workers, those involved experienced deskilling and separation from the means of production much more directly than the unskilled workers of today who take for granted wage labour and the private ownership of the means of production. Moreover, the occupation of their factories and the collective self-organisation of production through their councils meant that they understood only too well the meaning of capitalist exploitation. For Gramsci, whose experience of the working class was through the factory council movement, exploitation was hardly hidden and, on this occasion, the working class really did exhibit a good sense within the common sense. In Gramsci's eyes, the factory occupations failed because working-class *organs* – trade unions and the Socialist Party – were wedded to capitalism, i.e. their interests were coordinated with those of capital. For Gramsci, this 'betrayal' would have to be rectified by the development of a 'Modern Prince' – the Communist Party – that understood and challenged capitalist hegemony. There was nothing hidden or unconscious about the consent of parties and trade unions to capitalism.[5]

Bourdieu makes the opposite argument, namely that craft workers are not the most likely, but the least likely to see through their subjective experience to the objective truth of exploitation: 'It can be assumed that the subjective truth is that much further removed from the objective truth when the worker has greater control over his own labour' (2000 [1997]: 203). Curiously, Bourdieu is at his most Marxist here in arguing that subjective truth converges with objective truth, and exploitation becomes transparent as labour is deskilled. As barriers to labour mobility are swept away, workers lose any attachment to their work and can no longer win for themselves the freedoms that bind them to work. Fearing such stripped and homogenised labour, modern management tries to recreate those freedoms through participatory management: 'It is on this principle that modern management theory, while taking care to keep control of the instruments of profit, leaves workers the freedom to organize their own work, thus helping to increase their well-being but also to displace their interest from the external profit of labour (the wage) to the intrinsic profit' (Bourdieu, 2000 [1997]: 204–5), i.e. the profits from partial control over work.

While Bourdieu seems to be following my argument about the mystification of social relations through compensatory game playing, he is actually saying something quite different. For him, the power of misrecognition is linked to the level of skill, whereas I argue it has to do with the political and ideological apparatuses of production. Thus, in my case, the internal labour market and internal state create attachments to the employer and restrictions on employer interventions, so workers will be able to carve out those workplace games that give them their subjective sense of freedom. That is to say, hegemonic regimes are the necessary and sufficient condition for the mystification of exploitation, no matter how unskilled the work may be. Indeed, the more labour is unskilled, the more important become the games of work as compensation for arduousness and estrangement.

In short, for Bourdieu the convergence of the objective truth (exploitation) and the worker's subjective experience of work *increases* with the degradation of work, whereas I argue the opposite. The craft worker of the 19th century, as described by E. P. Thompson (1963), exhibits deeper class awareness of exploitation than the autoworker of the 20th century. Behind our differences lies a very different analysis of the basis of domination and subjugation.

CONDITIONS OF DOMINATION: INSTITUTIONS OR DISPOSITIONS

Instead of exploring the *institutional conditions* of mystification – the political and ideological apparatuses of the enterprise – Bourdieu turns to the *dispositional conditions* of misrecognition – 'the effect of these structural factors obviously depends on workers' dispositions' (2000 [1997]: 203). In an earlier piece, he is most explicit:

Differences in dispositions, like differences in position (to which they are often linked), engender real differences in perception and appreciation. Thus the recent changes in factory work, toward the limit predicted by Marx, with the disappearance of 'job satisfaction', 'responsibility' and 'skill' (and all the corresponding hierarchies), are appreciated and accepted very differently by different groups of workers. Those whose roots are in the industrial working class, who possess skills and relative 'privileges', are inclined to defend past gains, i.e., job satisfaction, skills and hierarchies and therefore a form of established order; those who have nothing to lose because they have no skills, who are in a sense a working-class embodiment of the populist chimera, such as young people who have stayed at school longer than their elders, are more inclined to radicalize their struggles and challenge the whole system: other, equally disadvantaged workers, such as first-generation industrial workers, women, and especially immigrants, have a tolerance of exploitation which seems to belong to another age (Bourdieu, 1981: 315).

The propensity to submission is not an invariant, but depends on the inculcated habitus. Those who have been socialised to industrial work or who come from oppressed conditions accommodate to it; those young people who have few skills but extended education and nothing to lose are likely to 'radicalize their struggles and challenge the whole system', while immigrants and women are supposedly submissive beyond the pale. What sort of folk sociology is this, dependent on conventional wisdom and belied by history? We know that immigrants and women are quite capable of being militant and of organising themselves into strong trade unions, whether this be in South Africa, China, Brazil or the United States. Since we have no way of measuring 'disposition' or 'habitus' independent of behaviour, the argument is simply tautological – immigrants and women are submissive because of their habitus of submission as demonstrated by their submissiveness.

The argument of *Manufacturing Consent* was directly opposed to this commonsense or 'spontaneous' sociology. I tried to bend the stick in the other direction, showing that externally derived dispositions made no difference to the way people responded to production or to the intensity with which they were drawn into the game of making out. Our experience on the shop floor was more or less the same, irrespective of our 'habitus'. Thus, I was struck by my own absorption into the game that I knew to be furthering my exploitation. I was not coerced into hard work. As my day man told me on my first shift, 'no one pushes you around here', and he was right. Nor could the extra money explain my devotion to hard work. Rather, it was the symbolic rewards and emotional satisfaction of making out that drove the rhythm of work.

Using quantitative and qualitative data, I showed that race, age, marital status and education had little to do with performance at work, whereas the workplace attributes of seniority and experience made a significant difference (Burawoy, 1979: chap. 9). Observing interactions on the shop floor, I argued that joking relations established between races underscored that differences in background, and racial prejudices were not relevant within the workplace, even as they were relevant with regard to the institutional racism beyond the workplace. I contrasted the situation in a Chicago factory with the mining industry in Zambia, where racism was, indeed, institutionalised *within* the workplace in the form of the colour bar, differential pay scales and differential legal codes. I described that system as one of colonial despotism, many of whose elements continued into the post-colonial era, despite the democratisation of the political sphere. While there is no denying that racial mindsets continue to exist, their significance at the point of production depends on the racial form of the political regime of production.

So we arrive at my crucial difference with Bourdieu. In contrast to Gramsci, both of us recognise a fundamental gap between the objective and subjective truth of labour, but for Bourdieu this is achieved through *misrecognition* rooted in the individual's habitus, whereas I claim it is achieved through *mystification* rooted in the social relations into which men and women enter – a mystification that operates on all individuals, independently of their inherited dispositions. Symbolic domination through misrecognition rests on the bodily inculcation of social structure and the formation of a deep, unconscious habitus. There is no need for any concept of hegemony, because we are programmed to act out the social structure. Mystification, on the other hand, rests on individuals being inserted into specific social relations. Mystification is the necessary condition for a stable hegemony, i.e. for the organisation of consent to domination.

If this is the difference that separates us, then examining consent/submission under different institutional complexes could corroborate or disconfirm our different theories. Thus, state socialism becomes a laboratory for the adjudication of our two theories. I will try to show that intensive inculcation from the party state and its institutions does not produce misrecognition, because these self-same institutions generate a transparency in their functioning. Without mystification, hegemony is not sustainable.

In other words, as I will now show, the contradictions sowed by its institutions prove stronger than the incorporation of habitus.

THE PRECARIOUS HEGEMONY OF STATE SOCIALISM

I went in search of factory work in Hungary for two reasons. The first is that I missed the boat with the Polish Solidarity movement, 1980–81, which had absorbed my attention as an extraordinary working-class movement. When General Jaruzelski got there before I had packed my bags, I did the next best thing – took up jobs in Hungary and asked why the Solidarity movement took place in Poland rather than Hungary, and, more broadly, why in state socialism rather than advanced capitalism. What were the possibilities for a democratic socialism to emerge from such struggles against state socialism? The second reason to draw me to the socialist world was the specificity of my Chicago experience – was it the product of capitalism or of industrialism? Would I find the same work organisation, factory regime and working-class consciousness in the industries of state socialism?

Between 1982 and 1989 I spent my summers and three sabbatical semesters studying and working in Hungarian factories (Burawoy & Lukács, 1992). I began in a champagne factory on a collective farm and moved to a textile factory on an agricultural cooperative, before graduating to industrial work in a machine shop very similar to the Chicago plant. Finally, I would spend about 11 months in three separate stints working as a furnace man in the Lenin Steel Works of Miskolc. Based on this research, I concluded that the workplace regimes of advanced capitalism and state socialism were indeed very different: if the former produced consent, the latter produced dissent, which was the disposition that fired the Polish Solidarity movement, but also the collective mobilisation in East Germany in 1953, in Poland and Hungary in 1956, and even in Czechoslovakia in 1968.

The argument was a simple one: unlike capitalism, the appropriation of surplus under state socialism is a transparent process, recognised as such by all. The party, the trade union and management are all extensions of the state at the point of production – extensions designed to maximise the appropriation of surplus for the fulfilment of plans. Being transparent, exploitation is justified as being in the interests of all. Like any process of legitimation, it is susceptible to being challenged on its own terms – the party state is vulnerable to the accusation that it is not delivering on its promises of serving the universal interest. Whereas under capitalism legitimation is secondary, because exploitation is hidden, under state socialism it is primary, necessary to justify the open exploitation of state socialism, but also the latter's undoing.

Thus, the party state organises rituals on the shop floor (what I called painting socialism) that celebrate its virtues – efficiency, justice, equality – yet all around workers see inefficiency, injustice and inequality. Workers turn the ruling ideology against the rulers, demanding that they realise the claims of their socialist propaganda. The state socialist bureaucratic regime of production sows the seeds of dissent rather than consent. As regards the organisation of work itself, the key games that dominate work are those involving the negotiation with management over the fulfillment of plan targets, so that the relations of exploitation are not obscured, but define the relations among the players. Furthermore, given the shortage economy – shortages of materials, their poor quality, the breakdown of machinery and so forth, all of which stem from the central administration of the economy – the games at work aimed to cope with those shortages, demonstrating the hollowness of official claims about the efficiency of state socialism. Moreover, this adaptation to shortages required far more autonomy than the bureaucratic apparatus regulating production would allow. Work games were transposed into games directed at the system of planning, bringing the shop floor into opposition to the production regime and the party state.

Far from social structure indelibly imprinting itself on the habitus of the worker and thus inducing doxic submission, the state socialist regime systematically produces the opposite – dissent rather than consent; even counter-hegemonic organisation to despotic controls. Indeed, more broadly, state socialism generated its own counter-socialisms from below – the cooperative movement in Hungary, Solidarity in Poland and the civics in *perestroika* Russia. From the beginning, state socialism was a far more unstable order, not because its socialising agencies were weaker – far from it – but because of the contradictions generated by the institutions themselves. State socialism was held together by a precarious hegemony that was always in danger of slipping back into a despotism that relied on secret police, tanks, prisons and show trials. In other words, where advanced capitalism organised simultaneously the mystification of exploitation and the consent to domination, so now we see how the hegemony of state socialism – the attempt to present the interests of the party state as the interests of all – is a fragile edifice that was always threatened by the transparency of exploitation.

Bourdieu's notion of symbolic domination assured through a deeply inscribed misrecognition cannot explain the instability of state socialism.

Within Bourdieu's framework of internalisation, there is no reason to believe that symbolic domination through misrecognition is any shallower or weaker in state socialism than in advanced capitalism. Quite the contrary: the coordination among fields – economic, educational, political and cultural – should have led to a far more coherent and submissive habitus than under capitalism, where such fields have far greater autonomy and are more contradictory in their effects. An analysis of the logic of institutions and their immediate effects on the individual and on collective experience goes much further in explaining the fragility of state socialist hegemony.

FOLLOWING BOURDIEU: THE POWER OF FIELDS

Bourdieu never paid much theoretical attention to one of the signal events of his time – the collapse of the Soviet Union. I have found only one sociological writing by him on state socialism – the four-page text of an address he gave in East Berlin on 25 October 1989, just two weeks before the fall of the Berlin Wall, amid massive demonstrations. Curiously, according to the published article, Bourdieu invoked the concepts of political and cultural capital to describe the tensions among the communist elites (Bourdieu, 1998 [1989]). Still, his notion of field can help us explain the dramatic demise of communism, so long as we drop the notion of habitus.[6]

Recall that Bourdieu's theory of social change rests on the discrepancy between position and disposition, between opportunities and expectations within a given field.[7] This is precisely what I described above for Hungarian workers – they were led to expect the wonders of socialism, yet they found themselves in a world of its inversions. Not only they, but the dominant class, trying as it might in reform after reform, could not bring reality into conformity with its ideology. The discrepancy was not due to some psychic lag between an inherited habitus and a rigid field ('hysteresis', as Bourdieu might call it), but was generated by the field itself. State socialism created expectations it could not fulfil. As the gap between official ideology and reality widens, and as attempts to reduce the gap violated that official ideology (as in market reforms), so the ruling class lost confidence in its capacity to rule and the enactment of socialist ideology became a meaningless ritual. Without capacity or belief, the dominant class's hegemony collapses. Again, there is no need to resort to the existence of a deep-seated habitus that resists change.

This line of argument can also be used to shed light on the timing of the collapse. To understand the dynamics of 1989 we have to look at the Soviet bloc as a transnational political field dominated by the Soviet Union, which defined the terms of competition among the dependent states – much as the state defines the terms of competition among elites. This certainly captures the way in which state socialism dissolves. The Soviet Union changed the rules of the game and then the national governments (themselves divided) acted in anticipation of the reaction of the others. Thus, the Hungarian government of Németh, being the first to determine how the rules had changed, opened its border with Austria, allowing East Germans to flood into the West. Honecker's East German government reacted by requesting the Czechoslovakian government to bottle up East German nationals, but then transported them to the West in a sealed train that went across Germany. Influenced by Solidarity sweeping the Polish elections and the movements in Hungary, as well as huge demonstrations against the party state, Egon Krenz realised that Honecker had to go, but in so doing laid the basis of his own burial in the rubble of the Berlin Wall. All this inspired the Czechoslovakian people to assemble in Wenceslas Square in their hundreds of thousands to listen to Havel and other dissidents. After the Czechoslovakian party had wilted, only Romania's Ceausescu remained obdurate, putting down protest with violence and ultimately succumbing to a palace coup that put an end to his dictatorship. This thumbnail sketch of the events of 1989 shows how national actors acted strategically in a common transnational field. Strategy, as Bourdieu insists, only becomes conscious in exceptional crisis times when rules are in flux.

This would require much further elaboration, but it indicates the importance of studying the *interaction* of fields – something Bourdieu never addresses systematically – in this case the field of transnational relations within the Soviet bloc (itself nested in a larger field of international relations) and the political field within each nation. Underlying these inter-field dynamics, however, is the underlying instability of the state socialist order, unable to create a stable hegemony due to the palpable transparency of exploitation and domination.

FOLLOWING GRAMSCI: THE GOOD SENSE OF SOCIALIST WORKERS

Just as Bourdieu's field analysis can be usefully reconstructed to shed light on the unfolding crisis of the Soviet empire, so reconstructing Gramsci also illuminates what transpired in 1989. Let me return to the shop floor and to the methodological issues raised by Bourdieu in the epigraph that opened this conversation. There, Bourdieu writes of the double truth of labour and that it was not enough to construct the objective truth by breaking with common sense (first reversal), but it was also necessary to break with this objective truth to understand how common sense both produced and concealed the objective truth (second reversal). That was how I approached the Chicago factory, first recognising the underlying truth of surplus labour and then trying to understand how that surplus labour was experienced subjectively in a way that explained its production. Unpaid labour was simultaneously obscured, but also secured through constituting work as a game, itself made possible by the internal labour market and internal state.

Like Bourdieu, I did not believe that my fellow workers grasped the conditions of their subordination in the way a sociologist might, but even if they did, it would have made little difference. In other words, I did not find any Gramscian good sense within the common sense of workers, so instead of trying to convince my fellow workers of my Marxist theory – a daunting project indeed – I sought to persuade my fellow academics of the superiority of my theory of the labour process and of manufacturing consent. This was so very different from my experience in Hungary where my fellow workers – no less hostile to Marxism – nonetheless were possessed of 'good sense', not because they were superior beings, but because the institutions created the basis of good sense. Therefore, I did not have to make a *break* with common sense, but instead I *elaborated* its kernel of good sense, including the immanent critique of state socialism, through dialogue with my fellow operators, contextualising it in terms of the political economy of state socialism.

Here in Hungary, Bourdieu's strict opposition of science and common sense was replaced by Gramsci's (1971: 333) account of the dual consciousness, i.e. a practical consciousness stemming from production and an ideological consciousness superimposed by the party state or inherited from the past. I was riveted to the practical consciousness of my fellow workers 'implicit' in their activity and which united them 'in the practical transformation of the real world', paying less attention to the ideologies 'superficially explicit or verbal … inherited from the past and uncritically absorbed', which included racist, sexist, religious and localist sentiments. Yet it is true that these latter sentiments formed powerful bonds among workers, often overwhelming their incipient class consciousness.

Together with my collaborator, János Lukács, we focused on the capacity and necessity of workers to autonomously and flexibly organise production in the face of shortages. We defended this practice to managers who strove to impose bureaucratic controls over production. Infuriated by our claims, they insisted that we redo our study. This was not just a struggle within the consciousness of workers, but between workers and management, and once again it would be the explicit and verbal consciousness perpetrated and perpetuated by management that ultimately prevailed. By the time Hungarian socialism entered its final years, bombarded by bureaucratic managers, workers had lost any confidence in the very idea of socialism and certainly had little imagination of an alternative democratic socialism, even though it had been implicit in the logic of their own practice. Inspired by the 'good sense' of workers, and what he saw as a great potential for some sort of worker-owned enterprises, in the immediate years after the collapse of state socialism, Lukács tried to work with labour collectives to create the foundations of an alternative to capitalism, but this withered on the vine as capitalist ideology gained the upper hand.

In short, the analysis of state socialism – how it generated dissent and ultimately collapsed – does not call for a theory of deep-seated habitus, but can remain at the level of social relations of production. It could not sustain its precarious hegemony, and the attempts to shore up such an hegemony only hastened its demise. By the same token, as we saw earlier, the reproduction of durable domination under capitalism does not require the *inculcation* of social structure. Such submission that exists can be explained by the configuration of institutions that elicit consent to domination based on the mystification of exploitation. *Homo habitus* is not necessary to explain submission and resistance; *homo ludens* is sufficient.

THE LOGIC OF PRACTICE: BEYOND GRAMSCI AND BOURDIEU

We can summarise my argument by referring back to the notion of *false consciousness*. For Gramsci, the problem with false consciousness lies not with consciousness, but with its falseness. That is to say, Gramsci believed that workers actively, deliberately, and consciously collaborate in the reproduction of capitalism and consent to a domination defined as hegemony. They understand what they are doing; they simply have difficulty appreciating that there could be anything beyond capitalism. Domination was not mystified, but naturalised, eternalised. Yet at the same time, by virtue of their position in production, workers also possessed a critical perspective on capitalism and an embryonic sense of an alternative – one that could be jointly elaborated in dialogue with intellectuals. They have a *dual* consciousness rather than a *false* consciousness.

If for Gramsci the questionable part of false consciousness was its 'falseness', for Bourdieu the problem lies not with 'falseness', but with 'consciousness' that denies the depth of symbolic domination – a domination that settles within the unconscious through the accumulated sedimentations of social structure.

> In the notion of 'false consciousness' which some Marxists invoke to explain the effect of symbolic domination, it is the word 'consciousness' which is excessive; and to speak of 'ideology' is to place in the order of *representations*, capable of being transformed by the intellectual conversion that is called the 'awakening of consciouness', what belongs to the order of *beliefs*, that is, at the deepest level of bodily dispositions (Bourdieu 2000 [1997]: 177).

Similarly, for Bourdieu, consent is far too thin a notion to express submission to domination and must be replaced by the idea of misrecognition, which is embedded within the habitus.[8] Because the dominated internalise the social structure in which they exist, they do not recognise it as such. They have, in Gramscian terms, only bad sense. Only the dominators – and then only privileged intellectuals – can distance themselves from, and thus objectivise, their relation to social structure. Only they can have access to its secrets. And not all intellectuals, to be sure – only those who are reflexive about their luxurious place in the world and who use that reflexivity to examine the lives of others can understand domination.

In adjudicating between these positions, I have argued that both are problematic. Gramsci does not recognise the mystification of exploitation upon which hegemony – i.e. consent to domination – rests. In other words, capitalist workers do suffer from 'false consciousness', but this falseness emanates from the social structure itself, which is where I depart from Bourdieu. Insofar as we participate in capitalist relations of production, we all experience the obscuring of surplus labour, independent of our habitus. Mystification is a product of the social structure itself and is not so deeply implanted within the individual that it cannot be undone, whereas Bourdieu's misrecognition is lodged deep within the individual psyche, assuring the harmonisation of habitus and field.

Accordingly, Bourdieu cannot explain why symbolic domination is effective in some societies, but not in others. Thus, why did state socialism, where one would have expected submission to be most deeply embedded, systematically produce dissent? For Bourdieu, social change, if it occurs at all, springs from the mismatch of habitus and field, but there is no systematic account of how this mismatch is produced, whether it is produced *situationally* through a cultural lag (hysteresis) – i.e. through habitus cultivated in one field clashing with the logic of another field – or *processually* through the very dynamics of social structure. Nor is there an analysis of the consequences of that mismatch in terms of whether it produces accommodation or rebellion. In other words, Bourdieu points to the *possibility* of social change, but has no *theory* of social change.

In the final analysis, habitus is an intuitively appealing concept that can explain any behaviour, precisely because it is unknowable and unverifiable. Bourdieu never gives us the tools to examine what a given individual's habitus might be. It's a black box. We infer the habitus from behaviour – a shop lifter is a shop lifter because he/she has the habitus of a shop lifter. We only know the habitus from its effects; there is no theory of its components or how they are formed as in psychoanalytical theory. In short, habitus is not a scientific concept, but a folk concept with a fancy name – a concept without content that might equally well be translated as character or personality.

Far more than Bourdieu, Gramsci is concerned with social transformation. He sees this as taking place through the breakdown of hegemony and the creation of a new subaltern hegemony, whether this comes through organic crises (balance of class forces) or through the war of position mounted from below on the basis of the kernel of good sense, or, what is more likely, a combination of the two. What my research suggests is that there is more to hegemony than the concrete coordination of interests or the ties linking state and civil society – there is more to hegemony than consent. There are non-hegemonic foundations of hegemony, namely the mystification of exploitation, which is why hegemony is so effective in advanced capitalism and so precarious in state socialism.

Because exploitation was so transparent in state socialism, it gave far more scope for intellectuals to engage with workers in the elaboration of alternative 'hegemonies' from below – the Hungarian worker councils in 1956, the Prague Spring of 1968, the Polish Solidarity Movement of 1980–81, the market socialism of Hungary's reform period of the 1980s, the effervescence of civil society under Soviet *perestroika*. These counter-hegemonies were formed by different configurations of intellectuals and workers. They were eventually swept away, but they did provide the embryos of alternative socialist social orders.

We live in depressing times of capitalist entrenchment when the failure of actually existing socialism buttresses dominant ideologies. We should not compound the forcefulness and eternalisation of the present by subscribing to unsubstantiated claims about the deep internalisation of social structure, reminiscent of the structural functionalism of the 1950s and its 'oversocialised man'. Remember, those theories were overthrown by a critical collective effervescence that structural functionalism did not, but also could not, anticipate. Each era has its own Cairo.

KARL VON HOLDT

The Margin of Freedom

Pascalian Meditations is, as Michael points out, Bourdieu's ' culminating theoretical work', in which he draws together and elaborates on the core concepts developed in a lifetime's research and reflection, referring back as he does so to his wide-ranging empirical studies. The main force of the book's arguments is to explain the stability and durability of social order: field, habitus and symbolic violence form an interlocking whole that ensures the reproduction of existing hierarchies and social orders.

Yet there is an undercurrent to the main argument, or a counter-current, that emerges briefly but vividly at certain points – a probing of the conditions under which the weight of social order may be destabilised or challenged. Some of these concern the potential of a destabilised field, or a contradictory habitus, to generate dynamics of change; Michael and I touch on these in some of the pieces in this book. However, in the final chapter of *Pascalian Meditations*, Bourdieu returns to symbolic struggle, and in this account he introduces an entirely new dimension: the symbolic order constitutes *a space of relative autonomy with a margin of freedom for redefining the world* and opening up new possibilities:

> But there is also the relative autonomy of the symbolic order, which, in all circumstances and especially in periods in which expectations and chances fall out of line, can leave a margin of freedom for political action aimed at reopening the space of possibles. Symbolic power, which can

manipulate hopes and expectations, especially through a more or less inspired and uplifting performative evocation of the future – prophecy, forecast or prediction – can introduce a degree of play into the correspondence between expectations and chances and open up a space of freedom through the more or less voluntarist positioning of more less improbable possibles – utopia, project, programme or plan – which the pure logic of probabilities would lead one to regard as practically excluded (Bourdieu, 2000 [1997]: 234).

The symbolic order introduces a crucial new dimension into an analysis of social reality dominated by the concepts of field and habitus, i.e. a flexibility or freedom through which the determinism of structure can be challenged by imagining alternatives. It is worth exploring Bourdieu's meaning as far as possible:

> ... symbolic power ... intervenes in that uncertain site of social existence where practice is converted into signs, symbols, discourses, and it introduces a margin of freedom between their objective chances, or the implicit dispositions that are tacitly adjusted to them, and *explicit aspirations*, people's representations and manifestations (Bourdieu, 2000 [1997]: 235).

That is, symbolic power implies 'a margin of freedom' between habitus and field, a space for interpretation and therefore contestation. This becomes a site of 'twofold uncertainty', because the meaning of the social structure remains open to several interpretations at the same time as agents are capable of multiple ways of understanding their actions. In other words, both habitus and field become sites of uncertainty, in radical contrast to the full and forceful weight of Bourdieu's main line of argument:

> This margin of freedom is the basis of the autonomy of struggles over the sense of the social world, its meaning and orientation, its present and its future, one of the major stakes in symbolic struggles. The belief that this or that future, either desired or feared, is possible, probable or inevitable can, in some historical conditions, mobilise a group around it and so help to favour or prevent the coming of that future (Bourdieu, 2000 [1997]: 235).

This account differs from those summarised elsewhere in this book in that it does not end with the alienated, maladjusted individual left disoriented by changing fields, nor does it rely on the intellectual who has the power to unmask domination to mobilise the masses, but rather suggests a significant indeterminacy in which a group can mobilise to shape the future. Here we have collective agency to imagine a different future and disrupt the social order. Finally

> ... the discourses or actions of subversion ... have the functions and in any case the effect of showing in practice that it is possible to transgress the limits imposed, in particular the most inflexible ones, which are set in people's minds ... The symbolic transgression of a social frontier has a liberatory effect in its own right because it enacts the unthinkable (Bourdieu, 2000 [1997]: 236).

Bourdieu was evidently grappling with the different possibilities for disruption and change available in different locations within his interlocking system of concepts, and in the passages quoted here finds in the indeterminacy of symbolic order a possibility of critical consciousness on the part of the dominated, resting on the ability to *imagine* an alternative future. Imagination calls forth a potential agency beyond the determinism of structure, although, to be comprehensible rather than 'unreal and foolhardy' (Bourdieu, 2000 [1997]: 236), it has to call on dispositions and structural possibilities that already exist in the world. These passages hold the clues we require in bringing Bourdieu to bear on South Africa – or in bringing South Africa to bear on Bourdieu.

THE RESISTANCE

It would be difficult to understand the re-emergence of resistance to apartheid in the 1970s and 1980s in terms of the dynamic between field and habitus. Certainly, changing social structures – the rapid growth of a mass semi-skilled working class based in the expansion of manufacturing, and the dramatic increase in the student population concentrated in township secondary schools and in 'bush universities' – meant that sectors of the black population had increased structural power in the economy and in communities, while the capitalist expansion of the 1950s and 1960s was mired in structural constraints.

These factors provided the material foundation for the formation of the two key forces in the new resistance – the black working class and its new trade unions, and the students and their organisations. In both cases, though, the substance of their struggles was a challenge to the symbolic order of apartheid. For workers, the trade union struggle was a struggle to be treated as a *human being*: 'Today I see myself as a human being because of the union', said one illiterate steelworker; and, 'Now you can actually tell the white man what you want, you can speak for yourself; those things were impossible in the dark years of the past, especially for the people before us, our fathers', said another (Von Holdt, 2003: 299).

For students, there was the elaboration of Black Consciousness as a symbolic counter-discourse to the racism of apartheid, and then the revolt against apartheid schooling triggered by the imposition of Afrikaans as a medium of instruction – again, a highly charged moment of symbolic struggle. To the extent that these assertions of agency could be said to involve habitus, the crucial factor is the 'margin of freedom' that symbolic struggle over the definition of social reality afforded first activists and then growing numbers of supporters to reimagine themselves – to 'see [themselves] as a human being' against a system that denigrated and commodified blacks.

And, as Bourdieu writes, the 'symbolic transgression of a social frontier has a liberatory effect in its own right because it enacts the unthinkable' (2000 [1997]: 236) – and, indeed, with every such transgression, the popular movement won wider support and the granite-like solidity of the apartheid system was seen to be illusory. By the late 1970s and early 1980s the popular movement was increasingly drawing on the symbolic resources provided by earlier waves of mass resistance. I well remember the public meeting in the Western Cape in 1981 where the symbols of the banned ANC were first displayed. At the entrances into the hall, young activists proffered baskets of ANC ribbons, and soon the audience of 3,000 was wearing ANC colours. Halfway through the meeting, three young activists, their identities concealed with balaclavas, marched the ANC flag down the aisle and onto the stage in a moment of extraordinarily potent political symbolism as the popular movement 'unbanned' an organisation that was at the time illegal, exiled, and prosecuting an underground political and military struggle against the regime. This was 'symbolic transgression' at its most charged.[9]

Symbolic transgression and mobilisation were profoundly *embodied*, from the ritual raising of clenched fists and call-and-response salute of '*amandla!*', answered with '*ngawethu!*', to the chanting of freedom songs and marching to their rhythms, a practice that reached its apogee with the toyi-toyi, a militant, chanted battle dance that originated in the Umkhonto we Sizwe camps outside the country and rapidly spread through the internal popular movement. Such rituals, songs and dances conveyed both exuberance and resolve, welding huge gatherings of people in halls, factories, mines, streets, and funerals into mass phalanxes of resistance and insurgency. Indeed, public performance was a central dimension of the popular movement's power. Every death led to a funeral that became a mass theatre of community unity and refusal to submit. It could be said that a new habitus, a habitus composed of dispositions to resistance, bravery and defiance, was forged out of these bodily performances – and that such a habitus was necessary if people were to face the hazards of bullets, detention and torture that the struggle entailed.

Public performance of the popular movement also provided the arena in which was forged a new symbolic universe ordered around ideas of freedom, democracy, non-racialism, people's power, women's rights, workers' rights, socialism, armed struggle, making apartheid 'ungovernable' and so on. In the face of this symbolic universe and the organisational power that underlay it, the symbolic order of apartheid lost its hold and coherence and in the end the regime became less and less able to speak and therefore unable to act, beyond the spasmodic bouts of repression facilitated by national states of emergency.

Habitus does not seem able to explain the emergence of resistance to apartheid; rather, habitus provided one location – uncertain and contested – among others for symbolic struggle between the embodied submission demanded by apartheid and the embodied defiance evoked by resistance and democracy. In explaining the large-scale durability or overthrow of regimes, habitus can only be a secondary concept; of central importance are symbolic order and resistance, and their relation to structural and material power in the economy and society.

TRANSITION AND AFTER

The symbolic struggle between the popular movement and the apartheid regime continued through the process of negotiated transition and was stabilised in the form of the new democratic constitution, which laid the basis for the emergence of a new symbolic order centred on the idea of democracy and the transformation of the social structures of racial domination in the economy and society.

While at one level the new constitutional order backed by broader national consensus did appear to stabilise the symbolic universe of a new South Africa, at other levels it opened up new arenas of contestation, particularly racial contestation over institutional and economic transformation. Contestation within the state has already been discussed in

Conversation 3 (pp 68–70). But the destabilisation of symbolic order is not confined to racial contestation over the meaning of social reality in post-apartheid South Africa. Side by side with these transformations has gone a rapid process of black elite formation out of which a new black middle class, a new black business class and a political elite are emerging. At the same time, the growth of unemployment and the expansion of insecure work has driven the fragmentation of the working class and the formation of the poor, condemned to informal substance activities or idleness.

The formation of historically new classes is not simply a material process of accumulation, on the one hand, and dispossession, on the other, of struggles to enter one class or avoid being forced into another, and of attendant social dislocation; it also entails the disturbance or disruption of the existing symbolic order, and formative projects to reconstitute symbolic order so as to make sense of new hierarchies and distinctions, new interests, and new social distances.

How will it be known who has power, who is a member of the elite, who has status? This is a particularly urgent question when elite formation is so rapid and the trajectory from poverty and subaltern status to powerful elite is so steep. A long-established ruling class or a long-drawn-out intergenerational process of class formation may evolve more discrete or subtle expressions of status and distinction, but a class or classes that tear themselves forth from the subalterns through internecine struggles and in which individuals remain subject to sudden reversals of fortune necessarily have to rely on more robust, and even brash, assertions of status. This is doubly so in South Africa, given the nature of apartheid, which consistently denigrated and undermined the capabilities of black South Africans. Hence what Jacob Dlamini (2011) calls 'the politics of excess': conspicuous consumption, the emphasis on marks of distinction that bear witness to high levels of disposable income – designer clothes, powerful cars, large homes, expensive parties, and largesse to friends and associates. These are the signs through which the new elite attempts to stabilise its power and assuage its uncertainties.

The emerging symbolic order of the new elite is oppressive – and contested – in other ways too. Young male protesters in one town related angrily how the mayor had publicly dismissed the protesters as 'unemployed, unwashed boys who smoke dagga, *abongcolingcoli* [puppets] who are not members of the community'. They pointed out, as did many others, that the mayor herself did not live in the town and that she had minimal schooling (Langa, Dlamini & Von Holdt, 2011).

In a second town, the mayor refused to meet the community, and when she did she told them that residents were like Eno digestive salts: they might bubble up in protest, but that would quickly die away. Councillors 'disdained us, and said *asiphucukanga, sizohlala singaphucukanga* [we are not civilised, we shall remain uncivilised]'. But as in the first town, the mayor herself is disdained because she was for years a 'tea-girl' in the post office and had only reached grade 4 at school (Dlamini, 2011). Evident in these stories is the destabilisation of the symbolic order and uncertainties over the meaning of different markers of status. While insecure members of the new elite seek to establish their status in the symbolic order by denigrating subalterns – i.e. by establishing the terms of symbolic violence against them – subalterns counter with efforts to contest and undermine the oppressive terms of the symbolic order articulated by the elite.

While much of this subaltern contestation of the symbolic order takes place in language, it becomes most explicit through the insurgent citizenship claims that are articulated in direct protest action (Holston, 2008). So, for example, elite targets of protest claim that the youth protesters have been bought by disgruntled faction leaders who have their own agendas. Young protesters respond angrily:

> It is an insult to my intelligence for people to think we are marching because someone has bought us liquor. We are not mindless. People, especially you who are educated, think we are marching because we are bored. We are dealing with real issues here. Like today we don't have electricity. We have not had water for the whole week (Langa, 2011: 61).

Insurgent citizenship in this context is defined by its claim for work and housing, for an improvement in municipal services, and to be heard and recognised. An end to corruption also features. The repertoires of protest resemble those that were used in the struggle for full citizenship rights against the racially closed citizenship defined by apartheid, and the protesters in post-apartheid South Africa explicitly claim the rights of democracy and citizenship, especially in relation to police violence against their protests:

> The Freedom Charter says people shall govern, but now we are not governing, we are being governed (Langa, 2011: 51).

> The constitution says we have rights. Freedom of speech, freedom of religion .... We have many freedoms ... but we get shot at for walking around at night (Langa, Dlamini & Von Holdt, 2011: 24).

The police want us to be in bed by midnight. It's taking us to the old days of curfews against blacks. What if I have been paid and want to enjoy my money? (Langa, Dlamini & Von Holdt, 2011: 51).

The elite engages in symbolic struggle in order to stabilise the material inequality between classes – what Holston calls 'differential citizenship' in the form of the differential access to basic services, housing, jobs and incomes between the underclass and the elite – and render it normal. However, the normality and justice of this state of things is contested by subalterns who qualify and reject the discourse of the elite, countering it with their own notions of a fair and just hierarchy and markers of status. The protest movements constitute an insurgent citizenship that demands the expansion of citizenship rights in the form of services and jobs, as well as in the form of respect by authority for all citizens, and protest action is itself a disruption of the symbolic order of the elite that controls the state.

The breakdown of the symbolic order of apartheid and contestation over its reconstruction go to the heart of many disputes in contemporary South Africa. Corruption, for example, is a lightning conductor for disputes over the meaning of the state and the legitimacy of elite formation. While the government and ANC routinely denounce corruption, their actual practices suggest that they are unwilling or unable to consistently crack down on it. So, when the chairman of the Northern Province ANC and MEC for finance was recently charged together with others for fraud amounting to over R100 million, both the Northern Cape ANC and the ANC Youth League immediately declared their support for him and it was announced that he would not be suspended from either of his two offices – a position that was later reversed. On the other hand, COSATU, formally in political alliance with the ANC, repeatedly lambasts the 'political hyenas' and 'predatory elite' in the ruling party, and challenges its leadership to undergo 'lifestyle audits'.

Likewise, the conflict between the ANC and COSATU over the latter's strategy of developing alliances with independent organisations in civil society: the ANC secretary-general attacked COSATU for 'betraying' the ANC and planning to establish a new anti-ANC political party. This outburst suggests that the ANC's conception of democracy – i.e. that it has a monopoly on political legitimacy for representing the black majority and that independent organisations in civil society are a threat to that legitimacy – is fundamentally at odds with the concept of democracy enshrined in the constitution. Meanwhile, young protesters at the end of their tether about the corruption and unresponsiveness of local politicians celebrate when their protests result in their (ANC) protest leaders winning local by-elections, but warn that they will resort to violence if the new councillors in turn betray them, as 'violence is the only language the government understands' (Langa, Dlamini & Von Holdt, 2011: 49).

These disputes are not simply spats between different political organisations or factions; they constitute heated disagreement over the nature of democracy and the new political order. They are, in other words, symbolic struggles over the meaning of social reality. The ANC itself is unstable and paralysed, not only by the rivalry between competing political factions for high office and access to patronage networks, but also because of its inability to speak for or invoke a consistent notion of symbolic order.

The current situation may be better described as a symbolic or classification crisis rather than a straightforward symbolic or classification struggle. There is, indeed, a widespread anxiety in South Africa about the breakdown of authority – within the ANC, within government, within schools and within the family. Crime is a lightning rod for this anxiety: while citizens bemoan their insecurity and berate government for not doing enough to protect them, each new police minister promises to use force to restore order. And indeed, while an average of about 100 police officers per year have been killed on duty over the past two years, an average of 590 people died as a result of police action over the same period, an average of 1,600 were assaulted by police, and over a one-year period 294 died in police custody, seven of them after torture and 90 due to 'injuries sustained in custody' (*Mail & Guardian*, 27 May–2 June 2011). The policing of protests and strikes has also been increasingly confrontational and violent over the same period, with the unprovoked killing of Andries Tatela in Ficksburg only the most recent.

It is not clear how this impasse will be resolved. Will one or other coalition of social forces gradually prevail in assembling sufficient symbolic power to dominate the process of forging a new hegemonic symbolic order? Will the current stalemate between contending social forces persist indefinitely, producing a kind of institutionalised and chronic disorder across society and the state? Will the state resort to a strategy of force to reinstall order and establish its monopoly over symbolic violence and symbolic power – demonstrating in the process the necessary relationship between physical violence and symbolic violence?

HABITUS: AN INTERMEDIATE CONCEPT?

As Michael argues, though, what is clear is the inability of the concept habitus to explain the durability or fragility of social order, notwithstanding Bourdieu's (2000 [1997]: 231) claim that it is 'no doubt one of the most powerful factors of conservation of the established order'. The concepts of symbolic power, symbolic order and symbolic struggle, I have tried to show, provide considerably more insight into exploration of order, disruption, resistance and disorder. It is these that restore indeterminacy to social structure and habitus, creating a 'margin of freedom', as Bourdieu describes it. In the light of this, it seems to me that Michael's analysis of the transparency of social structure and its role in the collapse of the state socialist order could be expanded. After all, the collapse took place not only in the workplace, but at the borders of countries and in their public squares – sites of tremendous symbolic force in the life of any nation.

Finally, I'm not sure that the inability of habitus to explain social change is sufficient reason to abandon the concept altogether, as Michael concludes. What do we do, then, with the insights into various forms of domination by some of the key Marxist thinkers whose engagement with Bourdieu through the medium of Michael makes these conversations so productive? How do we understand the symbolic violence of racial oppression explored by Fanon (or, indeed, by Steve Biko), or the symbolic violence of male domination explored by Beauvoir, without some kind of concept of an interiority, which is what Bourdieu attempts to map out with habitus? Is it sufficient to say that these forms of symbolic violence reside only in exterior social structures and that we do not need to understand how they inhabit our psyches in any way?

Without habitus, how do we think about Bourdieu's insight into the embodied nature of domination, the way in which submission, deference, and resistance are inscribed in the body and its stance and postures, as much as in the mind? Think here of the intersection between Bourdieu and Gramsci as they analyse the physical discipline that correlates to mental discipline as it is taught in the schools of the sanctified culture. Is the idea of social structure sufficient to grasp the physicality or corporeality of social relations and social repertoires?

Perhaps habitus is a useful concept at a more intermediate level of analysis. I'm thinking here of how the dispositions of defiance, bravery, and rebellion were embodied in the chants and dances of the toyi-toyi. This involved a kind of physical and emotional 'countertraining' in resistance (Bourdieu 2000 [1997]:172; see discussion in Conversation 2).

The toyi-toyi persists in the repertoires of strikes and protests in post-apartheid South Africa. Past dispositions and bodily repertoires have an ambiguous durability even in a substantially changed political context. Strikers and protesters explain that the toyi-toyi does not have the same meaning as in the past, when it marshalled insurrectionary struggles to overthrow the state; but, nonetheless, its current meaning partakes of the symbolism of violence and warfare, disrupting the authority of the state in order to call attention to the grievances of the people.

In the time of negotiated transition, a shop steward was referring to the depth of this habitus when he told me that 'a culture of resistance is inherent in the hearts and minds of the workers; I am sure to change that culture there has to be a process of learning' (Von Holdt, 2003: 194). And in 2008, discussing strike violence in the recent public service strike, a former shop steward said:

> Since I was born, I have seen all strikes are violent. There are no such strikes as peaceful strikes. Some workers do not join a strike because of fear. By force they must join the strike. Otherwise anybody would do their own thing (Von Holdt, 2010b: 141).

This worker draws attention to a process of historical habituation through which a strike gathers certain meanings and bodily repertoires that are reproduced in new historical situations. Even more significant is the way youthful protesters in community protests, who are too young to have any direct experience of the toyi-toyi of the 1980s, have adopted exactly the same repertoires, chanting the same songs to the same bodily movements as they gather, throw stones at the police, barricade streets and burn down municipal buildings. They describe the excitement, bravery and fighting spirit that are involved in these confrontations.

In the light of these durable and embodied practices and the emotions they involve, habitus may be a useful concept for exploring the interplay of symbolic power and symbolic order with the individual psyche. It also suggests ways in which historically established repertoires of symbolic challenge may establish a durable presence in the life of a society. Such repertoires may become more or less stylised or ritualised over time, but in conditions of symbolic contestation and of the clash between contending symbolic orders such as exist today in South Africa, they remain a resonant and widely understood element in the struggle over the structures of domination.

NOTES

1 An earlier version of this conversation was published in *Sociology*. I am borrowing the term '*homo habitus*' from correspondence with Bridget Kenny, who coined it to express Bourdieu's deeply pessimistic view of human nature. '*Homo ludens*' comes from the famous Dutch theorist Johan Huizinga.

2 I would later call the internal state 'the political and ideological apparatuses of production' or 'the regime of production' (Burawoy, 1985).

3 There is no shortage of studies that suggest the ubiquity of games. For some outstanding recent examples, see Ofer Sharone's (2004) study of software engineers, Jeffrey Sallaz's (2002) study of casino dealers, Rachel Sherman's (2007) study of hotel workers and Adam Reich's (2010) study of juvenile prisoners.

4 It was while working and teaching with Adam Przeworski at the University of Chicago that I developed the idea of social structure as a game. It was during this time that he was developing his Gramscian theory of electoral politics in which party competition could be thought of as an absorbing game in which the struggle was over the distribution of economic resources at the margin, thereby eclipsing the fundamental inequality upon which the game was based (Przeworski, 1985).

5 Indeed, Przeworski (1985) has shown just how rational it is for socialist parties to fight for immediate material gains in order to attract the votes necessary to gain and then keep power.

6 Interestingly, the major Bourdieusian analysis of the transition in Eastern Europe – Eyal, Szelenyi and Townsley (2001) – is not an analysis of the collapse, but of the (dis)continuity of elites in Hungary, Poland and the Czech Republic. Again, it is an examination of the inheritance, fate and the distribution of different forms of socialist capital (economic, cultural and political) in the post-socialist era.

7 This is most systematically elaborated in Bourdieu's (1988 [1984]) account of the crisis of May 1968, where he examines the consequences of the declining opportunities for expanding numbers of university graduates and the way the crisis in the university field dovetailed with the crisis in the wider political field.

8 '... knowledge and recognition have to be rooted in practical dispositions of acceptance and submission, which, because they do not pass through deliberation and decision, escape the dilemmas of consent or constraint' (Bourdieu, 2000 [1997]: 198).

9 This meeting was preceded by fierce struggles within the organising committee between activists who supported 'Congress' and those who favoured more 'workerist' political ideologies, and precipitated a split in the community movement and tensions with the trade unions; nonetheless, 'Congress' rapidly became the hegemonic force in the popular movement, partly because of the potency of its symbolic resources.

EPILOGUE
Travelling Theory

MICHAEL BURAWOY

In her *Southern Theory* (2007), Raewyn Connell problematises the canonical works of metropolitan theory – from the so-called classics of Marx, Weber and Durkheim to the contemporary theories of James Coleman, Anthony Giddens and Pierre Bourdieu. Their silence on the Global South, Connell argues, portends a distinctively Northern perspective, albeit disguised as universalism. In reaction to Northern theory, Connell presents us with a 'counter-hegemonic' project that foregrounds social thinkers from the South who have not made it into the conventional sociological tradition – from the Middle East, three Iranian thinkers: al-Afghani, Al-e Ahmad and the more contemporary Ali Shariati; from Latin America, the Argentinian economist Raúl Prebisch, the Brazilian sociologist Fernando Enrique Cardoso and the Mexican anthropologist García Canclini; and from South Asia, subaltern thinker Ranajit Guha, anthropologist Veena Das and public intellectual Ashis Nandy. From Africa, she chooses the Dahomeyan philosopher Paulin Hountontdji and the South African writer, politician, historian and newspaper editor Sol Plaatje. He was the first general secretary of the ANC and author of *Native Life in South Africa*, a denunciation of the 1913 Natives' Land Act. Around such forgotten or overlooked thinkers, Connell proposes to build an alternative social theory.

There is no doubt about the importance of her intervention – the latest in a long history of challenges to the hegemony of Northern sociology. Connell perhaps goes further than others in combining an assault on 'classical theory' with a global search for alternatives to Western and Northern social theory. She thereby underlines just how narrow are the geographical origins of 'recognised' or 'legitimate' sociological theory, both in their canonical and contemporary incarnations. Theory building appears to be the monopoly of the few, situated in elite universities of the Global North.

Important though her critique of the canon is, her sketch of 'Southern theory' is not without problems of its own. How feasible is an alternative Southern theory in the face of the unevenness of the distribution of resources – the concentration of the most lavishly funded universities and research establishments in the North, where working conditions are incomparably superior to anywhere else? As the more privileged nations in the South seek to develop their own 'world-class' universities, they reinforce existing global prestige hierarchies, channelling faculty publications into 'world-class' journals that are also generally located in the North and that publish in English, and thereby exacerbate the divide between centre and metropolis, both globally but, no less importantly, within countries. Poorer nations are increasingly dispensing with their own universities, and instead are sponsoring the training of their own scholars and experts abroad, i.e. usually in the North, or simply importing them from the North. Apart from anything else, the risk is that they will never return to their home countries. In the global division of knowledge production, can theory challenge and run ahead of the material conditions that it expresses? However tempting it may be, to opt out of this unequal world order is to risk invisibility, poverty and isolation, reproducing rather than challenging the selfsame hegemony.

To transcend the dominance of the North is a Sisyphean task, so we must avoid illusory solutions, the substitution of dream for reality. There is no easy escape from domination – that is the meaning of both hegemony and symbolic violence. So, even Connell's chosen Southern theorists, if they were not trained in the North, spent a lot of time there. As postcolonial theory has insisted, between Global North and Global South, just as between metropolis and colony, there has always been a circulation of social theory. Thus, Bourdieu's social theory is inspired by his experiences in Algeria and by his collaborations with Algerian intellectuals, just as many of the Indian subalternists got their degrees in the North, and, later, even settling into academic positions there, especially as their thinking became fashionable the world over. Furthermore, the distinction between North and South, or West and East, overlooks the underdeveloped regions within Northern academia, just as it overlooks the divide between centre and periphery within the South, especially within countries. The hierarchy of higher education in South Africa is but one example of the increasing knowledge divide *within* countries, drawing elite sectors into a global conversation that is ever more divorced from the weight of massified higher education and from the population at large.

Moreover, divisions within regions and countries refer not just to status and resources, but also to the content of social theory itself, so that we can say that Northern theory contains multiple strands, many of which contest dominant tropes – Connell herself has made major contributions to feminist theory that challenges mainstream orthodoxy. Moreover, Pierre Bourdieu was very much the critical sociologist, attacking pillars of hegemonic thinking in France and elsewhere. In placing all Northern sociology in the same rubbish bin, Connell risks committing the very error of which she accuses Northern sociology, namely false generalisation. Equally, in the South, the field of sociology, like other academic fields, is a terrain of conflict, reflecting serious divisions within nations and within regions – terrains that Connell ignores as she plucks her chosen theorists out of their historical and political context.

While resurrecting Southern theorists demonstrates that the soil of Southern theory is not barren, Connell's focus on individuals leads her to overlook the truly distinctive bodies of social theory that have developed deep roots in the South, social theory that grounds the work of an institute like SWOP.[1] Indeed, SWOP's distinctiveness lies in the way it appropriated Northern theory – even the more conservative social theory associated with the functions of conflict – in order to deploy it against the apartheid state. Edward Webster, for example, spent a lifetime arguing that violence can only be constrained if institutions, such as trade unions, are created to channel grievances. Thus, apparently innocuous Western theory about the institutionalisation of conflict became, in the hands of South African sociologists, a radical challenge to apartheid South Africa. Indeed, the defence of such theories proved so subversive that the state would place Webster on trial. Others were assassinated for their adoption and dissemination of critical Western theories. When theories travel, as Edward Said noted long ago, their meaning can be transformed in a radical or conservative direction, depending not only on the theory, but also on the context of reception. Indeed, when Southern theories travel north they often lose their radical edge, becoming domesticated in the jaws of the metropolitan university. This suggests that the real battle is not *against* reigning hegemonies but *on the terrain* of these hegemonies, appropriating, reordering and reconstructing them in new contexts. The problem is not so much with Northern theory, but with what we do with it once it arrives in the South.

In this regard, the spread of Marxism – a mobile theory if ever there were one – is especially interesting. Just think of the role of Marxism in South Africa: how a century ago it became a vehicle of a white supremacist labour aristocracy and later the supporter of a 'Native Republic'. Then it developed theories of internal colonialism and of the relation between race and class, as well as original theories about the articulation of modes of production and the elaboration of the formation of dominant classes. There was always tension between the orthodoxy emanating from the Comintern and the demands of the South African situation, and it was this tension that gave rise to an original Marxism. Indeed, Marxism became a field of productive contestation not only within the South African Communist Party, but no less so outside, within the ranks of the black and white working class. To be sure, there has always been an orthodox Marxism-Leninism that mechanically applies Marxism to the South African context, a Marxism of ritual incantation that dispenses with the dynamic interaction of theory and practice. The present period, in particular, calls for novel theorising. Bringing Marxism into dialogue with sociology, not least with the work of Pierre Bourdieu, is intended as a contribution to the revitalisation of Marxism not just here in South Africa, but elsewhere too, just as the dialogue with Weber, Simmel, Freud and Croce earlier revitalised Western Marxism.

All of which is to underline the importance of the dialogic moment and to suggest that struggle can as well take place on the terrain of Northern hegemony as in overturning Northern hegemony. In the context of our conversations with Bourdieu, we recognise, therefore, a dual dialogue – with the Marxism from which Bourdieu's opus draws its meaning as a silent antagonist, but also with the material context of its reception. I have dwelt on the first, while Karl has dwelt on the second, even as we simultaneously created our own conversation.

As Bourdieu himself insists, theories position themselves in relation to other theories within the same 'field'. So I have tried to elucidate a particular lens on Bourdieu by bringing his writings into dialogue with Marxism, especially the Marxisms that engage the three central pillars of Bourdieu's work, i.e. symbolic domination, social reflexivity and public engagement. Bourdieu and Marxism clash most fundamentally over their divergent understandings of domination and the possibility of the dominated recognising and contesting their subjugation. Notwithstanding internal inconsistencies, in the final analysis, for Bourdieu, cultural domination is deeper than it is for Marxism. The former denies the possibility of the working class achieving an understanding of its subjugation, let alone acting on its imperative. This has consequences for divergent understandings of the intellectual: in Marxism, intellectuals do not themselves form a class, but are the allies of classes, whose class consciousness they foster, whereas for Bourdieu, intellectuals are best viewed as universalising their own interests in reason.

My conversations between Marxism and Bourdieu set the stage for Karl's adjudication of the two bodies of theory as applied to South Africa. Instead of seeking an alternative Southern sociology, Karl's approach is to critically engage Marxism and Bourdieu on the terrain of South Africa. He challenges Bourdieu with the lived realities of South Africa, problematising what he takes for granted – assumptions that then also reverberate back into a critique of Bourdieu's understanding of France. As Karl says, ostensibly Bourdieu's concern with social order cemented through symbolic violence sits uneasily with a society like South Africa. There is not the stable symbolic order that Bourdieu claims for France; rather, we have a society in which the symbolic order is in perpetual crisis. But it is in crisis not only because different fractions of the dominant class are fighting for supremacy within the field of power (Bourdieu), but also because there are insurgent symbolic orders emanating from below. Karl describes the culture of resistance in townships, where many residents see all too little difference from the old apartheid order and so turn the old rituals, songs, dances that were so effective in the previous era against the new administration. Nor does the state have a monopoly of legitimate means of symbolic violence, as Bourdieu presumes. Karl shows only too clearly how the state crumbles from within as it becomes an arena of struggle between proponents of racial justice, on the one hand, and bureaucratic and professional expertise, on the other. While Bourdieu makes much of the idea of classification struggle, he rarely gives the notion any empirical support. For that he would have needed to come to South Africa or some such country undergoing transformation. Karl gives flesh and bones to the notion of classification struggle.

The continuity of social order, at the heart of Bourdieu's theory, presumes a dovetailing of habitus and structure, which is difficult to make sense of in a country like South Africa that has undergone such an upheaval in the last 30 years. Indeed, observing insurgencies from below, Karl asks whether apartheid inculcated a *habitus of defiance* as much as a habitus of submission – a habitus that still flourishes in the New South Africa. Here Karl finds more useful the Marxist analysis of dual consciousness found in Freire, Fanon and Gramsci, where domination creates competition between an inner authentic self and an outer inauthentic self, or between Gramsci's good sense and his bad sense deriving from ideology. In combing Bourdieu's culminating theoretical work, *Pascalian Meditations*, for a habitus of the dominated that produces not shame and humiliation, but defiance and rebellion, Karl finds very little. The concept of habitus may be necessary, but it has to be revamped if it is to explain the abiding struggles of the South African working class. The Arab uprisings of 2011 give ample support to the idea of a habitus of defiance, a habitus that today seems to spread with astonishing speed.

In South Africa, where physical violence is so commonplace, how can one justify the Bourdieusian focus on symbolic violence? Here Karl makes a brilliant move, informed by his research, which insists on examining the *interdependence* of symbolic and physical violence. He shows how displays of symbolic domination by new elites inspire township residents to react with physical violence. Perhaps even more than under apartheid, residents show their displeasure by burning down symbols of their new-found dispossession – libraries without books, clinics without medicine, community centres without communities. Their rage is uncontrollable as they confront a new order that violates their hopes and their sense of justice. In other words, physical violence is necessarily bound up with symbolic violence. Such eruptions – simultaneously physical and symbolic – easily spread to other localities, regions or even countries as the life of the dominated becomes more precarious in both North and South, as wage labour shrinks so that being exploited becomes a privilege of the few, and as the majority not only become, but also recognise themselves as, 'the wretched of the earth'.

Karl pursues this linkage of the physical and symbolic into the realm of masculinity, pointing to the existence of a progressive constitution and a wide array of laws protecting women, alongside pervasive brutal male physical violence. Indeed, it seems that when the symbolic domination of earlier patriarchal orders is threatened – for example, when they no longer command access to material resources – men often resort to physical violence. Again, this calls into question Bourdieu's presumption that symbolic violence works smoothly without leading or having recourse to physical violence. When the symbolic world is in crisis, physical violence all too easily fills the vacuum. Democratisation can unleash physical violence when it closes rather than opens institutional channels for self-expression and grievances – when it dashes the very hopes it nurtures.

At the heart of Bourdieu's theory of symbolic domination lies education. Here again Karl tries to work with and against Bourdieu. Thus, in his critique of Freire and in his endorsement of Gramsci, Karl insists that effective education requires more than symbolic violence, but a structural violence – an ongoing discipline of the body as well as the mind, a discipline that is necessary for the development of a critical consciousness. Bourdieu not only sees no alternative to conventional education – the inculcation of legitimate culture – but, even more bleakly, he cannot conceive of education as a realm of meaningful contestation. By contrast, drawing on the example of missionary education, Karl shows how legitimate culture can be turned against the domination it purportedly serves. Many of the leaders of the liberation movement, not least Nelson Mandela and Oliver Tambo, learned how to turn legitimate culture to their own advantage and in this way furthered the struggles against apartheid. When the apartheid regime replaced missionary education with Bantu education, it liquidated those opportunities and fomented violent student revolt, as in Soweto in 1976. If education fosters symbolic domination, it can also foster rebellion against that domination. If it can happen in South Africa, it can happen in France.

Extending his examination of education to the tertiary level, Karl takes up the second pillar of Bourdieu's edifice, namely reflexivity, i.e. the importance of examining the conditions of the production of knowledge. Here, Karl notes the continuing domination in South Africa of white academics who have an interest, not necessarily conscious, in their domination through the continuing supremacy of Western canonical thinking. Karl warns that they may be in for a shock as students begin to challenge the hegemony of Western thought, and this will be all to the good, so long as dialogue continues to be possible. We had better sharpen our critical tools when reconstructing Northern theory if sociologists are not going to become irrelevant.

Equally, Karl interrogates Bourdieu's conception of the public sociologist as someone who pursues the Realpolitik of reason, engaging in rational, enlightened discourse in some public sphere. Bourdieu clings to the potential of such discourse as denaturalising and defatalising the taken-for-granted, 'spontaneous sociology' of the people. His commitment to the progressive rationality of reason is not deterred by the imperialism of reason – reason deployed to both mystify and advance the interests of the dominant. Bourdieu wants to have his cake and eat it too – for him, reason is both emancipatory and justificatory. He is able to hold on to this contradictory position because his conception of public sociology is a traditional one – one that does not engage pre-existing conversations, that does not engage discourses that are firmly held by partisan publics. This is consistent with Bourdieu's separation of the logic of theory from the logic of practice, but it leaves the sociologist in the stratosphere. Karl argues that by standing aloof from their constituencies, public sociologists or public intellectuals condemn themselves to irrelevance. If they are to communicate, public sociologists have to take seriously existing political currents and their carriers, and also learn to compete with other voices in the public sphere. South African academics learned this lesson early on – they had a choice to be in direct conversation with various publics and compromise their independence or defend their independence by retreating behind academic walls, where they might nonetheless educate the organic intellectuals of tomorrow. There is a place for both traditional and organic public sociologies – indeed, they have to be interdependent, as Karl suggests.

Here, indeed, we might take Karl's insistence on dialogue between theory and practice even further. We have noted time and again the gap between Bourdieu's theory and his practice: how he warns others against direct engagement with publics, yet frequently does just that himself; how he recognises the role of culture in symbolic domination and in establishing distinction, but nonetheless vigorously defends that same culture against the market; how his call for reflexivity leads him to deploy it against others by reducing them to their position in an intellectual space, but refuses to analyse his own position as a source of his own sociology. Theory and practice never come together – they are always out of kilter, the one outpacing the other – but this is no reason not to place them in dialogue. Even if one believes, as Bourdieu does, that there should be an epistemological break between the two, this is still no justification for not attempting a conversation of mutual enlightenment, as he did in *The Weight of the World*.

Indeed, Bourdieu's separation of the logic of theory and the logic of practice places the theorist above the people being theorised. In bringing Bourdieu to South Africa, we are making him earn his distinction, forcing him to restore the connection of theory to practice. By putting him into conversation with both Marxist theories and South Africa's social reality, we are unsettling his foundations, while pointing, perhaps, to rebuilding his edifice. Just as Bourdieu's first visit to Africa turned a philosopher into a sociologist, we now have to see how his imaginary passage to Africa – this time to South Africa, not Algeria – will transform his writings, and what visions will be sent back to the metropolis. But we will see, first, whether he can survive the journey, whether he can flourish in the southern tip of Africa as he did on its northern coast. There is no meaningful Northern theory insulated from Southern theory, but only theory that circulates between North and South – and the best critical theory transforms itself as it traverses the globe, turning itself against itself.

NOTES

1   Society, Work and Development Institute at the University of Witwatersrand, Johannesburg, which has a history of engaged social research going back to 1983. Edward Webster was its founder and longtime director.

BIBLIOGRAPHY

Adkins, Lisa & Beverley Skeggs (eds). 2004. *Feminism after Bourdieu*. Cambridge: Blackwell.

Ally, Shireen. 2005. 'Oppositional intellectualism as reflection, not rejection, of power: Wits Sociology, 1975–1989.' *Transformation: Critical Perspectives on South Africa 59*: 66–97.

Anderson, Elija. 2002. 'The ideologically driven critique.' *American Journal of Sociology*, 107(6): 1533–50.

Beauvoir, Simone de. 1956. *The Mandarins*. New York: World Publishing.

——. 1964 [1963]. *Force of Circumstance*. New York: Putnam.

——. 1989 [1949]. *The Second Sex*. New York: Vintage.

Bourdieu, Pierre. 1962 [1961]. *The Algerians*. Boston: Beacon Press.

——. 1975. 'The specificity of the scientific field and the social conditions of the progress of reason.' *Social Science Information*, 14(6): 19–47.

——. 1977 [1972]. *Outline of a Theory of Practice*. Cambridge: Cambridge University Press.

——. 1979 [1963]. *Algeria, 1960*. Cambridge: Cambridge University Press.

——. 1981. 'Men and machines.' In K. Knorr-Cetina & A. Cicourel (eds), *Advances in Social Theory and Methodology*, pp. 304–17. Boston: Routledge & Kegan Paul.

——. 1984 [1979]. *Distinction: A Social Critique of the Judgment of Taste*. Cambridge, Mass.: Harvard University Press.

——. 1988 [1984]. *Homo Academicus*. Cambridge: Polity Press.

——. 1989. 'The corporatism of the universal: The role of intellectuals in the modern world.' *Telos*, 81: 99–110.

——. 1990 [1980]. *The Logic of Practice*. Cambridge: Polity Press.

——. 1990 [1982]. 'The uses of the "people".' In *In Other Words: Essays towards a Reflexive Sociology*, pp. 150–55. Stanford: Stanford University Press.

——. 1990 [1986]. 'Fieldwork in philosophy.' In *In Other Words: Essays towards a Reflexive Sociology*, pp. 3–33. Stanford: Stanford University Press.

——. 1990 [1987]. *In Other Words: Essays toward a Reflexive Sociology*. Stanford: Stanford University Press.

——. 1991. *Language and Symbolic Power*. Cambridge, Mass.: Harvard University Press.

——. 1991 [1984]. 'Social space and the genesis of "classes".' In *Language and Symbolic Power*, pp. 229–51. Cambridge, Mass.: Harvard University Press.

——. 1993 [1984]. 'Public opinion does not exist.' In *Sociology in Question*. London: Sage.

——. 1994. 'Rethinking the state: Genesis and structure of the bureaucratic field.' *Sociological Theory*, 12(1), March: 1–19.

——. 1995. 'Apologie pour une femme rangée.' Preface to Toril Moi, *Simone de Beauvoir: conflicts d'une intellectuelle*, trans. Ana Villarreal, pp. vi–x. Paris: Diderot Éditeur.

——. 1996 [1992]. *Rules of Art: Genesis and Structure of the Literary Field*. Stanford: Stanford University Press.

——. 1996 [1989]. *State Nobility: Elite Schools in the Field of Power*. Stanford: Stanford University Press.

——. 1998 [1998]. *Acts of Resistance: Against the Tyranny of the Market*. New York: New Press.

——. 1998 [1989]. 'The Soviet variant and political capital.' In *Practical Reason: On the Theory of Action*, pp.14–18. Stanford: Stanford University Press.

——. 1998 [1994]. *Practical Reason: On the Theory of Action*. Stanford: Stanford University Press.

——. 1999 [1996]. *On Television*, New York: New Press.

——. 2000. 'Making the economic habitus: Algerian workers revisited.' *Ethnography*, 1(1): 17–41.

——. 2000 [1997]. *Pascalian Meditations*. Stanford: Stanford University Press.

——. 2001 [1998]. *Masculine Domination*. Stanford: Stanford University Press.

——. 2003 [2001]. *Firing Back: Against the Tyranny of the Market*. New York: New Press.

——. 2004 [2001]. *Science of Science and Reflexivity*. Chicago: Chicago University Press.

——. 2005. *The Social Structures of the Economy*. Cambridge: Polity Press.

——. 2007 [2004]. *Sketch for a Self-analysis*. Chicago: University of Chicago Press.

——. 2008 [1977]. 'Giving voice to the voiceless.' In *Political Interventions: Social Science and Political Action*, pp. 70–77. London: Verso.

——. 2008 [2000]. 'A retrospective on the Algerian experience.' In *Political Interventions: Social Science and Political Action*, pp. 20–24. London: Verso.

——. 2008a [2002]. *The Bachelors' Ball*. Chicago: University of Chicago Press.

——. 2008b [2002]. *Political Interventions: Social Science and Political Action*. London: Verso.

Bourdieu, Pierre et al. 1999 [1993]. *The Weight of the World: Social Suffering in Contemporary Society*. Stanford: Stanford University Press.

Bourdieu, Pierre, Alain Darbel, Jean-Pierre Rivet & Claude Seibel. 1963. *Travail et travailleurs en Algérie*. Paris: Mouton.

Bourdieu, Pierre & Jean-Claude Passeron. 1977 [1970]. *Reproduction in Education, Society and Culture*. London: Sage.
——. 1979 [1964]. *The Inheritors: French Students and Their Relation to Culture*. Chicago: University of Chicago Press.
Bourdieu, Pierre, Jean-Claude Passeron & Jean-Claude Chamboredon. 1991 [1968]. *The Craft of Sociology: Epistemological Preliminaries*. New York: Aldine de Gruyter.
Bourdieu, Pierre & Adbelmalek Sayad. 1964. *Le déracinement: la crise de l'agriculture traditionnelle en Algérie*. Paris: Editions de Minuit.
Bourdieu, Pierre & Loïc Wacquant. 1992. *An Invitation to Reflexive Sociology*. Chicago: University of Chicago Press.
Buhlungu, Sakhela. 2006. 'Rebels without a cause of their own? The contradictory location of white officials in black unions in South Africa, 1973–1994.' *Current Sociology*, 54: 427–51.
Burawoy, Michael. 1979. *Manufacturing Consent: Changes in the Labor Process under Monopoly Capitalism*. Chicago: University of Chicago Press.
——. 1985. *The Politics of Production: Factory Regimes under Capitalism and Socialism*. London: Verso.
——. 2010. 'Southern windmill: The life and work of Edward Webster.' *Transformation: Critical Perspectives on Southern Africa*, 72/73: 1–25.
Burawoy, Michael & János Lukács. 1992. *The Radiant Past: Ideology and Reality in Hungary's Road to Capitalism*. Chicago: University of Chicago Press.
Cameron, Dan, Christine Christov-Bakargiev and J. M. Coetzee. 1999. *William Kentridge*. London & New York: Phaidon Press.
Chakrabarty, Dipesh. 2000. *Provincialising Europe: Postcolonial Thought and Historical Difference*. Princeton & Oxford: Princeton University Press.
Chatterjee, Partha (2004) *The Politics of the Governed: Reflections on Popular Politics in most of the World*. New York: Columbia University Press.
Chodorow, Nancy. 1978. *The Reproduction of Mothering: Psychoanalysis and the Sociology of Gender*. Berkeley: University of California Press.
Chun, Jennifer. 2009. *Organising at the Margins: The Symbolic Politics of Labour in South Korea and the United States*. Ithaca & London: ILR Press & Cornell University Press.
Collins, Patricia Hill. 1986. 'Learning from the outsider within: The sociological significance of black feminist thought.' *Social Problems*, 33(6): 14–32.
——. 1990. *Black Feminist Thought: Knowledge, Consciousness, and the Politics of Empowerment*. Boston: Unwin Ghyman.
——. 1998. *Fighting Words: Black Women and the Search for Justice*. Minneapolis: University of Minnesota.
Colonna, Fanny. 2009. 'The phantom of dispossessions: From *The Uprooting* to *The Weight of the World*.' In Jane Goodman & Paul Silverstein (eds), *Bourdieu in Algeria*, pp. 63–93. Lincoln, NE & London: University of Nebraska Press.
Connell, Raewyn. 2007. *Southern Theory: The Global Dynamics of Knowledge in Social Science*. Australia: Allen & Unwin.
Dlamini, Jacob. 2011. 'Voortrekker: The smoke that calls.' In Karl von Holdt,

Malose Langa, Sepetla Molapo, Nomfundo Mogapi, Kindiza Ngubeni, Jacob Dlamini & Adele Kirsten. *The Smoke that Calls: Insurgent Citizenship, Collective Violence and the Struggle for a Place in the New South Africa*, pp. 33–44. Johannesburg: CSVR & SWOP.

Du Bois, William Edward Burghardt. 1903. *The Souls of Black Folk*. New York: McClurg.

———. 1996 [1899]. *The Philadelphia Negro*. Philadelphia: University of Pennsylvania Press.

Duneier, Mitchell. 2002. 'What kind of combat sport is sociology?' *American Journal of Sociology*, 107(6): 1551–75.

Durkheim, Émile. 1965. *The Elementary Forms of Religious Life*. New York: Free Press.

Eyal, Gil, Ivan Szelenyi & Eleanor Townsley. 2001. *Making Capitalism without Capitalists: The New Ruling Elites in Eastern Europe*. London: Verso.

Fanon, Frantz. 1963 [1961]. *The Wretched of the Earth*. New York: Grove Press.

———. 1967 [1952]. *Black Skin, White Masks*. New York: Grove Press.

———. 2004 [1961]. *The Wretched of the Earth*. New York: Grove Press.

Freire, Paulo. 1970. *Pedagogy of the Oppressed*. New York: Continuum.

Friedan, Betty. 1963. *The Feminine Mystique*. New York: Norton.

Fung, Archon & Erik Wright (eds). 2003. *Deepening Democracy: Institutional Innovations in Empowered Participatory Governance*. London: Verso.

Gerth, Hans & Charles Wright Mills (eds). 1946. *From Max Weber: Essays in Sociology*. New York: Oxford University Press.

———. 1954. *Character and Social Structure: The Psychology of Social Institutions*. London: Routledge & Kegan Paul.

Goodman, Jane & Paul Silverstein (eds). 2009. *Bourdieu in Algeria*. Lincoln, NE & London: University of Nebraska Press.

Gouldner, Alvin. 1970. *The Coming Crisis of Western Sociology*. New York: Basic Books.

———. 1979. *The Future of the Intellectuals and the Rise of the New Class*. New York: Seabury Press.

Gramsci, Antonio. 1971. *Selections from the Prison Notebooks*. New York: International.

———. 1977. *Selections from Political Writings, 1910–1920*. London: Lawrence & Wishart.

Habermas, Jürgen. 1984. *The Theory of Communicative Action*. Boston: Beacon Press.

Hochschild, Arlie. 1983. *The Managed Heart*. Berkeley: University of California Press.

Holston, James. 2008. *Insurgent Citizenship: Disjunctions of Democracy and Modernity in Brazil*. Princeton & Oxford: Princeton University Press.

Kirsten, Adele. 2008. *A Nation without Guns? The Story of Gun Free South Africa*. Scottsville: University of KwaZulu-Natal Press.

Lamont, Michèle. 2009. *How Professors Think: Inside the Curious World of Academic Judgment*. Cambridge: Cambridge University Press.

Langa, Malose. 2011. 'Azania: Violence is the only language that this government knows.' In Karl von Holdt, Malose Langa, Sepetla Molapo, Nomfundo

Mogapi, Kindiza Ngubeni, Jacob Dlamini & Adele Kirsten. *The Smoke that Calls: Insurgent Citizenship, Collective Violence and the Struggle for a Place in the New South Africa*, pp. 57–69. Johannesburg: CSVR & SWOP.

Langa, Malose, Jacob Dlamini & Karl von Holdt. 2010. *Case Study 1/Town 1: Sending a Message to the Top*. Unpublished research report.

——. 2011. 'Kungcatsha: Sending a message to the top.' In Karl von Holdt, Malose Langa, Sepetla Molapo, Nomfundo Mogapi, Kindiza Ngubeni, Jacob Dlamini & Adele Kirsten. *The Smoke that Calls: Insurgent Citizenship, Collective Violence and the Struggle for a Place in the New South Africa*, pp. 45–56. Johannesburg: CSVR & SWOP.

Langa, Malose & Karl von Holdt. 2011, 'Bokfontein amazes the nations: Community Work Programme (CWP) heals a traumatised community.' *New South African Review 2*. Johannesburg: Wits University Press.

Lerner, Daniel. 1958. *The Passing of Traditional Society: Modernizing the Middle East*. Glencoe: Free Press.

Le Sueur, James. 2001. *Uncivil War: Intellectuals and Identity Politics during the Decolonization of Algeria*. Philadelphia: University of Pennsylvania Press.

Lévi-Strauss, Claude. 1969. *The Elementary Structures of Kinship*. Boston: Beacon Press.

Lynd, Robert. 1939. *Knowledge for What? The Place of Social Sciences in American Culture*. Princeton: Princeton University Press.

Macey, David. 2000. *Frantz Fanon: A Biography*. New York: Picador.

Marx, Karl & Friedrich Engels. 1978 [1845–46]. *The German Ideology*. In R. Tucker (ed.), *The Marx-Engels Reader*, pp. 146–200. New York: Norton.

——. 1978 [1848]. *The Manifesto of the Communist Party*. In R. Tucker (ed.), *The Marx-Engels Reader*, pp. 469–511. New York: Norton.

——. 1978 [1845–46]. 'The Holy Family.' In R. Tucker (ed.), *The Marx-Engels Reader*, pp. 594–616. New York: Norton.

Merton, Robert. 1968 [1947]. 'Social structure and anomie.' In *Social Theory and Social Structure*, pp. 185–214. New York: Free Press.

——. 1973 [1942]. 'The normative structure of science.' In *The Sociology of Science*, pp. 267–78. Chicago: University of Chicago Press.

Mills, Charles Wright. 1948. *The New Men of Power: America's Labor Leaders*. New York: Harcourt.

——. 1951. *White Collar: The American Middle Classes*. New York: Oxford University Press.

——. 1956. *The Power Elite*. New York: Oxford University Press.

——. 1958. The *Causes of World War Three*. New York: Ballantine Books.

——. 1959. *The Sociological Imagination*. New York: Oxford University Press.

——. 1960. *Listen, Yankee*. New York: Ballantine Books.

Moi, Toril. 1994. *Simone de Beauvoir: The Making of an Intellectual Woman*. Cambridge: Blackwell.

——. 1999. 'Appropriating Bourdieu: Feminist theory and Pierre Bourdieu's sociology of culture.' In *What Is a Woman? and Other Essays*, pp. 264–99. Oxford: Oxford University Press.

——. 2002. 'While we wait: The English translation of *The Second Sex*.' *Signs*, 27(4): 1005–35.

Morphet, Tony. 1990. '"Brushing history against the grain": Oppositional discourse in South Africa.' *Theoria: A Journal of Studies in the Arts, Humanities and Social Sciences*, 76, October: 89–99.

Mosoetsa, Sarah. 2011. *Eating from One Pot: The Dynamics of Survival in Poor South African Households*. Johannesburg: Wits University Press.

Naidoo, Prishani. 2010. 'Three thousand words on race.' *South African Review of Sociology*, 41(1): 120–26.

Newman, Katherine. 2002. 'No shame: The view from the Left Bank.' *American Journal of Sociology*, 107(6): 1576–98.

Parsons, Talcott. 1937. *The Structure of Social Action*. New York: McGraw-Hill.

——. 1967. *Sociological Theory and Modern Society*. New York: Free Press.

Pillay, Suren. 2009. 'Translating "South Africa": Race, colonialism and challenges of critical thought after apartheid.' In Heather Jacklin and Peter Vale (eds). *Reimagining the social in South Africa*, pp. 235–68. Scottsville: University of KwaZulu-Natal Press.

Poulantzas, Nicos. 1973. *Political Power and Social Classes*. London: New Left Books.

Przeworski, Adam. 1985. *Capitalism and Social Democracy*. Cambridge: Cambridge University Press.

Przeworski, Adam & John Sprague. 1986. *Paper Stones: A History of Electoral Socialism*. Chicago: University of Chicago Press.

Reich, Adam. 2010. *Hidden Truth: Young Men Navigating Lives in and out of Juvenile Prison*. Berkeley: University of California Press.

Rubin, Gayle. 1975. 'The traffic in women: Notes on the "political economy" of sex.' In Rayna Reiter (ed.), *Toward an Anthropology of Women*, pp. 157–210. New York: Monthly Review Press.

Sallaz, Jeffrey. 2002. 'The house rules: Autonomy and interests among contemporary casino croupiers.' *Work and Occupations*, 29(4): 394–427.

Sartre, Jean-Paul. 1948 [1946]. *Anti-Semite and Jew*. New York: Shocken Books.

Schwarzer, Alice. 1984. *Simone de Beauvoir Today: Conversations, 1972–1982*. London: Hogarth Press.

Scott, James C. 1990. *Domination and Arts of Resistance: Hidden Transcripts*. New Haven & London: Yale University Press.

Sharone, Ofer. 2004. 'Engineering overwork: Bell-curve management at a high-tech firm.' In Cynthia Fuchs Epstein & Arne L. Kalleberg (eds), *Fighting for Time: Shifting Boundaries of Work and Social Life*, pp. 191–208. New York: Russell Sage Foundation.

Sherman, Rachel. 2007. *Class Acts: Service and Inequality in Luxury Hotels*. Berkeley: University of California Press.

Silverstein, Paul. 2004. 'Of rooting and uprooting: Kabyle habitus, domesticity and structural nostalgia.' *Ethnography*, 5(4): 553–78.

Thompson, Edward P. 1963. *The Making of the English Working Class*. London: Victor Gollancz.

Toyana, Mbali. 2011. 'Dying to be: Gender-based violence.' *SA Labour Bulletin*, 35(2): 35–37.

Veblen, Thorstein. 1953 [1899]. *The Theory of the Leisure Class*. New York: New American Library.

Vetten, Lisa. 2007. 'Violence against women in South Africa.' In Sakhela Buhlungu, John Daniel, Roger Southall & Jessica Lutchman (eds). *State of the Nation: South Africa 2007*, pp. 425–47. Cape Town: HSRC Press.

Von Holdt, Karl. 1990. 'The Mercedes-Benz sleep-in.' *South African Labour Bulletin*, 15(4): 15–44.

———. 2003. *Transition from Below: Forging Trade Unionism and Workplace Change in South Africa*. Scottsville: Natal University Press.

———. 2010a. 'Nationalism, bureaucracy and the developmental state: The South African case?' *South African Review of Sociology*, 41(1): 4–27.

———. 2010b. 'Institutionalisation, strike violence and local moral orders.' *Transformation: Critical Perspectives on Southern Africa*, 72/73: 127–51.

———. 2011a. 'Overview: Insurgent citizenship and collective violence: Analysis of case studies.' In Karl von Holdt, Malose Langa, Sepetla Molapo, Kindiza Ngubeni, Jacob Dlamini & Adele Kirsten. *The Smoke that Calls: Insurgent Citizenship, Collective Violence and the Struggle for a Place in the New South Africa*, pp. 5–32. Johannesburg: CSVR & SWOP.

———. 2011b. 'Trouble: Mobilising against xenophobic attacks.' In Karl von Holdt, Malose Langa, Sepetla Molapo, Nomfundo Mogapi, Kindiza Ngubeni, Jacob Dlamini & Adele Kirsten. *The Smoke that Calls: Insurgent Citizenship, Collective Violence and the Struggle for a Place in the New South Africa*, pp. 97–105. Johannesburg: CSVR & SWOP.

Von Holdt, Karl, Malose Langa, Sepetla Molapo, Nomfundo Mogapi, Kindiza Ngubeni, Jacob Dlamini & Adele Kirsten. *The Smoke that Calls: Insurgent Citizenship, Collective Violence and the Struggle for a Place in the New South Africa*. Johannesburg: CSVR & SWOP.

Von Holdt, Karl & Bethuel Maserumule. 2005 'After apartheid: Decay or reconstruction in a public hospital?' In Edward Webster & Karl von Holdt (eds). *Beyond the Apartheid Workplace: Studies in Transition*, pp. 435–59. Scottsville: University of KwaZulu-Natal Press.

Wacquant, Loïc. 2002. 'Scrutinizing the street: Poverty, morality, and the pitfalls of urban ethniography.' *American Journal of Sociology*, 107(6): 1468–532.

———. 2004. 'Following Pierre Bourdieu into the field.' *Ethnography*, 5(4): 387–414.

——— (ed.). 2005. *Pierre Bourdieu and Democratic Politics*. Cambridge: Polity Press.

Weber, Max. 1946. 'Religious rejections of the world and their directions.' In Hans Gerth & C. Wright Mills (eds), *From Max Weber: Essays in Sociology*, pp. 323–69. New York: Oxford University Press.

———. 1970. *The Protestant Ethic and the Spirit of Capitalism*. London: Allen & Unwin.

Webster, Eddie. 1993. 'Moral decay and social reconstruction: Richard Turner and radical reform.' *Theoria: A Journal of Studies in the Arts, Humanities and Social Sciences*, 81/82, October: 1–13.

Willis, Paul. 1977. *Learning to Labour: How Working Class Kids Get Working Class Jobs*. Westmead: Saxon House.

Woolf, Virginia. 1927. *To the Lighthouse*. London: Hogarth Press.

Yongle, Zhang. 2010. 'The future of the past: On Wang Hui's rise of modern Chinese thought.' *New Left Review*, 62, March/April: 47–83.

INDEX